KT-498-963

CAMBRIDGE COMPANIONS TO CULTURE

The Cambridge Companion to Modern German Culture
edited by Eva Kolinsky and Wilfried van der Will

The Cambridge Companion to Modern Russian Culture
edited by Nicholas Rzhevsky

The Cambridge Companion to Modern Spanish Culture
edited by David T. Gies

Title page of Ben Jonson's *Works*, 1616.
Reproduced by permission of the Huntington Library, San Marino, California.

Ben Jonson is, in many ways, the figure of greatest centrality to literary study of the Elizabethan and Jacobean period. He wrote in virtually every literary genre: in drama, comedy, tragedy, and masque; in poetry, epigram, and epistle; in prose, literary criticism, and English grammar. He became the most visible poet of his age, honored more than even William Shakespeare, and his dramatic works, in particular his major comedies, continue to be performed today. This Companion brings together leading scholars from both sides of the Atlantic to provide an accessible and up-to-date introduction to Jonson's life and works. It represents an invaluable guide to current critical perspectives, providing generous coverage not only of his plays but also of his non-dramatic works. The volume is informed by the latest developments in Jonson scholarship and will therefore appeal to scholars and teachers as well as newcomers to his work.

Richard Harp is Professor of English at the University of Nevada, Las Vegas. He has published a number of articles on Renaissance literature and on Irish literature, and is the editor of the forthcoming *Norton Critical Edition of Jonson's Plays and Masques*. He has also edited Thomas Percy's *Life of Dr. Oliver Goldsmith, Dr. Johnson's Critical Vocabulary*, and, with Robert Evans, *Frank O'Connor: New Perspectives* and the forthcoming *Companion to Brian Friel*.

Stanley Stewart is Distinguished Professor of English at the University of California, Riverside, and the author of numerous books, essays, and reviews, including *The Enclosed Garden: The Tradition and the Image in Seventeenth Century Poetry, The Expanded Voice: The Art of Thomas Traherne, George Herbert*, and, most recently, *"Renaissance" Talk: Ordinary Language and the Mystique of Critical Problems*. He is also co-author, with Bernd Magnus and Jean-Pierre Mileur, of *Nietzsche's Case: Philosophy as/and Literature* and, with James A. Riddell, of *Jonson's Spenser: Evidence and Historical Criticism*.

Richard Harp and Stanley Stewart are also the founders and editors, with Robert Evans, of *The Ben Jonson Journal*, which began publication in 1994.

CAMBRIDGE COMPANIONS TO LITERATURE

The Cambridge Companion to Greek Tragedy
edited by P. E. Easterling

The Cambridge Companion to Virgil
edited by Charles Martindale

*The Cambridge Companion to Old English
Literature*
edited by Malcolm Godden and Michael
Lapidge

The Cambridge Companion to Dante
edited by Rachel Jacoff

The Cambridge Chaucer Companion
edited by Piero Boitani and Jill Mann

*The Cambridge Companion to Medieval English
Theatre*
edited by Richard Beadle

*The Cambridge Companion to Shakespeare
Studies*
edited by Stanley Wells

*The Cambridge Companion to English
Renaissance Drama*
edited by A. R. Braunmuller and Michael
Hattaway

*The Cambridge Companion to English Poetry,
Donne to Marvell*
edited by Thomas N. Corns

The Cambridge Companion to Milton
edited by Dennis Danielson

*The Cambridge Companion to British
Romanticism*
edited by Stuart Curran

The Cambridge Companion to James Joyce
edited by Derek Attridge

The Cambridge Companion to Ibsen
edited by James McFarlane

The Cambridge Companion to Brecht
edited by Peter Thomason and Glendyr Sacks

The Cambridge Companion to Beckett
edited by John Pilling

The Cambridge Companion to T. S. Eliot
edited by A. David Moody

*The Cambridge Companion to Renaissance
Humanism*
edited by Jill Kraye

The Cambridge Companion to Joseph Conrad
edited by J. H. Stape

The Cambridge Companion to William Faulkner
edited by Philip M. Weinstein

*The Cambridge Companion to Henry David
Thoreau*
edited by Joel Myerson

The Cambridge Companion to Edith Wharton
edited by Millicent Bell

*The Cambridge Companion to American Realism
and Naturalism*
edited by Donald Pizer

The Cambridge Companion to Mark Twain
edited by Forrest G. Robinson

The Cambridge Companion to Walt Whitman
edited by Ezra Greenspan

The Cambridge Companion to Ernest Hemingway
edited by Scott Donaldson

*The Cambridge Companion to the Eighteenth-
Century Novel*
edited by John Richetti

The Cambridge Companion to Jane Austen
edited by Edward Copeland and Juliet
McMaster

The Cambridge Companion to Samuel Johnson
edited by Greg Clingham

The Cambridge Companion to Oscar Wilde
edited by Peter Raby

*The Cambridge Companion to Tennessee
Williams*
edited by Matthew C. Roudané

The Cambridge Companion to Arthur Miller
edited by Christopher Bigsby

*The Cambridge Companion to the French Novel:
from 1800 to the Present*
edited by Timothy Unwin

*The Cambridge Companion to the Classic Russian
Novel*
edited by Malcolm V. Jones and
Robin Feuer Miller

*The Cambridge Companion to English Literature,
1650–1740*
edited by Steven N. Zwicker

The Cambridge Companion to Eugene O'Neill
edited by Michael Manheim

*The Cambridge Companion to George
Bernard Shaw*
edited by Christopher Innes

The Cambridge Companion to Ezra Pound
edited by Ira Nadel

The Cambridge Companion to Modernism
edited by Michael Levenson

The Cambridge Companion to Thomas Hardy
edited by Dale Kramer

*The Cambridge Companion to American Women
Playwrights*
edited by Brenda Murphy

The Cambridge Companion to Virginia Woolf
edited by Sue Roe and Susan Sellers

The Cambridge Companion to Chekhov
edited by Vera Gottlieb and Paul Allain

THE CAMBRIDGE
COMPANION TO

BEN JONSON

EDITED BY
RICHARD HARP AND STANLEY STEWART

CAMBRIDGE
UNIVERSITY PRESS

PUBLISHED BY THE PRESS SYNDICATE OF THE UNIVERSITY OF CAMBRIDGE
The Pitt Building, Trumpington Street, Cambridge, United Kingdom

CAMBRIDGE UNIVERSITY PRESS
The Edinburgh Building, Cambridge CB2 2RU, UK   www.cup.cam.ac.uk
40 West 20th Street, New York, NY 10011-4211, USA   www.cup.org
10 Stamford Road, Oakleigh, Melbourne 3166, Australia
Ruiz de Alarcón 13, 28014 Madrid, Spain

First published 2000

Printed in the United Kingdom at the University Press, Cambridge

Typeface Monotype Sabon 10/13pt   *System* QuarkXpress® [SE]

A catalogue record for this book is available from the British Library

Library of Congress Cataloguing in Publication data

The Cambridge companion to Ben Jonson / edited by Richard Harp and Stanley Stewart.
p. cm. – (Cambridge companions to literature)
Includes bibliographical references and index.
ISBN 0 521 64113 6 (hardback) ISBN 0 521 64678 2 (paperback)
1. Jonson, Ben, 1573?–1637.   2. Dramatists, English – Early modern,
1500–1700 – Biography.   I. Title: Companion to Ben Jonson.   II. Harp, Richard
III. Stewart, Stanley, 1931–   .   IV. Series

PR2631 .C35 2000
822′.3–dc21
[B]   00-08900

ISBN 0 521 64113 6 hardback
ISBN 0 521 64678 2 paperback

CONTENTS

NOTES ON CONTRIBUTORS

DAVID BEVINGTON is the Phyllis Fay Horton Professor in the Humanities at the University of Chicago, where he has taught since 1967. His studies include *From "Mankind" to Marlowe* (1962), *Tudor Drama and Politics* (1968), and *Action Is Eloquence: Shakespeare's Language of Gesture* (1985). He is also the editor of *Medieval Drama* (Houghton Mifflin, 1975); *The Bantam Shakespeare* (in 29 paperback volumes, 1988); and *The Complete Works of Shakespeare* (HarperCollins, 1992 [updated, Longman, 1997]), as well as the Oxford *1 Henry IV* (1987), the Cambridge *Antony and Cleopatra* (1990), and the Arden *Troilus and Cressida* (1998). He is the general editor of the Revels Student Editions, and is an editor of the Revels Plays and of the forthcoming *Cambridge Edition of the Works of Ben Jonson*.

MARTIN BUTLER is Professor of English Renaissance Drama at the University of Leeds. He has recently edited *Re-Presenting Ben Jonson: Text, History, Performance* (Macmillan, 1999), and, with Ian Donaldson and David Bevington, is a general editor of the forthcoming *Cambridge Edition of the Works of Ben Jonson*.

IAN DONALDSON is Fellow of King's College and Grace I Professor of English, Cambridge University. He has edited Jonson's poetry and other writings for Oxford University Press, and is a general editor of the *Cambridge Edition of the Works of Ben Jonson*. He is currently completing a life of Ben Jonson for Oxford University Press.

RICHARD DUTTON is Professor of English and Associate Dean for Research in the Faculty of Arts and Humanities at Lancaster University. He is the author most recently of *Ben Jonson: Authority: Criticism*, and has also been invited to edit Jonson's *Epicœne* for the Revels Plays. He has also written *Ben Jonson: to the First Folio* and *Mastering the Revels: the Regulations and Censorship of English Renaissance Drama*.

ROBERT C. EVANS is University Alumni Professor at Auburn University at Montgomery. His books include volumes on Ben Jonson, Frank O'Connor, Kate Chopin, short fiction, and the Renaissance poet Martha Moulsworth.

RUSS MCDONALD is Professor of English at the University of North Carolina at Greensboro and the author of *Shakespeare and Jonson/Jonson and Shakespeare*. Among his other publications are editions of four plays in the new Pelican Shakespeare series, *Shakespeare and the Arts of Language* (forthcoming from Oxford), and the widely adopted *Bedford Companion to Shakespeare*.

LEAH S. MARCUS is Edwin Mims Professor of English at Vanderbilt University. Her books include *Childhood and Cultural Despair* (1978), *The Politics of Mirth* (1986), *Puzzling Shakespeare* (1988), *Unediting the Renaissance* (1996), and *Queen Elizabeth I: Collected Works* (co-edited with Janel Mueller and Mary Beth Rose, 2000).

JOHN MULRYAN is Distinguished Professor of English at St. Bonaventure University and editor of *Cithara*. His books include *Milton and the Middle Ages* and, most recently, *Through a Glass Darkly: Milton's Reinvention of the Mythological Tradition*. He has also recently completed a translation of Natalis Conti's *Mythologiae, sive Explicationis Fabularum*.

STEPHEN ORGEL is the Jackson Eli Reynolds Professor of Humanities at Stanford. His most recent book is *Impersonations: The Performance of Gender in Shakespeare's England* (Cambridge, 1996). He has edited Jonson's masques for the Yale Ben Jonson, and *The Tempest* and *The Winter's Tale* for the Oxford Shakespeare.

JAMES A. RIDDELL is the co-author, with Stanley Stewart, of *Jonson's Spenser: Evidence and Historical Criticism* and has published two dozen articles in journals such as *The Library* and *Studies in Bibliography*. Most recently he has published "Jonson and the Blushing Maid" in *English Language Notes*.

SARA VAN DEN BERG is Associate Professor of English at the University of Washington. She is the author of *The Action of Ben Jonson's Poetry*, and of essays on Shakespeare, Jonson, Dekker, Milton, Keats and Freud.

R. V. YOUNG is Professor of English and Director of Graduate Programs in English at North Carolina State University. He is co-founder and co-editor of the *John Donne Journal* and has served as President of the John Donne Society. His most recent books are *At War with the Word: Literary Theory and Liberal Education* (ISI Books, 1999) and *Doctrine and Devotion in Seventeenth-Century Poetry* (Boydell & Brewer, 1999).

PREFACE

Although the contributors in this volume are Jonson specialists, this book is not an encyclopedia of accepted wisdom in Jonson studies. These critics might not even agree that consensus on this complex figure is a desirable goal. Raised the stepson of a bricklayer, Ben Jonson, whose career as a writer spanned the reigns of Elizabeth I, James I, and Charles I, became the most visible poet of his age, honored more than even William Shakespeare, whom he admired just "this side of idolatry." In many ways, Ben Jonson is the literary figure of the greatest centrality of his time. He began his career in the last decade of Elizabeth's reign, was the dominant writer for the stage in the Jacobean period, and went on writing well into the reign of Charles I. He died in the year that Milton's *Lycidas* appeared in a volume of verse commemorating the death of a fellow student at Cambridge. During that forty-year literary career, Jonson took a hand at writing tragedy as well as comedy, for which he is largely remembered, and in which he was a great innovator. In poetry, he wrote in virtually every received genre and mode – so successfully, in fact, that an entire generation of poets sought to associate their names with his style. Jonson's versatility was never at the expense of his intensity and combativeness, which mark many of his social and professional relations. Ben Jonson was not only long-lived, but complex: bricklayer, artisan, artist, poet, playwright, writer of masques, translator, literary critic, scholar, moralist, criminal, prisoner, editor, husband, father, drunk, Protestant, Catholic, traveler, tutor, actor, opportunist, court entertainer, brawler, antiquarian, book-collector, book-seller, irrepressible reader, loyal friend, relentless foe. So if these essays seem to move off in different, even contradictory, directions, we need to remember the variegated life and interests of the subject, Ben Jonson.

Without any claim, then, to a definitive treatment of Ben Jonson, this volume undertakes a fresh introduction to Jonson's literary world, his achievement, and his impact. First, contributors lay out what is known of his life as others saw it and as we see it represented in his work. Since Jonson was a man of the theatre, contributors describe the London theatres of his times, as well as the city and court that sponsored them, and the circle of playwrights with whom Jonson worked, drank, and competed. We know that, during the sixteenth and seventeenth centuries, actors and theatres were viewed with suspicion, unless the actors happened to be aristocrats performing masques or entertainments for privileged audiences. So Jonson's professional relations to the court are, in this context, as important as his acquaintance with London. Then, too, as anyone who has read "An Execration upon Vulcan" will recall, Jonson was a man of learning, who thought of books as an integral part of friendship and conversation. Jonson's achievement in satire is very much a part of the swiftly changing world of London, the lively new theatre, and Jonson's erudition. With these contexts in mind, contributors discuss Johnson's major comedies, his minor plays, his understanding and employment of the related arts, and his relationship to William Shakespeare.

Since, above all, Jonson thought of his poetry as his likeliest claim to inclusion in that pantheon with such poets as Horace, Martial, Catullus, and Persius, the volume includes a generous treatment of "Jonson's Poetry." In his famous 1616 Folio edition of his Works, we can see Jonson's ambition to place his literary efforts in the tradition of classical authors. Jonson's interest in what we call the "classics" is integral to his understanding of his poetic vocation. So contributors discuss Jonson's editorial practices, the Renaissance understanding of the classical writers so important to Jonson's conception of his literary vocation, as well as his mastery of the classical languages. In Jonson's literary criticism, many of the themes already established converge; Jonson thought proper judgment in reading integral to achievement as a poet, and his erudition served as the keystone of his critical theory. Although the designation "Sons of Ben" is almost synonymous with "Cavalier Poets," in the end, Jonson was remembered through the ensuing centuries as a successful dramatist in the satiric (moral) mode.

The editors wish to thank the staffs of the British Library and the Huntington Library for their help in obtaining materials for this book. We also thank Joe McCullough, John Bowers, and John Ganim for their support, as well as the Center for Advanced Research at the University of Nevada, Las Vegas (Ron Smith, Director) and the Research Committee of the Academic Senate at the University of California, Riverside. Jon Bauch provided editorial help of many different kinds. Our thanks also to the anonymous readers of the Cambridge University Press, who helped shape this project at an early stage, and to the reader who reviewed so expertly the final draft of the manuscript. Susan Watkins, our copyeditor, was careful and always helpful, and Victoria Cooper was a patient, sympathetic, and always intelligent editor, for all of which we are very grateful. Margaret Harp and Barbara Stewart were, as always, crucial in their forbearance and understanding of the project.

ABBREVIATIONS

The following abbreviations are used in referring to Jonson's works:

Alch.	*The Alchemist*
Cat.	*Catiline*
Conv. Dr.	*Conversations with William Drummond of Hawthornden*
EMI	*Every Man in his Humour*
EMO	*Every Man out of his Humour*
Epig.	*Epigrams*
For.	*The Forest*
NI	*The New Inn*
P.H. Barr.	*The Speeches at Prince Henry's Barriers*
Queens	*The Masque of Queens*
Sej.	*Sejanus*
S. of N.	*The Staple of News*
Und.	*The Underwood*
UV	*Ungathered Verse*
Volp.	*Volpone*

Editions of Jonson

Donaldson	*Ben Jonson*, edited by Ian Donaldson (Oxford: Oxford University Press, 1985).
HS	*Ben Jonson*, edited by C. H. Herford and Percy and Evelyn Simpson, 11 vols. (Oxford: Oxford University Press, 1925–52).

CHRONOLOGY

1572	Born in Westminster, a month after the death of his father; his mother remarries a bricklayer.
1588	Leaves Westminster School, where he had studied with the famous teacher, William Camden.
1591–2	Enlists as a soldier in Holland and Belgium, where he kills an enemy in single combat in front of both armies.
1594	Marries Anne Lewis.
1597	Acting in and writing plays by this date for Philip Henslowe. Imprisoned for his share in a lost play, *The Isle of Dogs*.
1598	Imprisoned for killing the actor Gabriel Spencer in a duel but released when he claims "benefit of clergy" (he is able to recite a Bible verse in Latin); is converted to Roman Catholicism while in prison, most likely by the Jesuit priest Father Thomas Wright, and remains a Catholic for twelve years. *The Case Is Altered* *Every Man in his Humour*
1599	*Every Man out of his Humour*
1600–1	"War of the Theatres" with playwrights Thomas Dekker and John Marston. *Cynthia's Revels* (1600) *Poetaster* (1601)
1601	Paid by producer Henslowe for additions to Thomas Kyd's *The Spanish Tragedy*.
1603	Death of Queen Elizabeth; accession of James I. Death of son Benjamin from the plague. Accused by the Earl of Northampton of popery and treason and called before the Privy Council. *Sejanus* *The Entertainment at Althorpe* *A Panegyre*

xiv

1604	*King's Coronation Entertainment*
	The Entertainment at Highgate
1605	Gunpowder Plot; Jonson offers to gather information for Lord Salisbury about the Plot but is ultimately unable to do so.
	Eastward Ho! (collaboration with George Chapman and Marston; authors imprisoned for politically unwise satire against the Scots).
	The Masque of Blackness (begins Jonson's association with architect Inigo Jones).
1606	*Hymenæi*
	Barriers
	The Entertainment of the Two Kings at Theobalds
	Volpone
1607	*The Entertainment of King James and Queen Anne at Theobalds*
1608	*The Masque of Beauty*
	The Haddington Masque
1609	*Epicœne*
	The Masque of Queens
1610	*The Alchemist*
	Prince Henry's Barriers
1611	*Oberon, the Fairy Prince*
	Love Freed from Ignorance and Folly
	Catiline
1612–13	Travels to France as tutor to Sir Walter Raleigh's son.
	Love Restored (1612)
1613–14	*A Challenge at Tilt* (December/January)
	The Irish Masque (29 December, 3 January)
1614	*Bartholomew Fair*
1615	*Mercury Vindicated from the Alchemists at Court*
1616	Granted a hundred-mark pension by the King.
	Works published in a Folio edition; contains poetry collections.
	Epigrams and *The Forest* in addition to plays.
	The Golden Age Restored
	Christmas, his Masque
	The Devil Is an Ass
1617	*Lovers Made Men*
	The Vision of Delight
1618	Walking trip to Scotland, where he visits William Drummond and others.
	Drummond makes a record of their conversations.
	Pleasure Reconciled to Virtue

	For the Honour of Wales
1619	Honorary degree of Master of Arts from Oxford.
1620	*Pan's Anniversary*
	The Entertainment at Blackfriars
1620–3	Deputy Professor of Rhetoric at Gresham College, London.
1621	*News from the New World*
	The Gypsies Metamorphosed
1622	*The Masque of Augurs*
1623	His personal library and manuscripts destroyed by fire.
	Time Vindicated
1624	*Neptune's Triumph*
	The Masque of Owls
1625	Death of King James; accession of King Charles I.
	The Fortunate Isles
1626	*The Staple of News*
1628	Jonson suffers a stroke that paralyzes him; appointed City Chronologer.
1629	*The New Inn*
1630	Annual pension increased to a hundred pounds and a tierce of royal sack.
1631	*Love's Triumph Through Callipolis*
	Chloridia
1632	*The Magnetic Lady*
1633	*The King's Entertainment at Welbeck*
	A Tale of a Tub
1634	*Love's Welcome at Bolsover*
1637	Dies in Westminster, August 6, and is buried in Westminster Abbey. A marble plaque marking his burial spot is inscribed "O rare Ben Jonson."
	The Sad Shepherd
	Mortimer his Fall
1638	Posthumously published book of poetic tributes to Jonson entitled *Jonsonus Virbius*.
1640	A second Folio edition of Jonson's *Works* is published, including the poetry collection, *The Underwood*, assembled by his literary executor Sir Kenelm Digby.

I

SARA VAN DEN BERG

True relation: the life and career of Ben Jonson

Because Ben Jonson creates such a powerful representation of himself in his poetry and in the prologues to his plays, he seems to stand before us a stable and knowable self. Abraham van Blyenberch's painting of Jonson in the National Portrait Gallery shows a man alone, without any symbolic accoutrements. Jonson's enormous head and shoulders fill the canvas: there is nothing to see but Jonson, plainly dressed, large featured, deep eyed, craggy faced. To describe Jonson's life means to fill in the blank background of the canvas, to show all we can of the relationships that created and constituted what Jonson terms the "gathered self." Even a brief sketch of his life requires attention to the way relationships were crucial to him, both in his life and in his work. There are few personal lyrics among his poems, no soliloquies in his plays: his is an art of community and contest. It is also a professional art: Jonson was the first Englishman to earn his living as a writer, exploiting every form of the literary medium to address private, public, and courtly audiences. This brief account of his life will focus on his relationships with his family, friends, rivals, patrons, and audience, setting his works in that dynamic context.

Born in 1572, Jonson rose to prominence as a playwright and man of letters, only to lose popularity, suffer a stroke, and die in relative obscurity in 1637. Little is known about his family beyond what William Drummond records in their *Conversations* (1619):

> His grandfather came from Carlisle and he thought from Annandale to it; he served Henry VIII, and was a Gentleman. His father lost all his estate under Queen Mary; having been cast in prison and forfeited, at last turned minister. So he was a minister's son. He himself was posthumous born a month after his father's decease; brought up poorly. (Donaldson 600)

Of his mother only one incident is reported in the *Conversations*. Jonson, Chapman, and Marston were imprisoned for writing "something against the Scots" in *Eastward Ho!*, and it was feared "they should then had their ears cut and noses." When the three men were released unharmed, Jonson feasted all his friends, and "at the midst of the feast his old mother drank to him, & show[ed] him a paper which she had, if the Sentence had taken execution, to have mixed in the prison among his drink, which was full of lusty strong poison. And that she was no churl, she told she minded first to have drunk of it herself" (Donaldson 601). The bond between mother and son, it seems, had endured despite her marriage to a bricklayer, perhaps Robert Brett (Warden and Master of the Tile and Bricklayers Company), whose trade the boy Ben "could not endure."[1] Jonson married Anne Lewis in 1594, when he was only twenty-two years old and halfway through his loathed apprenticeship as a bricklayer. Their first child, Benjamin, was born in 1596; by that time Jonson had terminated his apprenticeship and found employment as a journeyman player. By 1599, when Anne gave birth to Joseph, their second child, Jonson had seized the opportunity to pursue a new and risky career as a playwright, and had already been imprisoned for his part in writing *The Isle of Dogs*. Their third child, Mary, born in 1600, lived only six months. Jonson's tender epitaph describes her as "the daughter of their youth" (*Epig.* 22) and implies that something of their youthful exuberance and hope died with her. We hear no more about Anne's tears, but only Jonson's gruff comment to Drummond that "she was a shrew, yet honest" – faithful despite the five years he was absent from her in the house of Lord d'Aubigny (HS 1:139). Jonson not only lost his father but his firstborn son as well. According to Drummond, Jonson was away from home when the plague broke out in 1604, just as King James was entering England for his coronation, and the poet had a vision of his eldest son "w[i]t[h] the mark of a bloody cross on his forehead, as if it had been cutted w[i]t[h]a sword." The next day "comes th[e]r[e] letters from his wife of the death of th[a]t boy in the plague. He appeared to him, he said, of a manly shape, and of th[a]t growth that he thinks he shall be at the resurrection" (Donaldson 601). Jonson expressed his enormous sorrow in an epitaph for his son, exhausting all the familiar consolations and crying out, in a pun that expresses both the fullness of his grief and the futile wish he could somehow escape it, "Oh could I lose all father now" (*Epig.* 45). By the time he visited Drummond, Jonson lived alone, depending on friends for comfort and community. The *Conversations with Drummond* begin with gossip about his friends and comments about the London literary scene; the intimate revelations about his family come in the center of the text; and subsequent comments indicate Jonson's withdrawal into "narratives of great ones" and bawdy jokes. Although the organization of the *Conversations* may be Drummond's design, it is also plausible to speculate that Jonson's most personal revelations came in the midst of the two men's encounter, and that Jonson then pulled back into impersonal commentary, perhaps realizing that Drummond was not especially sympathetic to him.

Drummond's own assessment of Jonson is less than admiring:

> He is a great lover and praiser of himself, a contemner and scorner of others, given rather to lose a friend than a jest, jealous of every word and action of those about him (especially after drink, which is one of the elements in which he liveth), a dissembler of ill parts which reign in him, a bragger of some good that he wanteth, thinketh nothing well but what either he himself, or some of his friends and countrymen hath said or done. He is passionately kind and angry, careless either to gaine or keep, vindicative, but, if he be well answered, at himself.
>
> (Donaldson 611)

Drummond's comments make it clear that the encounter between the two men was an abortive attempt at friendship. Despite Drummond's strictures, his remarks indicate that Jonson greatly valued friendship, and indeed he was the first English poet to make that theme central to his art. As a man without the advantages of family, rank, or privilege, Jonson considered friendship not only an ideal but a necessity. Among his friends he counted men who were his fellow writers, men who led the intellectual life he valued, and powerful aristocratic men and women who were his readers and patrons. The loss of a friendship or the failure of a relationship roused him to anger, and he made art of rage and betrayal, of envy and contempt, as well as of affection and respect.

Jonson's friends included many of the finest writers of his day: privileged men and women who circulated their works in manuscript, professionals who depended on public sales and private patronage, and scholars who published books (both their own and the translations of others) in order to disseminate humanist learning. Jonson devoted one cluster of his epigrams and many poems in *The Forest* to the Sidney–Pembroke circle, the most important aristocratic circle of literary patrons in England at the time. Jonson praises the Countess of Rutland, daughter of Sir Philip Sidney, for her poetry (*Epig.* 79; also *For.* 12 and *Und.* 50); Lady Mary Wroth, author of *Urania* and *Pamphilia to Amphilanthus* (*Epig.* 103, 105; also *Und.* 28); the Countess of Montgomery, to whom Wroth dedicated *Urania* (*Epig.* 104); Sir Robert Wroth (*For.* 3), husband of Lady Mary Wroth; William Herbert, Earl of Pembroke, who was Lady Wroth's lover and the "Amphilanthus" of her sonnet sequence (*Epig.* 102); Sir Robert and Lady Barbara Sidney, whose estate is celebrated in "To Penshurst" (*For.* 2); their eldest son, Sir William Sidney, who died before Jonson's birthday ode to him was published (*For.* 14); Edward Herbert, later Lord Herbert of Cherbury, a poet and philosopher best known today as the brother of the poet George Herbert (*Epig.* 106); and Benjamin Rudyerd (*Epig.* 121, 122, 123), poet and friend of Pembroke. Another of Pembroke's friends, the pastoral poet William Browne, is also the subject of a complimentary epigram (*UV* 21). Other poems praise John Donne

3

(*Epig.* 23) and his circle, notably Christopher Brooke (*UV* 19), Sir John Beaumont (*UV* 32), Sir Henry Goodyere (*Epig.* 85, 86) and Lucy Harington, Countess of Bedford (*Epig.* 76, 84, 94). Goodyere and the Countess of Bedford are praised as readers who value learning and appreciate sophisticated poetry; not writers themselves, they are friends to poetry and poets. Late in his life, Jonson praised another woman, Mrs. Alice Sutcliffe, for her *Divine Meditations* (*UV* 40), as well as several young writers, including Joseph Rutter (*UV* 42) and Robert Dover (*UV* 43). Jonson composed complimentary epigrams to his fellow professionals as well – Francis Beaumont (*Epig.* 55), John Fletcher (*UV* 18), George Chapman (*UV* 23), Richard Brome (*UV* 38) – and to the actor Edward Alleyn (*Epig.* 89), who acted major parts in Jonson's plays; to the musician Alphonso Ferrabosco (*Epig.* 130, 131), who composed the music for Jonson's masques; and to the lyricist-translator Edward Filmer (*UV* 33). Katherine Duncan-Jones has recently discovered an epitaph Jonson wrote for Thomas Nashe,[2] and one of Jonson's most important poems is the tribute to William Shakespeare prefixed to the First Folio (*UV* 26).

The first group of poems returns repeatedly to issues of the poet's sincerity and the subject's superiority; in the poems to fellow professionals Jonson copes with his own envy and with the general question of the artist's vulnerability. In at least one of these poems, "The Vision of Ben Jonson, On the Muses of His Friend M. Drayton" (*UV* 30), it is impossible to decide the poet's answer to his initial premise: "It hath been questioned, Michael, if I be / A friend at all; or, if at all, to thee." Jonson had competed with Drayton for patronage, and the poem is saturated with a sense of tension, resentment set against affection. Jonson praises Drayton's book, yet labels it a "strange Mooncalf." Rather than exorcizing his envy, as he does in most poems to friends and rivals, Jonson transfers it to the world which envies him and must judge him. Envy remains, and the poem concludes with what seems self-serving rather than selfless praise.

The third group of complimentary poems is addressed to scholars, men of humanist learning who translated classical texts and published their own scholarly works. These scholars include the historian Henry Savile (*Epig.* 95); Clement Edmondes, author of *Observations* upon Caesar's *De Bello Gallico* (*Epig.* 110, 111); Thomas May, translator of Lucan's *Pharsalia* (*UV* 29); and John Selden, a noted jurist and scholar of Hebraic law (*Und.* 14). Jonson praises these men for their knowledge, wisdom, and good judgment. He does not presume to be their rivals, so envy is not an issue in these poems.

It must be noted that these three groups were not entirely separate. Many members of the Pembroke circle, the newly professional writers, and the men of learning were associates at the Inns of Court. Members of the legal community known to associate with Ben Jonson include Benjamin Rudyerd, Thomas Overbury, and Sir John Beaumont of the Middle Temple; Francis Bacon and

Henry Goodyere of Gray's Inn; Sir John Harington, Christopher Brooke, and John Donne of Lincoln's Inn; and John Selden and Francis Beaumont of the Inner Temple.[3] A two-part poem (*Und.* 52), written to Sir William Burlase, should be linked to the legal community among whom Jonson found so many friends. Herford and Simpson mistakenly conclude that Jonson addresses the Sir William Burlase who was Sheriff of Buckinghamshire. It is far more likely that the poem was written to his son, a man of Jonson's own age who lived in London and associated with many of Jonson's friends.

Jonson's poems to all three groups develop the theme of friendship. To the Countess of Bedford he sends a copy of Donne's satires, commenting that "Rare poems ask rare friends." Or to another friend, "Yet when of friendship I would draw the face, / A lettered mind and a large heart would place / To all posterity: I will write *Burlase*." He celebrates other friendships as well: of John Selden and Edward Hayward, of Lucius Cary and the late Henry Morison (*Und.* 70). Indeed, the words "friend" and "friendship" in their various forms occur more than 124 times in Jonson's poetry. He works out the idea most thoroughly in his long poem, "On Inviting a Friend to Supper" (*Epig.* 101), developing Erasmian ideals of liberty, honesty, and simplicity as the foundation of true friendship. Every guest can speak freely; no spies will betray a confidence; nothing will be done or consumed to excess. He argues for personal integrity and mutual trust as well, most powerfully in the "Epistle Answering to One that Asked to be Sealed of the Tribe of Ben": ". . . First give me faith, who know / Myself a little. I will take you so, / As you have writ yourself" (*Und.* 47).

The "Tribe of Ben" epistle grows out of another situation too frequently the subject of his poetry: failed friendship. Drummond's criticism of Jonson was not entirely off the mark. Jonson in fact had a quick temper, which could escalate to violence and simmer over years. As a young man, Jonson killed another actor, Gabriel Spencer, in a brawl that probably had its origin when the two men were imprisoned for their part in *The Isle of Dogs* (now lost). Jonson was brought to trial, and narrowly avoided execution by pleading "benefit of clergy" (because he could read the prescribed "neck verse," a passage from Psalm 51). His later quarrel with two other playwrights, John Marston and Thomas Dekker, escalated onto the stage in the so-called War of the Theatres. Dekker resented the murder of Gabriel Spencer and attacked Jonson in *Satiromastix*. In *What You Will*, Marston ridiculed Ben Jonson, who responded by ridiculing Marson in *Every Man in his Humour* and again in *Cynthia's Revels*. These quarrels were at once personal and professional; putting their rivalries on stage was good box-office if nothing else. Failed friendships seem more painful in his poems to patrons and collaborators. "To my Muse" relates Jonson's rueful awareness of misplaced trust and unwarranted respect (*Epig.* 65). When he was disappointed in a woman, his contempt spilled into misogyny: "A woman's friendship! God whom I trust in, / Forgive me this one foolish deadly sin" (*Und.* 20). Feeling betrayed, he condemns his own failure as well as woman's perfidy: "Knew I all this afore? Had I perceived / That their whole life was wickedness, though weaved / Of many colours; outward, fresh from spots, / But their whole inside full of ends and knots?" This general rage against womankind yields to a specific attack: "Do not you ask to know her; she is worse / Than all the ingredients made into one curse, / And that poured out upon mankind, can be!" Jonson appropriates conventional misogynist attacks on Eve to attack a specific woman, most likely Cecilia Bulstrode, whom he mocks elsewhere in a bitter epigram (*Epig.* 79). She was a close friend of the Countess of Bedford, and Jonson seems to have changed his opinion, or at least thought better of it by the time Cecilia Bulstrode died, when he composed a generous, complimentary epitaph (*UV* 9).

The failure of his friendship with Inigo Jones caused Jonson his greatest anger and disappointment. The two men collaborated on masques at court, Jones designing sets and costumes, Jonson writing the script. Each man rose to prominence during the reign of King James (1603–25), but Jones slowly superseded the poet. In "An Epistle Answering to One that Asked to be Sealed of the Tribe of Ben" (*Und.* 47), composed in 1623, Jonson works through his feelings about Jones. Jones had excluded him from planning the festivities to welcome the Spanish Infanta to the English court. Although the Spanish Infanta never came and her planned marriage to Prince Charles never occurred, Jonson knew the slight to him was "a blow by which in time I may / Lose all my credit with . . . [the] animated porcelain of the court" (51–3). Jonson's quarrel with Jones reflected both personal animosity and the different aesthetic values of the two men. Jonson privileges the ear over the eye, language over spectacle.[4] He derides spectacle as transient and deceptive illusion, and makes Jones' sets into a metaphor for false friendship, contrasting "square, well-tagged, and permanent" friendships to those "built with canvas, paper, and false lights, / As are the glorious scenes at the great sights," all too soon revealed as mere "Oily expansions, or shrunk dirty folds" (64–8).

Although Jonson uses the "Tribe of Ben" epistle to overcome his bitterness and take a chance on commitment to a new friendship, he held a deep grudge against Jones for the rest of his life. After the two men quarreled again in 1631 because Jonson's name appeared first on the title page of a court masque, *Love's Triumph through Callipolis*, Jonson attacked Jones and his "mighty shows" in two vitriolic poems, "An Expostulation with Inigo Jones" (*UV* 34) and "To Inigo, Marquis Would-Be A Corollary" (*UV* 35). He also wrote caricatures of Jones into three works. The Master of the Revels required that Jonson omit "Vitruvius Hoop" from *A Tale of a Tub*, but Jonson contrived to keep "In-and-In Medlay," another gibe at Jones, in the script. He also inserted "Coronel Vitruvius" into *Love's Welcome at Bolsover* and "Damplay" into *The Magnetic Lady* (HS X.342n).

6

The "Tribe of Ben" epistle, like another long poem of 1623, "An Execration upon Vulcan," can be read as a poem of loss and resolution. Just as Jonson had suffered a blow at court, so he had also suffered the devastating loss of his extensive library and working papers in a fire. Jonson composed a third long poem in 1623, the eulogy for Shakespeare prefatory to the First Folio. Here, Jonson subdues his own values in order to praise a rival he respected. When these three long poems are taken together, the first can be characterized as a poem of introspection, the second of bitter recrimination, the third of admiration. In all three poems, Jonson takes the occasion of loss to spell out his own literary values, developing a humanist theory of art as high culture, both moral and learned.

The foundation of Jonson's humanist values can be traced to his education at Westminster School, made possible by its famous headmaster, the antiquarian scholar William Camden. Jonson thanks Camden in a lavish epigram:

> Camden, most reverend head, to whom I owe
>> All that I am in arts, all that I know,
> (How nothing's that?) to whom my country owes
>> The great renown and name wherewith she goes;
> Than thee the age sees not that thing more grave,
>> More high, more holy, that she more would crave.
> What name, what skill, what faith hast thou in things!
>> What sight in searching the most antique springs!
> What weight, and what authority in thy speech!
>> Man scarce can make that doubt, but thou canst teach.
> Pardon free truth, and let thy modesty,
>> Which conquers all, be once overcome by thee.
> Many of thine this better could than I;
>> But for their powers accept my piety.   (*Epig.* 14)

Jonson's comments about himself and what he learned, from arts to piety, frame his praise of Camden. The poet not only compliments his teacher, but by moving from pride to piety imitates Camden and enacts the education Camden gave him. The poet's highest compliment to Camden consists of dramatizing the Camden in himself. Camden is celebrated as the perfect teacher in style (grave, high, holy), knowledge (name, skill, faith, and research), and presentation (weight and authority in speech). Camden is also celebrated for his particular work. As an antiquarian, he sought to locate signs of the Roman occupation of Britain, and in two books – *Britannia* and *Remains of a Greater Work Concerning Britain* – popularized the Latinized name of the nation. The Latinized name, which can be traced in the writings of Cicero, Pliny, and Tacitus, testifies to the significance of Camden's work: he searches the "antique springs" of Roman history in England to show the continuity of the ancient and modern empires.

The method Camden applies in archaeology Jonson attempts in poetry: he appropriates two of Pliny's letters to shape his own complimentary poem. Jonson quotes Pliny's praise of Corellius, a learned man who advised him and helped him advance in society.[5] He also echoes Pliny's praise of Titius Aristo, an intimate friend.[6] Translating the spirit as well as the text of Pliny, Jonson affirms not only his debt to Camden but also their mutual link to the Roman past. Pliny's friendships live again in Jonson's poem, and Jonson's poem receives from Pliny the weight of authority and tradition.

Belief in the continuity of classical past and English present was not only a humanist ideal Jonson learned from Camden but also the governing principle of his dramatic practice.[7] The only one of his early plays to survive, *The Case is Altered*, was performed by the Children of the Chapel and published a decade later in quarto. Although it hardly seems stageworthy today, it shows the characteristics of his subsequent work: classical plotting, an Italian setting, effusive comic prose. Because Jonson did not include the play in the 1616 Folio edition of his works, critics have been somewhat hesitant to attribute it to him; those who do often dismiss the play as an early trial run, a work Jonson would just as soon have forgotten.[8] However, a reading of the play indicates that Jonson was following the fashion of the 1590s (as did Chapman and Shakespeare) by combining Plautine comedy, an Italian setting, and native English morality and jokes. Jonson develops his plot from two Plautine comedies, *Captivi* and *Aulularia*, and sets the action in Milan. *Captivi* provided sentiment, *Aulularia* satire. In Jonson's play, Count Ferneze of Milan has two daughters and a son named Paulo. A second son, Camillo, had been lost in infancy. When Paulo is captured on the battlefield, Camillo (in the guise of a commoner, Gasper) is about to exchange him for a French prisoner of war. Ultimately, of course, Camillo is recognized and both sons are reunited with their father. *Aulularia* provides a plot in which Jaques, a miser, has stolen gold from his French employer and moved to Milan with his daughter Rachel. Two servants, Juniper and Onion, steal his gold, and he is tricked into revealing his crimes. Every "case" or set of relationships in the play is "altered" as identities are restored and truth recognized. Gold is "muck," virtue golden. Like Shakespeare in *The Comedy of Errors*, Jonson doubles and redoubles his story and characters. What is most unusual is the invention of a second male friendship, between Paulo and a new character, the villainous Angelo, which ends in betrayal. Like so many Jonsonian comedies, *The Case is Altered* begins in lack and explodes into excess: plot is piled on plot, words on words.

In subsequent plays, Jonson slowly moves away from combining classical sources, Italian settings, and English jokes. *Every Man in his Humour* and *Every Man out of his Humour* were revised to transfer the action from Italy to London. In *Cynthia's Revels*, the raucous and gritty world of London constantly impinges on the world of courtly myth. *Poetaster* is set in the Rome of Horace and Ovid, without Italian decadence. *Volpone*, on the other hand, is immersed in Italian vice without a hint of Roman glory. Jonson's great city comedies – *Volpone*, *Epicœne*, and *The Alchemist* – were framed by two Roman tragedies, *Sejanus* (1603) and *Catiline* (1611). In *The Alchemist*, and in his subsequent city comedies *Bartholomew Fair* and *The Devil is an Ass*, Jonson turned from classical plots and Italian settings to place the action entirely and uproariously in the London just outside the theatre door. The combination of classical sources and Italian settings, raised to the level of myth, Jonson mostly transferred to his court masques. Despite his reverence for classical art, Jonson was a man of London. He knew its streets and its citizens, its noise, density, and energy. His audiences in the public theatres most wanted to see the image of themselves and their folly he set forth, and for that they would eagerly pay.

Jonson's relationship to his audience is made part of theatrical experience through his vivid prologues. *Every Man in his Humour* begins by admitting the poet's "need" as his motive for writing the play. *Volpone* promises to "mix (the poet's) profit with your pleasure." *The Alchemist* offers the audience a vision of London and its "natural follies": "No clime breeds better matter, for your whore / Bawd, squire, impostor, many persons more . . . which have still been subject for the rage / Or spleen of comic writers." *The Devil is an Ass*, in which the young devil Pug finally pleads to return to Hell – for Hell is but grammar school to London's university of vice – begins with the players' attack on the audience: "Anon, who worse than you the fault endures / That you yourselves make, when you will thrust and spurn, / And knock us o' the elbows, and bid, turn." The playwright's only hope, in *Bartholomew Fair*, is an elaborate contract with the audience, the first of the many "warrants" that structure the action and relationships in the play.

A comprehensive vision of the many audiences Jonson chose for his plays, poems, and masques is constructed in the 1616 Folio edition of his works. A man of the new print culture as well as of court entertainments and the popular stage, Jonson carefully edited his works, dedicating plays to specific people (William Camden, Lady Mary Wroth, Lord d'Aubigny, even "the two famous Universities"). After dedicating his *Epigrams* to the Earl of Pembroke, Jonson instructs the "Reader" in his first poem, and scatters through the collection poems on good and bad readers, good and bad writers. The court masques, originally visual spectacles, become dense texts, heavily annotated to explicate their visual and verbal symbolism.[9]

Just as Jonson felt betrayed by Inigo Jones, so he often felt betrayed by the audience, especially when they rejected *Sejanus* and *Catiline*, classical tragedies closely in accord with his humanist values, and later when *The New Inn* was

9

mocked off the stage. As early as *Poetaster*, the figure of the Author vows to "sing high and aloof, / Safe from the wolf's black jaw, and the dull ass's hoof." Jonson later made those lines the conclusion of "An Ode. To Himself," in which he berates himself for taking the unworthy judgments of the audience so seriously that he is unable to write, "Buried in ease and sloth" (*Und.* 23). His greatest rage against the audience, however, comes out in a second "Ode. To Himself" after the failure of *The New Inn* (1629), which followed the lukewarm reception of *The Staple of News* (1626). The old jokes did not work any more, and Jonson offered little the crowd wanted. Now he genuinely feared the loss of his career, protesting that the audience preferred garbage and junk food ("Husks, draff to drink, and swill") to true art. Rather than abandon writing, however, he advises himself to return to classic art, to "thine own Horace." Instead of trying to please the crowd, he vows to "sing / The glories of the King," so that everyone will know "no palsy's in [my] brain."

He did suffer from palsy, having had a stroke the year before. He subsisted on a small allowance from the King's Treasury (for which he occasionally had to beg) and a small stipend from the City of London. Although he received a gift of money from King Charles and saw his royal pension increased, his salary as City Chronologer was terminated late in 1631. It was only restored at the King's request in 1634. During these final years, three of his greatest plays were revived by the King's Men: *Volpone* (1630), *Every Man in his Humour* (1631), and *The Alchemist* (1631). He wrote one new play, *The Magnetic Lady*, and completed *A Tale of a Tub*. He also wrote two masques and two court entertainments, including his final public work, *Love's Welcome at Bolsover* (1634).

Jonson's final relationships were with the court and, especially, with his Catholic patrons, Sir William Cavendish and Sir Kenelm Digby. Jonson had converted to Catholicism in 1598 while he was in jail; in 1606 he and his wife had been officially charged with recusancy. Although he stopped practicing his Catholic religion, a number of poems in *Epigrams* and *Underwood* were written to praise English Catholics. It is widely recognized that he returned to Catholicism late in his life, and three "Poems of Devotion" at the beginning of *Underwood* have been dated after 1626.[10]

Jonson had a close relationship with the Cavendish family, for whom he wrote several poems, and with Digby, for whom he wrote *Eupheme*, a baroque sequence of poems commemorating Lady Venetia Digby. These poems show that Jonson was still able to write poetry in new ways, while retaining his old values. Just as he had argued the value of words over images in his quarrel with Inigo Jones and in his more congenial poem to Sir William Burlase, Jonson here stages a contest between himself and "the painter" (Van Dyck) who had been commissioned to paint two portraits of Venetia Digby. Unlike Jones, Van Dyck saw no threat in Jonson; at least, no response to Jonson's challenge has survived.

Digby seems to have been pleased both by Van Dyck's paintings and by Jonson's poems.

A poignant letter from Jonson to William Cavendish, Earl of Newcastle, dated 1631, shows the way the poet was forced to seek patronage during his last years:

I my self being no substance, am fain to trouble you with shadows; or (what is less) an apologue or fable in a dream. I being struck with the palsy in the year 1628, had by Sir Thomas Badger some few months since, a Fox sent me for a present; such creature, by handling, I endeavored to make tame, as well for the abating of my disease, as the delight I took in speculation of his Nature. It happened this present year 1631, and this very week, being the week ushering Christmas, and this Tuesday morning in a dream, (and morning dreams are truest) to have one of my servants come up to my Bedside, and tell me, Master, Master the Fox speaks. Whereat, (me thought) I started, and troubled, went down into the Yard, to witness the wonder; There I found my Reynard, in his tenement the Tub, I had hired for him, cynically expressing his own lot, to be condemned to the house of a poet, where nothing was to be seen but the bare walls, and not any thing heard but the noise of a saw, dividing billets all the week long, more to keep the family in exercise, then to comfort any person there with fire, save the paralytic master; and went on in this way as the fox seemed the better fabler of the two. I, his master, began to give him good words, and stroke him: but Reynard barking, told me those would not do, I must give him meat; I angry, called him stinking vermin. He replied, "Look into your cellar, which is your larder too, you'll find a worse vermin there." When presently calling for a light, me thought, I went down, & found all the floor turned up, as if a colony of moles had been there, or an army of salt-peter men; Whereupon I sent presently into Tuttle Street, for the King's most excellent mole-catcher to relieve me, & hunt them. But he when he came and viewed the place, and had well marked the Earth turned up, took a handful, smelt to it, and said, "Master it is not in my power to destroy this vermin; the K. or some good man of a Noble Nature must help you. This kind of mole is called a *want*, which will destroy you, and your family, if you prevent not the working of it in time, and therefore God keep you and send you health.

The interpretation both of the fable and dream is, that I waking do find want the worst, and most working vermin in a house, and therefore my noble lord, and next the King, my best Patron, I am necessitated to tell it you. I am not so impudent to borrow any sum of your Lordship, for I have no faculty to pay: but my needs are such, and so urging, as I do beg, what your bounty can give me, in the name of good letters, and the bond of an ever-grateful and acknowledging servant.

To your honor

Westminster. 20. Dec   B. Jonson

1631

Yesterday the barbarous Court of Aldermen
have withdrawn their Chanderly Pension,
for Verjuice, & Mustard.[11]

This letter shows none of the independence characteristic of Jonson's early epigrams. The only traits that remain are humor (in the devising of the "dream") and plain speaking (in its rueful "interpretation").

Jonson portrays himself in this letter as a shadow, a man without substance, wasting away. This is the last phase in his portrayal of himself – first as a man of intellect and judgment (in *Epigrams*), then as a man of letters (of "character"), then as a man massively physical, "fat and old, / Laden with belly" (*Und.* 56). It is in the third phase of his career that he depicts his body, which serves at once as a barrier to and a test of his Humanist ideals. The only portrait to depict Jonson late in life is an image recorded by David Piper.[12] In this "begging portrait," the poet holds the manuscript of some Skeltonic verses asking the clerk of the Exchequer to forward his overdue pension (*Und.* 57). In the lower left-hand corner is an inkstand, decorated with the figure of Fortune, which underlines the diminished condition of the poet and the humiliation that attended it. The portrait offers an image of the writer whose autonomy was compromised by his dependency as a man, forced to seek aid from his friends and patrons.

Throughout his career, Jonson celebrated and mocked the human body, a case that can and cannot be altered. That body became for him the necessary representation of the self. Two models of self contended in the Early Modern era: self as moral essence and self as social construction. In Jonson's works, both are figured as the body, and are set in tension through tricks of naming, deformity, cross-dressing, disguise and projection, all designed to augment the body and to satisfy its desires. Because the tension between these two models of selfhood is intensified rather than resolved in the ending of his major plays, the desires of the audience are also intensified rather than satisfied. The epilogue to *The Devil is an Ass*, for example, declares that the play may or may not end in a feast with the Poet, as the audience shall choose. Jonson's body was not thematized in the 1616 Folio of his works; indeed, he seems invisible in those works, present only in his assertions and judgments. In the latter half of his life, when Jonson took his own body as an image of himself, his ideal of a constant self was challenged by the model of the constructed self, constructed by enemies as well as friends. In psychoanalytic theory, the body is the primary locus of self, the basis for a stable personal identity. Yet the body constantly changes – growing, decaying – and responds to the body politic that surrounds and constructs it. Jonson took pride in being constant to himself despite the vagaries of fortune, but was also forced to acknowledge the necessity of relationship. As a writer, he needed a supportive and understanding audience. As a man, he needed the support of the society he judged.

Although Jonson had no one to care for him before he died except one paid servant woman who did little but drink with him, all the gentry and men of letters in London turned out for his funeral, and his friends arranged to have him buried in Westminster Abbey.[13] The Sons of Ben issued a copy of memorial poems, *Jonsonus Virbius*, comparing their literary father to the nephew of Daedalus, who was transformed into a partridge – a bird who chose to stay close to the ground rather than soar on dangerous wings.[14] Close to the ground he may have stayed, but by doing so he could keep in close touch with his world and his friends. In *Discoveries*, the reading notes he kept all his life, Jonson praised the community of writers, living and dead, as "the learned and the good." He kept that community alive, citing and imitating their works. A true relation of his life means telling the story of his relationships with his predecessors, with his contemporaries, and with the subsequent writers who took him as their poetic father.

NOTES

1 C. H. Herford, Percy and Evelyn Simpson, *Ben Jonson* (Oxford: Clarendon Press, 1925–1952), I. 139. On Thomas Brett, see W. David Kay, *Ben Jonson: A Literary Life* (London: Macmillan, 1995), 1–2.

2 Katherine Duncan-Jones, "Johnson's Epitaph on Nashe," *Times Literary Supplement,* 7 July 1995 (No. 4814), 4–7.

3 David Riggs, *Ben Jonson: A Life* (Cambridge, MA: Harvard University Press, 1989), 56.

4 See D. J. Gordon, "Poet and Architect: The Intellectual Setting of the Quarrel between Ben Jonson and Inigo Jones," *Journal of the Warburg and Courtauld Institutes* 12 (1949), 152–78.

5 Pliny, *Ep.* IV.xvii.4. Hutchinson, vol. I, 328–9: "Observatur oculis ille vir, quo mneminem aetas nostra graviorum, sanctiorem, subtiliorem denique tulit." (The image of that excellent person, than whom this age has not produced a man of greater dignity, rectitude, and penetration, rises to my mind's eye.)

6 Pliny, *Ep.* I. xxii. 2–3. Hutchinson, vol. I, 78–9: "nihil est enim illo gravius, sanctius, doctius; ut mihi non unus homo, sed litterae ipsae omnesque bonae artes in uno homine summum periculum adire videantur. Quam peritus ille et private iuris et publici! Quantum rerum, quantum exemplorum, quantum antiquitatis tenet!" (Virtue, knowledge, and good sense shine out with so superior a luster in this excellent man that learning herself and every valuable endowment seem involved in the danger of this one man. How consummate his knowledge of the private and public laws! How much he knows of things, precedents, history!)

7 An excellent introduction to Jonson's humanism is provided by H. A. Mason in the final chapter of *Humanism and Poetry in the Early Tudor Period* (London: Routledge and Kegan Paul, 1959). See also Katharine Eisaman Maus, *Ben Jonson and the Roman Frame of Mind* (Princeton: Princeton University Press, 1984).

8 John J. Enck, *Jonson and the Comic Truth* (Madison: University of Wisconsin Press, 1957), 21–32.

9 See *Ben Jonson's 1616 Folio,* ed. Jennifer Brady and W. H. Herendeen (Newark: University of Delaware Press, 1991) and Richard Newton, "Ben Jonson and the (Re)invention of the Book," in *Classic and Cavalier: Essays on Jonson and the Sons of Ben,* ed. Claude J. Summers and Ted-Larry Pebworth (Pittsburgh: University of Pittsburgh Press, 1982), 31–58.

10 Ian Donaldson, ed., *Ben Jonson: Poems* (Oxford: Oxford University Press, 1975), 125n, 127n.
11 HS I. 213–14.
12 David Piper, "The Development of the British Literary Portrait up to Samuel Johnson," *Proceedings of the British Academy* 54 (1968), 51–106, plate 9.
13 Riggs, *Ben Jonson: A Life*, 348.
14 Enck, *Jonson and the Comic Truth*, 3–4.

2

MARTIN BUTLER

Jonson's London and its theatres

Jonsonian topographies

Ben Jonson was one of the more traveled dramatists of the English Renaissance. He crossed the Channel twice, as a footsoldier in the Low Countries in the 1590s, and as chaperone for the visit of Sir Walter Raleigh's son to Paris in 1613. At home his most notable journey was his 1618–19 walk to Edinburgh and back, during which he laid plans for a Loch Lomond pastoral and a poem on the wonders of Scotland. Among other exploits, he visited Sir Robert Cotton in Huntingdonshire in 1603, and turned up in Rutland in 1621.[1] But it is entirely characteristic that while away from the city, his imagination harked back to it. In Scotland, he dubbed Edinburgh "Britain's other eye" (HS 1: 143), implying that England's capital was eye number one. Incidents from the Paris trip became source material for *Bartholomew Fair*. At Cotton's house, he was unable to forget the danger his family stood in from the plague, and was troubled by dreams of home (HS 1: 139–40). For Jonson was a writer who, however extensive his engagement with wider spheres, could not disengage himself from the city. His drama is deeply invested in the rhythms, meanings and structures of the metropolis, and his works are imbued with and shaped by urban topographies: the urban experience was the single most determining factor of his career. If Sir Thomas More was the first major English writer to be preoccupied with the idea of the city, Jonson is the second – only that imaginary space to which More gave the title "Utopia" Jonson called by its real name, "London."

Jonson was not born in London but in its sister city, Westminster. Here the English court had its principal residence, parliament and the law courts were held, and, in Westminster Abbey, monarchs were crowned. Hartshorn Lane, his childhood home, was at Charing Cross, where the Thames bends sharply eastwards. Westminster School, where he studied under Camden, lay in the Abbey precincts, and for the last decade of his life he lived close by, in the house (according to Aubrey) "under which you pass, as you go out of the churchyard into the old palace" (HS 1: 179). Westminster was the political heart of the nation, and as the writer of masques staged in the Banqueting House, client of the powerful and panegyrist to the Stuart state, Jonson must have taken this symbolic geography for granted. His masque *Time Vindicated* (1623) has the Banqueting House as the backdrop to its action, and he himself would be buried in the Abbey.

And yet much of Jonson's professional and social life was conducted a mile or two to the east, in the commercial city to which Westminster was neighbor and where he lived during his maturity. For two periods he resided inside London's wall as the houseguest of his patron Lord Aubigny, and unlike other dramatists, for whom London was often merely a lodging, he acquired city property, signing the epistle to *Volpone* "From my house in the Blackfriars." The Mermaid Tavern, which Francis Beaumont identified as the scene of meetings memorable for wit and drink, stood in Cheapside, at the very heart of commercial London. The Devil Tavern, where the Apollo room became a meeting-place for Jonson's circle, was at Temple Bar, close by the Inns of Court, at which many of his acquaintances lived. Jonson needed to be based here for the sake of proximity to theatres and court – the Exchequer Receipts for 1617 include payments to a messenger who summoned him from Blackfriars to Whitehall for business probably connected with a masque (HS 1: 232) – but his geographical situation expressed more than merely professional convenience. It allowed him an inner flexibility of position, an ability to set urban and court spaces against one another while reserving final allegiance to neither. This dialectic between the two cities is foundational to his writing. London and Westminster are the geographic and imaginative poles between which his life and works oscillate.

Though Jonson lived in London, he tried not to seem of it. Blackfriars lay within the walls, but it had long been a liberty, a territory that for historical reasons was outside mayoral jurisdiction. As a consequence, it had some legal and social autonomy, and here the King's Men were able to open an indoor playhouse despite the customary civic resistance to such institutions. *The Alchemist* celebrates this anomaly: it is set in Blackfriars, the same district in which the play was actually being performed, and makes complex self-referential fun with a group of cozeners who, though stereotypical urban products, are gloriously exempt from the normal restraints of city life. For Jonson the city was a vast reservoir of folly and crime, a panorama of enterprise and overreaching endlessly suitable for satirical dissection, and his situation in the liberties expressed a characteristic attitude of detachment from a metropolitan scene in which he was, nonetheless, a participant. However, these symbolic coordinates were not stable on the ground. In 1608 – a year after the *Volpone* epistle and two years before *The Alchemist* – James made a deal with the city that restored Blackfriars to London's jurisdiction, and the district's technical marginality was abrogated.[2] Despite this change, in *The Alchemist* Jonson presented the plague and the consequent absence of the gentleman in whose house the cozeners operate as confirming Blackfriars' status as an authority-free zone, allowing him to sustain his skepticism towards city institutions. At the end of the play, order is restored not by the local officers but by Lovewit's return, and Lovewit's main qualification for social leadership is his willingness, when it suits his interests, to be morally accommodating. He has all the urbanity of a gentleman accustomed to modern town life, but is mercifully free from civic bigotry or self-importance.

In Jonson's Folio volume of *Works* (1616), London is kept at a distance. The dedications to the Folio's component texts parade his links to gentlemen, scholars and great aristocrats, and the volume's organization leads towards the masques and entertainments, the court festivals which it situates as the culmination of his career. Yet Jonson's involvement with London was more intimate than the Folio acknowledges. His first substantial panegyrical work was not a Whitehall masque but a civic commission, the royal entry of March 1604, the occasion on which James I took symbolic possession of his principal city. For this Jonson designed three of the triumphal arches under which the King passed, and wrote accompanying speeches. Admittedly, he transformed the civic event after the manner of Europe's avant-garde festival culture, sidelining Dekker's and Middleton's arches by turning the stiff vernacular pageantry that he inherited into a sophisticated and dazzlingly learned celebration of the overwhelming power of Stuart kingship. His arches welcomed James as a peaceful monarch but also as a conqueror, who parades through the city in imperial triumph and lays it prostrate before his will. James' entrance to London is seen as irresistibly potent, an act of penetration which the city answers with testimonies of burning desire. The citizens themselves are represented in condescending terms. Their flood of zeal is praised – they "thirst to drink the nectar of thy sight," James is told (HS 7: 93) – but their acclamations seem redundant noise in comparison with the profound meanings which the poet identifies in this historical conjuncture, and to which only he and the King have access.[3] Yet while Jonson's words belittle the individual citizens, the corporation itself is aggrandized, and as expressions of civic goodwill towards the new monarch his arches must have seemed appropriately magnificent. The first arch presented James with the characters of Thamesis and the City's Genius, and it was crowned with a steepled and turreted representation of London as a new imperial city, a recovered Rome. Not surprisingly, when in 1625 the city companies needed arches to welcome the next Stuart monarch – an entry which in the event was canceled and from which no texts survive – it was Jonson to whom they again turned.[4]

Other texts which Jonson excluded from the canon suggest that his links with the city were more sustained than he chose to admit. In 1604 he was paid £12 – a substantial sum – for devising the pageant celebrating the election of Sir Thomas Lowe as lord mayor. In 1607, the Merchant Taylors' company gave him

£20 for a royal entertainment, which involved a ship suspended from the roof of their hall and a child dressed as an angel (HS 11: 586–7). In 1609, the Earl of Salisbury opened his shopping center in the Strand, Britain's Burse, with a presentation to the King written by Jonson.[5] And in 1616 Jonson prepared a show of dyers, clothdressers, and German craftsmen as a gift to the King from the powerful merchant Sir William Cockayne, whose monopoly of the English broadcloth trade was currently under attack.[6] Jonson included none of these in his collected works. He preferred to leave the impression that his career had developed without the city hackwork produced by dramatists who were more attuned to London's commercial ideology, such as Middleton, Dekker, and Heywood. Yet the *Entertainment at Britain's Burse*, the only one of these shows to survive, celebrates the expansion of British trade into Asian markets, and dwells approvingly on the luxury goods that could be bought from Salisbury's marvelous mall. The other shows could scarcely have avoided praising the values of industry. Evidently Jonson owed more than he cared to publicize to that civic enterprise from which, in his printed works, he tended to distance himself. In later life the connection continued. He seems to have lectured at London's Gresham college (HS 11: 582–5), and in 1628 was appointed City Chronologer, in succession to Middleton. Although his pension was withdrawn in 1631 because he failed to produce anything in London's honor, prompting him to exasperated splutterings about "the barbarous Court of Aldermen" and their "chanderly pension, for verjuice and mustard" (HS 1: 214), the aldermen must once have regarded him as a suitable candidate for patronage. Certainly he could celebrate civic institutions when he wanted. His "Speech according to Horace" (*Und.* 44) commemorates the activities of the trained bands at the Artillery Yard in 1626, and though it has often been deemed a satire, it praises city valor in terms that are, I believe, largely free from irony. In this, as in other matters, Jonson's satirical perspective on London concealed profoundly divided attitudes. Though ideologically at odds with the city's puritanical ethos, he was professionally and personally a product of modern civic life.

Giddy humor

In 1600, London was easily the biggest city in England, and was still growing at astonishing speed.[7] A century earlier, in comparison with other European conurbations, it had been a moderately sized and relatively unimportant town of some 60,000 souls. By 1600, it had more than trebled to 200,000 inhabitants, and by 1700 had more than doubled again, to around half a million. This was twenty times larger than Norwich, England's next most sizable city, and twice the size of all her other cities combined. To sustain this rate of increase, there had to be a net population influx – i.e. total expansion after subtraction of wastage through deaths, often well above average in the plague-ridden streets – of 8,000 persons a year, a figure equivalent to half the annual population increase for the whole of England and Wales. London was also expanding faster than the nation, for the percentage of the population living there doubled between 1600 and 1700: England was a small country increasingly dominated by its capital. Well before Jonson's birth, it was already acquiring the suburban sprawl that caused concern to mayors and monarchs. Upriver, towards Westminster, the streets were lined with palaces which bespoke the wealth of England's aristocracy, but northwards into Clerkenwell and eastwards towards Wapping were expanding communities where poverty was rife and where plague, when it struck, was especially virulent. Within the walls, the streets were densely populated, and congestion was increased by the subdivision of houses into tenements and by opportunistic development of the remaining empty spaces. Although the central parishes tended to be most prosperous, the social composition of the urbanized area as a whole was highly mixed. Rich and poor lived in immediate proximity, hovels and well-to-do households crowding together within a single neighborhood. The biggest houses were not segregated into their own quarters, and even the poorest parishes had some wealthy families taking advantage of cheaper land. Yet for all its populousness, London was geographically compact, and open countryside was in easy reach. The Tower in the east was only thirty minutes' walk from Ludgate in the west. Moorfields, where Brainworm accosts Knowell disguised as an unemployed soldier (*EMI* 2.5), was just outside the walls, and the rural villages around which the action of *A Tale of a Tub* ambles were only two or three miles to the north-west.

London was expanding so fast because it uniquely combined so many economic and political functions. In the nation at large, population growth and a shortage of land were pushing migrants towards the towns, and in the metropolis this created a huge pool of casual labor (or vagrants and criminals, depending on your perspective). Higher up the scale, apprentices flooded in, since London was the main center for vocational training. A bewildering variety of trades and crafts were pursued here, mostly in small, pre-industrial units operating out of domestic settings. As a major port, London had long outstripped Bristol as the country's main commercial outlet, controlling access to northern Europe, and attracting huge financial investments and reservoirs of cash. By the mid sixteenth century it had a virtual monopoly of the cloth trade, dominating the nation's principal product and export. In wider markets its global status was signaled by the building of Gresham's Exchange (1570), and by the establishment of trading companies to Russia (1555), the Levant (1581), the East Indies (1600), and Virginia (1606). The city oligarchy included some of the wealthiest men in the kingdom, and the publication of John Stow's *Survey of London* (1598) testified to an emerging confidence in the benefits of enterprise.

London also profited from being near the political and legal institutions based at Westminster. Since this was where the sovereign lived and where parliaments and the law courts convened, any gentleman with business to be done, careers to follow, cases to try, or wives to find needed to be in this neighborhood. England's legal community centered on the Inns of Court, where at any one time up to a thousand gentlemen might be in residence. Some of these were training seriously as lawyers, while others were just enjoying the sophisticated social and cultural life that the Inns fostered. Jonson was well known in these circles, and counted lawyers like John Selden and Richard Martin as his friends. When he dedicated *Every Man Out of his Humour* to the Inns, he called them "the noblest nurseries of humanity and liberty in the kingdom" (HS 3: 421). Even more influential in drawing social elites to London was the presence of the monarch, around whom congregated courtiers, gentlemen, functionaries, and the hundreds of service personnel that inevitably followed on. Elizabeth had an entourage of about 1,000 servants, while James and Charles, with their families, had well over twice that number. Under the Stuart monarchs the court went less frequently on progress, and this encouraged a significant proportion of the aristocracy to reside at London on a seasonal or semi-permanent basis, a development that meant the creation of households, lifestyles, and consumer industries to match. During Jonson's lifetime, increasingly large numbers of Londoners were engaged in supplying the new world of fashion, with its taste for luxury goods, pictures, gossip, gaming and entertainment. Genteel families were more frequently coming up for the pleasures of the season, and London had begun to signify as a tourist destination, visited simply for its own sake. These were habits that impacted on the urban topography, for during the seventeenth century a separation gradually arose between the city proper and the "Town," the fashionable community that gravitated towards elegant quarters in what is now the West End. Here, in Drury Lane and the Strand, midway between Whitehall and Cheapside and upwind of the city smoke, more select accommodation was beginning to appear. In the 1600s the Earl of Salisbury financed a series of luxury developments around the Strand, including Britain's Burse, for which Jonson wrote his entertainment. In *Epicœne*, Sir Amorous La-Fool lodges in the Strand (HS 5:174). Twenty years later, the Earl of Bedford's development of Covent Garden would be celebrated in plays by Richard Brome and Thomas Nabbes.

Jonson's London contemporaries were thus becoming habituated to one of the characteristic modes of modern life. The first English generation fully to enjoy the opportunities and disadvantages of a complex metropolitan coexistence, they were newly absorbing the material, social and psychological consequences of urbanity, and Jonson's plays, preoccupied as they are with pleasures and follies in a city setting, may be read as foundational texts in the emergence of a modern urban consciousness. It is important to realize that such a consciousness was only beginning to develop, as London's civic culture remained provisional and many-voiced. The pageants, histories and panoramas which celebrated city institutions, and the mayoral and monarchical proclamations complaining of its many inconveniences – vagrancy, crime, congestion, jerry-building, prices, plague – were not a unified discourse, and lagged behind the developments they sought to address. Early modern London also lacked the sedentarism of twentieth-century cities. With significant parts of its population only seasonally resident, and with such a high proportion of youthful incomers, many of its people were insecurely rooted, making it seem a city of migrants, pregnant with transformational possibilities. It is hardly surprising that Jonson's drama seized upon alchemical transformation as its characteristic metaphor for urban experience. His plays explore modes of behavior and forms of language that must have seemed only just in the process of crystallizing.

Jonson was certainly antagonistic to many aspects of London. His plays are merciless towards puritanism, double-edged on economic accumulation, caustic about gossip and the printing of "news," and withering over get-rich-quickery. The ideology of thrift, industry and godliness held few attractions for him. And yet the London setting is the ground of all his major comedies and the necessary precondition for their mechanics. If, in Gabriele Jackson's formulation, "a Jonson comic plot is a group of subplots collected in one place,"[8] it requires an urban world where suitably random gatherings of people can congregate. Unlike the situations of intrigue or romance, in which protagonists struggle with corporately inhabited structures of family or inheritance, Jonson's plots put together characters who are largely strangers to each other. A typical Jonson comedy consists of a fantastic project or magnetic center that draws together an assembly of individuals who have no other commonality or collective purposes, and who come from far-flung quarters of their play's world. They comprise a community merely by virtue of being in the same place on the same day, and their choices affect each other only casually. Whatever their individual successes or disasters, the life of the city continues unchanged. Where family ties do exist, as in *Bartholomew Fair*, events tend to dissolve them: the bonds uniting the Littlewit and Overdo households prove desperately frail when subjected to the confusions of the marketplace. More usually it is the separation of characters and the juxtaposition of unrelated types so characteristic of early modern London on which Jonson's distinctively urban comedy depends. In *Every Man in his Humour*, Matthew is surprised to find the would-be gentleman Bobadil lodging in the house of the poor citizen Cob, while the merchant Kitely, unsettled by the guests his brother-in-law attracts to his house, feels as though the whole city were violating his privacy:

> He makes my house here common as a mart,
> A theatre, a public receptacle
> For giddy humour and diseased riot;
> And here, as in a tavern or a stews,
> He and his wild associates spend their hours
> In repetition of lascivious jests,
> Swear, leap, drink, dance, and revel night by night,
> Control my servants; and indeed what not? (HS 3: 324–5)

In this play the only unifying agent is Cob the water-bearer, who has ingress and regress in all households by virtue of his profession. The cityscape has no encompassing principle stronger than that lowest common denominator, water.[9]

If the city is fluid, labyrinthine and contingent, the plays themselves hold together by strictly observing the boundaries of the urban day. The pattern is established early on, in *Every Man In*. This play begins at sunrise, with (in the revised text) a letter calling Edward Knowell up to London from Hogsden, just outside the walls. In 1.4 it is six o'clock in the city, and Cob is doing his pre-breakfast run. In 1.5, Matthew forces Bobadill out of bed by visiting him at 6.30, rather earlier than he expected, and in 2.2 Kitely's bell rings to breakfast; in the following scenes, the Knowells traipse to the Old Jewry over the fields. At 3.3.4 it is midmorning, "Exchange time," and Kitely sets off to work, leaving a house where, much to his distress, unwanted visitors are beginning to gather. At one o'clock (4.6) Brainworm takes Formal off to make him drunk; an hour later (4.8), in Formal's clothes, he brings Knowell Senior a false message. After farcical consequences in the city streets, the cast gradually reassembles at Justice Clement's in the late afternoon. In 5.3, a wedding banquet is proposed, and in 5.5 Clement concludes events by inviting most of the participants to supper. No previous English comedy had been plotted with such nice attention to the clock, while Kitely, dithering helplessly between the conflicting calls of home, the Exchange and Justice Clement's, is a recurrent Jonson character, someone who has more business on his hands than he can possibly cope with. Subsequent plays reiterate this design, *Epicœne*, *The Alchemist*, and *Bartholomew Fair* repeating its dawn to dusk structure with the same temporal rigor and the same illusion of overload. As Anne Barton observes, the effect of these rhythms is to evoke, in unprecedented detail, "the life of a great mercantile Renaissance city."[10] Inevitably, Jonson's hyperrealism is merely conventional: the twelve hours that pass on stage do not correspond to three hours in the theatre. But his sensitivity to mechanical time and its consequences for human behavior testifies to a new understanding of city pressures, the subjection of city populations to stress and the rigidly demarcated passage of the hours. With their existence parceled out by bells and clocks, and with more demands on their attention than they can comfortably handle, his are England's first fictional characters to be alienated by urban life.

The great instance of alienation is, of course, Morose, that character who perversely lives in the city even though he is morbidly allergic to noise. As Leo Salingar has demonstrated, it is London itself that persecutes Morose. The traffic, the chatter, the eddying crowds of tourists, women, braveries and wits combine to make his a quintessentially urban torment.[11] But if Morose is incapable of feeling at home in London, the historic function of Jonsonian comedy was to naturalize the city, to develop collective forms of representation suited to a metropolitan society of increasing complexity and self-awareness. To this process, Jonson gave the name "humors." As described in *Every Man out of his Humour*, the project of humors characterization is to co-ordinate psychology with ethics by explaining eccentric behavior as a physiological imbalance crying out for adjustment. Humors allow an individual's actions to be critiqued in terms of interior deficiencies and redundancy. But as is evident in set-pieces like the Paul's Walk scene (*EMO* 3.1–3.6), what signals a Jonsonian humor is not in fact an ethical flaw but a social mannerism. A humors character is one who deviates from socially-constituted norms, and reproduces as an affectation the behavioral protocols that everyone else has learned but pretends to inhabit as if they were natural. In the Paul's Walk scene – virtually the first quasi-realistic pastiche of everyday conversation in an identifiable city setting in any English play, and certainly the most elaborate[12] – Londoners meet in the middle aisle of the cathedral to gossip, do business and exchange news. As they cross and recross apparently at random, anything approaching a plot is suspended. Instead, their persons are paraded as performances, exposing their social selves as constructions, and focusing attention on their different levels of skill at the game of good manners, from excess to incompetence to mastery. This offers a spectacle of identity not as a characterological given but as an endlessly renegotiated process, and it required a new order of engagement from its spectators. Also a society in a state of becoming, Jonson's audiences saw games being played out on stage in which they too were implicated, so that in judging his characters, they were passing judgment on themselves.[13] In this respect, his drama opened the way to a new relationship between London and its theatres. So often figuring as opposites in the discourse of the time, the city and the theatre were yoked in his plays into a profound and historically momentous symbiosis.

The loathed stage

If Jonson was more at home in London than his plays seem to imply, his discomfort with the playhouses themselves can scarcely be doubted. It has become commonplace to see him as a playwright deeply at odds with the medium in which he worked.[14] One of the stage's most effective defenders, he was also one of its fiercest critics, and much of his creative energy went on putting blue water between himself and the rest of London's dramatists. His prefaces, prologues and inductions do indeed constitute a foundational defense of stage practice. The most considerable body of English critical writing about the drama before Dryden, they were crucial in establishing London's theatres as a legitimate artistic medium. Yet Jonson was an effective apologist for the stage precisely because he so readily granted the case against it, eagerly conceding that much that passed for drama in his day was beyond redemption. Although he savaged the views of those who opposed the stage on ideological grounds, he did not extend this argument into a general defense of current theatre. On the contrary, his typical maneuver was to associate himself with the theatre's critics, seeing the enemy without as less problematic than the poetaster within. In *Bartholomew Fair*, the puppet's demonstration that he is sexless gives the *coup de grâce* to puritan complaints about the immorality of acting, but the show to which he belongs is desperately cheap and sordid. The epistle to *Volpone* warned that today's playwrights produced mostly bastard writings: "it is certain, nor can it with any forehead be opposed, that the too much licence of poetasters in this time hath much deformed their mistress" (HS 5: 17). The preface to *The Alchemist* affirmed that audience tastes were little better, for "now the concupiscence of dances and antics so reigneth, as to run away from nature and be afraid of her is the only point of art that tickles the spectators" (HS 5: 291). As for the players, Jonson's poem to Edward Alleyn (*Epig.* 89) enthusiastically commends his acting, but in language that effaces contemporary London and evokes the theatre of classical Rome. More typical are the inductions to *Cynthia's Revels* and *Bartholomew Fair,* which ironically suggest that at some performances the author or his man might be hanging around backstage, anxiously policing actors who, if left to their own devices, were likely to mess up.

At every point, then, Jonson's apology for his art was accompanied by an ingrained skepticism about the circumstances of its performance. To a considerable degree, though, his anxieties about his medium were responses to the everyday conditions of playwriting: much that seems idiosyncratic or personal in his attitude was symptomatic of larger tensions within the structures of the Elizabethan stage. Although he sought to distinguish his work from his rivals', he was deeply embedded in London's theatrical world, and was subject, like everyone else, to its opportunities and constraints. Having begun his career as a jobbing dramatist under the impresario Philip Henslowe, collaborating with working playwrights such as Chettle, Dekker and Nashe, he would necessarily have been hardened to hackwork. The distinguishing feature of the Elizabethan repertory system was the astonishing turnover of new plays that it consumed. Since each company staged a different play every afternoon, at any moment it had to have some three dozen plays ready to perform. Although popular titles were frequently staged over a long period, plays were not repeated on successive days as they are today, but were continuously alternated with one another. New plays were staged every two weeks or so, and shelf-life was often short (perhaps a third would still be in the repertoire next season). As a consequence, plays did not qualify in the developing category of literature. Around three thousand were written in the years 1560–1642 but only a sixth have survived,[15] and when published they appeared in cheap sixpenny quartos, often badly printed and visibly ephemeral – Sir Thomas Bodley specifically banned playbooks from his library at Oxford. Moreover, the crippling rate of turnover required a small factory of writers to satisfy it, who had to be capable of working collaboratively and at speed. Not all were as prolific as Thomas Heywood, who said he had a hand "or at least a main finger" in 220 dramas, but since in the 1590s Henslowe only paid £6 a play, it was necessary to write rapidly if one were not to starve. Little wonder that Jonson was anxious about being stereotyped as a hack, or that his relations with other playwrights often seem competitive and self-assertive.

At the same time, London's theatres were slow to achieve respectability. Throughout Jonson's life, the city authorities were never fully reconciled to the presence of the new playhouses near London, but distrusted them for bringing crowds together, seducing citizens from their work and, so they thought, attracting prostitutes and thieves. Actors lacked a recognized vocation – under the 1572 statute, players without proper licence were punishable as vagabonds – and the erection of theatres around London was deemed dangerous to civic order. As a consequence, playhouses had to be built in locations that were within reach of big audiences but outside the city jurisdiction. Their geographical segregation to the suburbs of Shoreditch, Clerkenwell and Southwark, or to the liberties where the Mayor's writ did not run, helped to intensify the perception that theatre was a marginal activity. The playhouses themselves were substantial, diverse, and sometimes unruly places. The amphitheatre or "arena" houses, for which *Sejanus, Volpone, Bartholomew Fair* and the early humor plays were written, had a top capacity of some 3,000 spectators, and their audiences seem to have been socially heterogeneous. Since entry to the arenas could be had for merely a penny (one paid more for a seat in the galleries), it was theoretically possible for all but the poorest to get in, and contemporary descriptions amply testify to the audiences' inclusiveness. Although not a representative cross-section of London's populace, they were a wide sample nonetheless: here gentry mixed with apprentices, students, artisans, citizens, city wives and daughters, and the atmosphere was occasionally riotous. Only after 1600, with the establishment of companies of boy actors at the smaller indoor playhouses where admission prices began at sixpence, did the audience profile start to change. Their clientele was socially more exclusive and had more advanced theatrical tastes, and this development was accelerated by the move of the King's Men into the Blackfriars playhouse (1609) and by the building of new indoor theatres for adult companies in Drury

Lane (1617) and Salisbury Court (1629). By Jonson's death, a significant differential had arisen between the sophisticated drama staged at the hall theatres and the more old-fashioned styles still current in the arenas.

For all Jonson's disrespect towards the contemporary theatre, his dramaturgy was brilliantly attuned to its resources. The amphitheatres consisted of tiered galleries arranged in a polygon around a central space partly open to the sky, and their stages were spacious but simple platforms thrust forward into the arena from one side of the round. Spectators sat in the galleries or stood around the platform in the yard, so that the players performed in the very middle of the audience, in a situation far removed from the naturalism of later proscenium-arch theatres. Any illusion of "real" place had to be created imaginatively, or by the movement on and off the stage of large props, such as Volpone's bed or the booths of Bartholomew Fair. Jonson matched the openness of these platforms with a stagecraft that was correspondingly flexible and dynamic. Some plays, such as *Every Man Out* and *Bartholomew Fair*, are tidal constructions. Presenting large casts that ebb and flow unpredictably, they are governed by the economy of the group: although individual characters seem to act autonomously, their self-will merely manifests the patterns of collective momentum. Other plays adopt a structure of frames nested within frames that takes advantage of the stage's spaciousness by juxtaposing contrasted sets of characters. In *Sejanus* and the humor comedies, much of the action is overseen by figures who stand on the sidelines and comment satirically on the action, presenters mediating between the play and the spectators. They make a structural principle out of Jonson's dictum that "life is like a play, where every man . . . is in travail with expression of another" (HS 8: 597). But such complex architecture was less well adapted to the indoor playhouses, where space was more constricted, the atmosphere more refined and the audience's encroachment more emphatic. The Blackfriars stage was only half the size of the Globe's, but Jonson turned this disadvantage to a virtue by exploiting the aesthetic advantages of proximity. In *Epicœne* (written for Whitefriars), Morose's peaceful world is invaded by tormenting crowds, while in *The Alchemist* (a Blackfriars play) the effect is doubled since events are restricted to a single room and time is calibrated by the minute. Jonson had a predilection for unified structures, but such enclosed forms were ideally suited to the confined spaces of the indoor houses. The first English dramatist to discover the structural power of claustrophobia, his art was unlocked by the physical conditions for which he wrote.

Yet despite these successes, Jonson's attitude towards the theatre in which he worked remained deeply defensive. When discussing his own work, he repeatedly sought to emphasize its distance from the common currency of the professional stage, and even at the end of his career – when his status as a legitimate writer had long been established – signs of discomfort continued to surface. The epistle to *Volpone* carefully staked out Jonson's difference from other dramatists, calling him not a playwright but a "poet" and censuring the "ribaldry, profanation [and] blasphemy" produced by others (HS 5:18). In the *Eastward Ho!* affair, he lamented to Salisbury that he and Chapman had been imprisoned for so worthless thing as a play: "the word irks me, that our fortune hath necessitated us to so despised a course" (HS 1: 195). In 1619 he proudly told Drummond that playwriting had earned him less than £200 (HS 1: 148). One might have expected these anxieties to ease once Jonson was writing for the genteel hall theatres, but in fact the most spectacular loss of confidence was still to come, when *The New Inn* was hissed at the Blackfriars. Jonson's less than humble response was the thundering ode "Come leave the loathed stage," which accused the select Blackfriars audience of malice, pride, fastidiousness, ignorance and faction, and dismissed them as unworthy of his art. "Envy them not," the ode consoles its author, "their palate's with the swine" (HS 6: 492). Wounded *amour propre* must have motivated this astonishing diatribe against the playwright's own public, but it also demonstrates how fundamentally Jonson's ideal conception of himself conflicted with the commercial demands of the theatrical marketplace. His image of the author as an independent figure, an isolated producer working in protected space, not merely distanced him from the playhouses that he served but situated him as fundamentally at odds with their dangerous collectivity. Foregrounding the writer's demeaning subordination to the will of paying customers (envisaged by this definition as always being prone to misjudge), it was about as far as one could get from the prevailing conditions of the contemporary stage.

In the "Apologetical Dialogue" to *Poetaster*, the "Author" claims that "if I prove the pleasure but of one, / So he judicious be, he shall be alone / A theatre unto me" (HS 4: 324). To a considerable extent, Jonson did achieve a position of relative autonomy within the London theatre world. Unlike Shakespeare, who wrote two plays a year for the Chamberlain's Men, or Brome, who in the 1630s was contracted by the Salisbury Court for three, Jonson produced a play every two years or so and had them staged by five companies in all. G. E. Bentley's analysis of playwrights' careers classes Jonson as an "unattached professional," writing slowly and distributing his plays widely.[16] Yet the Apologetical Dialogue's fantasy of total independence from the market could never be completely realized: except perhaps at court, there never could be a theatre of one. On the contrary, the commercial theatre that Jonson represented as so threatening to his art was in fact its very ground and condition. The career about which he was so anxious was made possible only by the opportunities that the London theatres uniquely provided, and his plays are unimaginable without that large commercial public from which he was so eager to separate himself. Consequently Jonson's work expresses most fully the contradictions inherent in the new career of urban playwright. Hostile to the increasingly consumerist culture of his time yet empowered by the opportunities its markets created, he was perhaps more sensitized than any other contemporary writer to the ways the drama both unsettled the city's commerce and colluded in it.

Jonson's comedies are obsessed with situations in which business and theatre intersect. In *Volpone*, *Bartholomew Fair* and *The Alchemist*, the plays' rogues are also their greatest entertainers, whose skills at self-enrichment cannot be disentangled from their theatrical power. The artistry in illusions that makes Volpone and Face dangerous is also what makes them rich, and their theatrical abilities implicitly link their criminal gettings to the playhouses' own accumulation of profit. At the end of *The Alchemist*, Face apologizes to the spectators for his lies, but promises that if they forgive him, the "pelf" he has accumulated "rests / To feast you often, and invite new guests" (HS 5: 407). His joke implicitly acknowledges the continuity between his gains within the play and the income the King's Men have drawn from the regular customers who pay to see them act. No less than the gulls, the Blackfriars spectators have been alchemized, but what is crime in Face is, in the actors, only good business. The paradox that this joke proclaims is the subversive similarity between the world of the theatre and the world of the city, that for all their surface oppositions, moneymaking and art were profoundly linked. Although the playhouses of Jonson's London were geographically marginal, they were symbolically central. Joint-stock companies that sold a specialized product to mass audiences and depended for their prosperity on low wage costs and fluid capital, they were typical outgrowths of the developing city economy, reproducing in their operations that civic ethos to which they seemed such a threat. It was one of Jonson's main achievements to have intuited these complex subterranean connections, and explored so fully the market's theatrical potential and cultural consequences. In doing this, he was – if not always willingly – helping his contemporaries to internalize the ideologies of modern urban life.

NOTES

1 Changes made to *The Gypsies Metamorphosed* between its performances at Burley and Belvoir indicate that Jonson must have been present.

2 Stephen Mullaney's argument, in *The Place of the Stage* (Chicago: University of Chicago Press, 1988), that London's relationship to its playhouses was a straight opposition between authority and liberty, center and margins, simplifies the situation: see D. Bruster, *Drama and the Market in the Age of Shakespeare* (Cambridge: Cambridge University Press, 1992), 9–10.

3 See my "'Servant but not slave': Ben Jonson at the Stuart court," *Proceedings of the British Academy*, 90 (1995), 65–93.

4 See O. P. Grell, *Calvinist Exiles in Tudor and Stuart England* (Aldershot, 1996), 174–82.

5 J. Knowles, "Jonson's *Entertainment at Britain's Burse*," in *Re-Presenting Ben Jonson: Text, Performance, History*, ed. M. Butler (London: Macmillan, 1999), 114–51.

6 N. W. Bawcutt, "Ben Jonson's drunken Hamburgians," *Notes and Queries*, 242 (1997), 92–4.

7 Figures are from L. Stone, "The residential development of the West End of London in the 17th century," in *After the Reformation*, ed. B. C. Malament (Manchester: Manchester University Press, 1980), 166–212. See also *London 1500–1700*, eds. A. L. Beier and R. Finlay (London: Longman, 1986), 9–13 and 37–59; N. G. Brett-James, *The Growth of Stuart London* (London: G. Allen & Unwin, 1935); and S. Rappaport, *Worlds within Worlds: Structures of Life in Sixteenth-Century London* (Cambridge: Cambridge University Press, 1989).

8 *Every Man in his Humour*, ed. G. B. Jackson (New Haven: Yale University Press, 1969), 2.

9 See Lorna Hutson, "The displacement of the market in Jacobean city comedy," *The London Journal*, 14 (1989), 1–16.

10 A. Barton, *Ben Jonson, Dramatist* (Cambridge: Cambridge University Press, 1984), 46.

11 L. Salingar, *Dramatic Form in Shakespeare and the Jacobeans* (Cambridge: Cambridge University Press, 1986), 175–88.

12 The sole precedent is in Gilbert Haughton's *Englishmen for My Money* (1598).

13 See Helen Ostovich, "'To behold the scene full': seeing and judging in *Every Man Out of his Humour*," in Butler, ed., *Re-Presenting Ben Jonson*, 76–92.

14 The classic account is Jonas Barish's *The Anti-Theatrical Prejudice* (Berkeley: University of California Press, 1982), 132–54.

15 A. Gurr, *The Shakespearian Playing Companies* (Oxford: Oxford University Press, 1996), 26–7.

16 G. E. Bentley, *The Profession of Dramatist in Shakespeare's Time* (Princeton: Princeton University Press, 1971), 30–2.

3

LEAH S. MARCUS

Jonson and the court

In dedicating the 1616 Folio version of *Cynthia's Revels* to the court, Jonson addressed that body as "A bountiful and brave spring" that "waterest all the noble plants of this island. In thee, the whole kingdom dresseth itself, and is ambitious to use thee as her glass. Beware, then, thou render men's figures truly, and teach them no less to hate their deformities than to love their forms; for, to grace there should come reverence; and no man can call that lovely which is not also venerable."[1] If, as Jonson claimed, the court nurtured and sustained the whole island, it would be impossible to overestimate the importance of his self-appointed role as court reformer. Throughout his career, though in varying modes and intensities at different times, he assigned himself the gargantuan and foolhardy task of critiquing the foibles and vices of the court.

Jonson lived most of his life in close proximity to the English court at Whitehall, and the court figures prominently in his writings. But physical proximity is not the same thing as access. The court can be defined variously: as a bureaucratic and ceremonial structure sometimes located at Whitehall but accompanying the person of the monarch from one royal seat to another; or as the social group of those who had regular access to the monarch, not only in the royal presence chamber, where access was relatively unrestricted, but in the privy chamber, to which entry was much more difficult. Or the court can be defined much more loosely as a network of affiliations and a culture generated specifically by or for the bureaucratic structure and the social group that were also called the court. Only in the third and most capacious sense can Jonson be regarded as having been close to the court, and even there, our perception of his proximity to power is often grounded less in historical realities than in his own imaginative rendering of them. To the extent that Jonson's writings convey a sense of intimacy with the monarch and chief courtiers, that intimacy is often a carefully modulated construction. Part of the fascination of Jonson's literary portrayals of the court, the monarch, and the English subject's relationship to both, derives from our recognition of a significant gap between the standard contemporaneous views of this triangulation and Jonson's configurings of it.

Jonson's first known foray into satire upon the manners of the court appears to have ended unhappily: when he was still in his early twenties he was briefly imprisoned for his part in the daringly scurrilous *Isle of Dogs* (1597). The text of this play is lost, but it is titled after an island in the Thames where Queen Elizabeth I kenneled her hounds, and probably suggested likenesses between the Queen's canines and her courtiers. Two years later Jonson had recovered sufficient reputation to have a play performed at court. In the first performance of *Every Man out of his Humour* in the public theatre (1599), a boy actor impersonating Queen Elizabeth evidently appeared on stage at the end, abruptly terminating the display of wayward humors in the body of the play and also the asperity of its satirist figure, Malicente, identified closely with Jonson himself. At the performance before Elizabeth during the revelry of the 1599–1600 holiday season, a similar ending must surely have made use of the presence of the Queen at the end: she is the bright "sun" and clear flood of silver water who purifies the passions of the satirist and her other malcontent subjects. Indeed, *Every Man Out* may have been the play the Queen attended in 1601 when she is reported to have visited Blackfriars after a private dinner at the Lord Chamberlain's.

Elizabeth was known for her ability to create instant rapport with the populace, of whatever station and calling. Her "Golden Speech" of a year later repeatedly and memorably invoked her forty-year love affair with her people, "for above all earthly treasures I esteem my people's love, more than which I desire not to merit." Its delivery was an elaborate choreography of mutual bowings and exchanges of adoring respect between the Queen and members of Parliament. At much the same time that *Every Man out of his Humour* was performed at court, Dudley Carleton, who was temporarily in attendance there, reported that the Queen "played the goodfellow amongst us these holy-days at dancings and music . . ."[2] That is not the monarch portrayed in *Every Man out of his Humour*. The Elizabeth who intervenes at the end of Jonson's play is a distant, aloof figure who reforms her subjects not through love but through intimidation, through a remote power accessible only to the extent that it is assimilated to natural forces like sun and water.

Cynthia's Revels, or the Fountain of Self Love, written shortly after *Every Man Out*, performed publicly by the Children of Queen Elizabeth's Chapel during fall, 1600, and performed at court during the 1600–1 holiday season, offers a more complex working of the relationship between Elizabeth and her courtiers. In this play the setting is prudently distanced to "Gargaphie," a valley and spring sacred to Diana, and Elizabeth is imagined as "Queen and Huntress chaste and fair," the virgin goddess Cynthia, whose court and revels, like that of the moon she personifies, are only of the night. In *Cynthia's Revels* Jonson continues to portray the Queen as aloof from her people, but she has both reason and a plan for a cure: her erstwhile favorite Acteon (an allegorical depiction of the Earl of Essex, who had earned the Queen's displeasure through his military failures in Ireland and his insolent obliviousness to royal commands) has been punished and his adherents have breathed "black and envious slanders" against the Queen in reaction. Elizabeth/Cynthia proclaims a "solemn revels" at which she will ameliorate the appearance of austerity and distance by opening her court to outsiders and gracing it with her presence.

But even with this scenario established, Jonson does not display the Queen in the intimate, loving interaction with her subjects for which she was famous. Rather, he interposes another satirist figure – in this instance Crites (Criticus in the quarto version and probably in the play as performed), a low-born but stoically imperturbable scholar suspiciously like Jonson's idealized image of himself as corrector of his social betters. Crites' true peers are the inner circle of Cynthia's court and the monarch: among themselves, the three confer in blank verse, the verse form also employed by the classical divinities who appear within the play, while the less privileged courtiers in the play always blither in inchoate prose. After Crites has shown his mettle by critiquing their follies, Cynthia is prompted by Arete, one of her ladies in waiting (probably representing Jonson's patroness the Countess of Bedford, who held that role at court) to call for a masque of Crites' devising. Cynthia is awestruck by the masque's exquisite beauty and its mirroring of her own virtues. Thenceforth, Crites is chosen as a familiar and favorite: he is "our Crites; / Whom learning, virtue, and our favour last / Exempteth from the gloomy multitude" (5.8.32–3); he is entrusted, along with Arete, with the task of reforming the folly and self-love of the court.

To associate Crites with Jonson is impossible in view of the effrontery involved: Elizabeth was not known to admit any below the rank of the gentry as her intimates, and we have no evidence that Jonson succeeded where others had failed. But the association is also inescapable. In *Cynthia's Revels* Jonson constructs for himself, or at least for his own idealized self, a stoic persona "never moved nor stirred at anything," a fantasy of wish-fulfillment by which his learning and moral probity earn him the place of royal favorite – a much worthier successor to Essex who belongs to the Queen's inner circle and polices the court rather than encouraging it in excess and vice.

A subtext of this masque may well have been the controversy over monopolies. Elizabeth had already withdrawn Essex's monopoly of currants; a year later in her Golden Speech before members of the 1601 Parliament, she was to promise reform of the financial and other excesses she had permitted many of her courtiers through her tolerance of their abuse of monopolies. In *Cynthia's Revels* she similarly recognizes excesses she had previously overlooked, but it is Jonson/Crites who serves as her agent, interposing himself between the monarch and her subjects to ameliorate past abuses. Crites is not deformed by court life but becomes more himself insofar as he belongs to Cynthia (5.8.34); he can therefore offer himself as a peculiarly suitable delegate for restoring the courtiers to a similarly centered selfhood.

But the fantasy was only that: *Cynthia's Revels* was not "liked" at court, and its successor play *Poetaster*, in which the Jonsonian critic-figure became no less a personage than Horace, appears to have succeeded no better as a bid for employment and patronage, though the name seems to have stuck and Jonson was sometimes styled "our English Horace" by his admirers. In reality, as in his dramatic images of her, Elizabeth remained aloof: her unwillingness to spend the royal treasury on patronage rewards to poets (at a time when she was fighting an expensive war against Spain) caused her to appear cold and unnurturing to Jonson even while she was portrayed as warm, loving, and maternal in other contexts. Jonson had to wait for the advent of James I before he was to be adopted as artist-reformer at court, and then his chief medium was not the public theatre but private royal entertainments, similar to the masques embedded within *Cynthia's Revels*, which allowed him to bypass the awkward business of representing himself on stage.

Like other Englishmen to whom James I was to offer particular favor, Jonson went out of his way to praise the new King even before his installation in London: the "Entertainment at Althorp," performed before Queen Anne and Prince Henry on June 20, 1603, may have been written at the behest of the Countess of Bedford, already one of Anne's ladies in waiting, and hails James I, in a slight adjustment of Jonson's previous praise of Cynthia, as the successful reformer of a court that Elizabeth had allowed to fall into corruption. By 1604 Jonson had also published a volume of panegyric verses for James with copious, learned notes.[3] But if Jonson's portrayals of Elizabeth vis-a-vis her court and subjects can be characterized as the imposition of alienating distance, his portrayals of James do just the opposite – create a warmth and familiarity between monarch and subjects that was frequently missing in reality. It became increasingly evident during the early years of James' reign in England that he lacked Elizabeth's magic gift for achieving rapport with her people through the performance of mutual displays of affections. Contemporaries complained that he was silent, withdrawn, and impatient, and played his part in public entertainments with poor grace. Jonson's masques for James I succeeded in part because he designed them to fill a gap: they perform an intimacy between monarch and subjects that, especially over time, became increasingly absent in reality. However, the performance of Jacobean intimacy frequently involved Jonson in an uncomfortably congratulatory acknowledgment of the monarch's imperfections. As early as Jonson's *Private Entertainment of the King and Queen* at Highgate (Mayday 1604), Pan affectionately teased both King and Queen about personal foibles such as drunkenness and an inordinate love of hunting, and asserted that the pair "live safe in the love, rather than the fear, of your subjects."

It is highly likely, as David Riggs speculates, that Jonson owed to the Countess of Bedford his commission as masque-writer to Queen Anne in 1604, when he was chosen to devise *The Masque of Blackness*, performed at court on Twelfth Night 1605, in which Queen Anne and her ladies appeared rather scandalously as "blackamoors."[4] Much has been made of the difficulty of this assignment – Jonson had to argue for the beauty of blackness at the same time that he intimated a link between the color and a need for purification to be effected through the cleansing power of James I – but not enough has been made of this masque's vastly expanded vision, if contrasted with the much smaller, more localized, embedded masques in *Cynthia's Revels*. Queen Anne and her court had a significant degree of independence from James I, and even at times supported markedly different policy initiatives than he did, but in selecting the role of blackamoors they tapped into a theme that was dear to his heart: the idea of British Empire and the extension of royal power far beyond the traditional possessions of the English crown. In *Cynthia's Revels* Jonson had associated Queen Elizabeth with the sun and the purifying power of the Thames, but in *The Masque of Blackness,* and its sequel *The Masque of Beauty* performed on Twelfth Night 1608, James' reputation and healing rays are imagined as extending as far as the Niger River in Africa.

Even before he took the English crown, James I had thought of the British Isles as a single political entity. Great Britain, as James I liked to style it, was not officially created until the early eighteenth century, when England, Ireland, and Wales were officially united with Scotland, but it was promoted in a vocabulary and vision of empire from the beginning of James' reign in England. Jonson's language of colonial transformation in the Jacobean court masque enormously contributed to a new role played by entertainments in the court of James I: the masque became a vehicle for the conceptualization of empire and expanding colonial potential. Jonson's *Hymenæi*, performed for the marriage of the Earl of Essex and Frances Howard, daughter of the Earl of Suffolk, in 1606, celebrated the Union of England and Scotland that James I had effected (through his person as monarch of both realms, if not yet through parliamentary ratification), and figured that Union through a large "microcosm or globe" that was turned, according to one observer's account, by Ben Jonson himself.

Our poet was not, however, content to remain a mere turner of wheels behind the scenes: he had a strong thirst for public acclaim along with a continuing appetite – no doubt fueled in part by envy – for the excoriation of aristocratic vice. During the years that he was successfully producing masques at the Jacobean court, his plays for the public theatres regularly got him into trouble for satire against the very same court. After *Sejanus* was performed at court during the 1603–4 holiday season, Jonson was called before the Privy Council and accused of treason, presumably because of the play's highly negative portrayal of imperial power in the persons of Nero and Tiberius. He got in a far worse scrape for his part in *Eastward Ho!* (1605), which returned to the scene of the *Isle of Dogs* and ruthlessly satirized James I's Scottish courtiers, who had created enormous resentment among English aristocrats by taking the best appointments at court and freezing out English attempts to gain the familiar access to the monarch that they had enjoyed under Elizabeth. For his part in *Eastward Ho!* Jonson was thrown in prison and feared execution, though he was eventually released at the behest of some of his patrons. Thereafter, his plays for the public theatre tended to focus on city rather than aristocratic vice, and Jonson found a more felicitous device for perpetuating his role of Crites for the Jacobean court.

In his preface to *The Masque of Queens*, performed in February 1609, Jonson credits Queen Anne with calling for "some dance or show that might precede hers and have the place of a foil or false masque." He fulfilled her request by devising an antimasque of witches who served as false versions of the idealized procession of queens enacted by Queen Anne and her ladies in the main masque. This bifurcation of masque structure between a negative antimasque and its banishment or reformation in the main masque became the prototype for more ambitious, even reckless antimasques later on by which he was able to satirize court, and sometimes royal, vice at the same time that he celebrated the beneficent rule of the King. *The Masque of Queens*, casting Anne as Bel-Anna, Queen of the Oceans, was apparently the final masque Jonson devised specifically at the command of Queen Anne. For the next decade, Jonson's masques took on subjects that centered far more directly on the power and policies of the King, Prince Henry, and Prince Charles. It is highly suggestive that the development of the satiric antimasque in the *Masque of Queens* was followed closely by a shift to masques that celebrated specific achievements in the public lives of male members of the royal family. Could it be that James recognized the propaganda potential of the form and wished to bring it more directly under his control? James was clearly interested in the masque as a literary type – he had devised a masque of his own in Scotland – but the extent to which he involved himself personally in the specific subject matter of his masques is an issue about which scholars are in disagreement. Whatever the explanation for the shift, from 1610 on the court ladies played a more subservient role in Jonson's masques, representing virtues and attributes centering more directly upon the person and policy of the King; the antimasques during the same period honed in with increased intensity on vices associated with James I as well as members of his court.

The satiric potential of the antimasques is not particularly visible in *Oberon the Fairy Prince* (1611), which featured Prince Henry's debut as chief masquer, or in *The Lords' Masque* (1613), which celebrated the marriage of Princess Elizabeth to Frederick, Elector Palatine, but becomes unmistakable in *Mercury Vindicated from the Alchemists at Court* (1616), which celebrates the King for his successful undoing of sinister alchemical perversions of humanity produced by his favorites, but also glances with some asperity at James' own "making of men" through his scandalous sale of aristocratic titles and consequent debasement of their previous value. Not coincidentally, Jonson's patron the Earl of Pembroke had assumed the office of Lord Chamberlain during 1615, and that office included among its duties the management of court entertainments. The banner year of 1616, in which both James I and Jonson himself published Folio volumes of their respective *Works*, and in which Jonson was officially appointed poet laureate to the court and offered an annual pension, was also the year in which Jonson became unprecedentedly direct in his antimasque critiques of court vices. If the government thought they could subdue his satiric virulence by buying him off with a pension, they were sadly mistaken. With Pembroke as Lord Chamberlain, Jonson apparently felt assured of support in his portrayal and excoriation of vices that flourished at court. Jonson's masques from 1616 onward celebrate policy initiatives of the King's to reform various abuses, and use the court as a microcosmic laboratory to display their impact on the nation at large. Frequently, the very courtiers satirized in the antimasque would actually dance in the main masque, enacting Jonson's vision of the court as a "bountiful spring" that "waterest" the island as a whole. By displaying their transformation, the courtiers would promulgate a mimetic process by which they themselves had been transformed. Such, at least, was the theory.

The Vision of Delight (1617) celebrates James' policy initiative, articulated with particular forcefulness in a 1616 speech before Star Chamber that was published at the end of his 1616 *Works*, to decrease crowding and disease in London by setting strict limits on new construction and ordering nobles and gentry without specific business in London to return to their country estates to keep hospitality and restore the depopulated countryside. *The Vision of Delight* parallels the King's speech in evoking the fatal attractions of a swollen, overgrown London: the first antimasque represents a city street dominated by grotesque inchoate forms that incarnate urban excess. But the second antimasque of "Phantasms" and nighttime revelry strongly suggests the court as an equally virulent fountain of excess. Even as Jonson celebrates James I's initiative to reduce London and restore the countryside, he calls attention to the court as one of the chief magnets attracting the upper classes to London: insofar as the "bounteous and brave spring" of the court itself is polluted, its emulators learn deformity from its own "glass." The main masque symbolically restored the countryside by taking the courtiers out of harm's way and placing them in a rural "bower of Zephyrus." Beginning in 1616, Jonson's masques typically end in visions of a pastoral countryside rather than a city or a reformed court, thereby acknowledging the King's own "anti-court" initiatives to revitalize the countryside by dispersing the crowds of would-be suitors at Whitehall. But Jonson managed to have it both ways: the portrayal of courtly corruptions in the antimasques of these entertainments demonstrated the wisdom of royal efforts at reform, but simultaneously offered ammunition to those contemporaries who saw the court and its manners under James as hopelessly corrupt.

In his next masque Jonson was bolder: *Pleasure Reconciled to Virtue* (1618) celebrates James I's visit to Scotland during summer 1617, his attempts to replace the authority of the Scottish Kirk with that of the Church of England, and his publication of a declaration that became known as the *Book of Sports* – yet another initiative designed to revitalize the countryside by encouraging traditional sports and pastimes that had been suppressed or fallen into disuse. Jonson brilliantly unites these separate policy initiatives by portraying them as instances of James I's favorite self-portrayal as a bringer of the "middle way" in all things. *Pleasure Reconciled to Virtue* shows royal power in the form of Hercules vanquishing excess at both the extremes of Catholic superfluity and Puritan denial in order to revitalize the countryside and the nation as a newly-balanced whole. The dances of the main masque demonstrate the courtiers' internalization of Hercules' lessons in moderation and end with Prince Charles and the other masquers poised to take on the demanding role of Hercules for themselves. But the antimasques' visions of excess are specifically tied to the King and his profligate favorites. Comus the belly-god and his drunken retinue are introduced by a Ganymede-figure, Hercules' cupbearer, who bears a strong resemblance to the King's beloved new favorite the Duke of Buckingham, and who acknowledges that it is Hercules' own cup that is being dishonored through Comus' drunken orgies. The fact that Ganymede is made spokesman for the King calls attention to James' fondness for young male favorites like the Duke of Buckingham, on whom he lavished extravagant affection and to whom, seemingly, he denied nothing. The King's own excess is purged along with that of his courtiers in the main masque of *Pleasure Reconciled to Virtue*, but perhaps less memorably than it is celebrated in the carnivalesque antimasque of Comus and the joys of the belly. Jonson's brilliant tour de force was not appreciated at court. Indeed, as one contemporary reported, Jonson's masque was so thoroughly disliked that "divers think fit he should return to his old trade of bricklaying again." Perhaps Jonson's portrayal of the royal favorites cut too close to the bone. When Jonson revised the masque to honor Prince Charles' recent investiture as Prince of Wales, he replaced the original antimasques with a much safer display of comical but loyal Welshmen.

The final shipwreck of Jonson's most strenuous phase of attempted reform came in *The Gypsies Metamorphosed* (1621), a masque commissioned by the Duke of Buckingham to celebrate James' visit to his estate in Rutland during that summer's royal progress. In this unusual production, the carnivalesque celebration of excess totally dominates the main masque. The chief courtiers are imagined as thieving gypsies under the captaincy of Buckingham himself. What Jonson might earlier have identified as vices to be reformed are here collectively celebrated through jests and coterie innuendo: James is welcomed to Buckingham's person as well as to his home, and there are numerous in-jokes about the penetrability of the "Devil's Arse," a cavelike structure in the north of England with obvious homoerotic connotations. *The Gypsies Metamorphosed* was a great success with the court, but a defeat for the Crites in Jonson who had made artistic capital out of bracing encounters between the squalor of an aristocracy gone to seed and the sublimity of its revitalization. Thereafter, Jonson's court entertainments increasingly turned from the domestic to the international scene, and his antimasques identified targets less patently associated with the court.

The dominant subject of Jonson's masques during the 1620s, beginning with *News from the New World Discovered in the Moon* (1620), is celebration of James I as a keeper of peace when most of Europe was at war. What was to become known as the Thirty Years' War had erupted in 1618, and England's involvement appeared inevitable after James' daughter Elizabeth and her husband Frederick, Elector Palatine, were ousted by Catholic Habsburg forces from the largely Protestant Kingdom of Bohemia, over which Frederick had unwisely accepted sovereignty in 1619. James' subjects clamored for news from the continent, and for English military aid to Frederick and the Protestant cause, but he steadfastly refused to intervene. *News from the New World*'s antimasques satirize various commercial agents by which the incipient war was reported in England and which James had attempted to suppress by proclamation: a Chronicler (or historian), a Printer, and a Factor (who was located abroad and paid to communicate the latest events via correspondence to his English subscribers). Over against this jangling and illicit "news," the main masque ascends to a new world that is unchanging: the mind and ethos of the King, portrayed as a universal primum mobile who remains in "perfection" and "pure harmony" despite the fantastical irregularities of the newsmongers he has silenced. In actuality, the court, like the nation, was severely divided over the proper national response to the Bohemian crisis; but in Jonson's masque they rally around the King and his pacifism with the grace and predictability of planetary bodies. Once again, we discover an incipient colonial vision, and a portrayal of the scope of royal power beyond anything depicted in Jonson's earlier masques. Through the fertile inventions of the masque poet, what many subjects saw as James' narrow, dangerous isolationism is recast as largeness of vision: the King is celebrated as the unmoved mover of all things – indeed, as a divinity – who presides over and controls a universe rather than a mere kingdom. Ensuing masques for James like *The Masque of Augurs* (1622), *Time Vindicated to Himself and to His Honors* (1623), and the unperformed *Neptune's Triumph for the Return of*

Albion (1624), similarly contrast a petty, commercialized, fragmented, and frequently war-mongering mini-culture in the antimasques with vast and peaceful evocations of royal power in the main masque.

In studies of the Jacobean era, there has been considerable confusion between the actual areas of authority claimed by the King and artistic renderings of universal royal power like those brought by Jonson to the masque. Scholars have tended to see Jonson in *News from the New World* and later masques of the 1620s as simply communicating James' own grandiose notions of royal absolutism. But it is worth noting that Jonson's visions go considerably beyond the King's own assertions of royal prerogative powers, particularly as those assertions have been reinterpreted by recent revisionist historians, who emphasize the limitation of James' power and his reliance on day-to-day negotiation and the painstaking balancing of various factions for successful government. It is Jonson, not James, who portrays royal power as absolute in its operation. Even Jonson's early masques for Queen Anne had celebrated James' transforming mana as international in scope and influence. With the passing of time Jonson's masques increasingly link that power with the "removed mysteries" of neoplatonic planetary magic, portraying it as divinely infinite, unitary, and infallible. Jonson was not, of course, the only English subject to be attracted by neoplatonic imagery of world domination, although he may have been one of the first to apply such notions to the King. In bringing neoplatonic astral imagery to the masque he was enormously aided by Inigo Jones' innovative uses of perspective in his staging designs for the masque, which increased the audience's visual perception of distance and thereby broadened the imaginable range of royal power and authority. For better or for worse, Jonson helped James I to expand his own understanding of the meaning and scope of royal power, and that, no doubt, was part of the fascination of Jonson's masques for early viewers at court.

Did Jonson assume that after the death of James I in 1625, his employment as Crites to the court would be continued under Charles I? In marked contrast to his warm reception of James, complete with a published volume of panegyric verses, Jonson left no known verses in honor of Charles' accession until a belated burst of them in 1629, after the assassination of the Duke of Buckingham, with whom Charles had become intimate after the death of James. Charles continued to pay Jonson's pension at least sporadically, but the poet's services were less frequently called upon at court, and Jonson himself was less able to perform them since he had suffered debilitating strokes in 1626 and 1628. Jonson wrote only a handful of large-scale entertainments explicitly for performance before Charles and his court: *Love's Triumph through Callipolis*, the King's Twelfth-Night masque for 1631; *Chloridia*, Queen Henrietta Maria's Shrovetide masque performed in February, 1631; and two rural entertainments for Charles I on progress, the *Entertainment at Welbeck* (1633) and *Love's Welcome at Bolsover*

(1634), both of these commissioned by the Earl of Newcastle, Jonson's most important patron after the death of the Earl of Pembroke in 1630.

The relative paucity of this Caroline court production is not the result of unadaptability on the part of the poet: his masques for Charles and Henrietta Maria chimed in with the ethos of the new court by exquisitely celebrating the pair's highly publicized cult of married chastity and Platonic love. But it is clear that Jonson felt unwelcome in some of the circles that had nurtured him earlier, and his attempts to create plays for court performance uniformly failed. *The Staple of News* (1626), which takes up many of the same subjects as *News from the New World Discovered in the Moon*, was not liked at court. In an epilogue to his play *The New Inn* (1628–9), which was intended for court performance but never staged there because of its utter failure at Blackfriars, Jonson blamed his waning productivity on neglect by Charles and his consort: "And had he lived the care of King and Queen, / His art in something more yet had been seen" (Epilogue, 21–2). In *The New Inn*, as much earlier in *Cynthia's Revels,* Jonson took the somewhat desperate measure of writing hmself into the action of the play as the balancer and corrector of a court-like community gone awry; the poet can be identified on some interpretive levels with the genial Host of the New Inn, who turns out to be a Lord in disguise. The strategy worked no better in *The New Inn* than it had in *Cynthia's Revels. The Tale of a Tub* had a little more success: it held the stage long enough to be performed at court in 1634, and was clearly designed to appeal to King Charles at least to the extent that it celebrated his renewal of his father's *Book of Sports* a year earlier. But at court *The Tale of a Tub* was not liked.

A partial explanation for the failure of these works may be Jonson's inability to let go of a quarrel begun more than a decade before. The art of Inigo Jones, the "master artificer" with whom he had collaborated in most of his masques, remained thriving and popular at the Caroline court while Jonson himself faded in influence, and the poet could not resist satirizing Jones and his "almighty shows" even in works like *The Tale of the Tub* in which his obsessive vendetta had no artistically credible place. Jonson's relentless hostility against Jones is a measure of the continuing importance of the court not only to his financial well being but also to his self-definition as an artist. Even at the end of his life, Jonson had not abandoned hope for gaining the respect under Charles I and Henrietta Maria that he had enjoyed under James. When he died in 1637, he left unfinished his elegaic *Sad Shepherd*, which was clearly designed to feed the seemingly insatiable appetite for pastoral drama at the Caroline court. In terms of his relations with the three monarchs under whom he lived and wrote, Jonson's dramatic production for the court takes on a certain melancholy symmetry: under Elizabeth and then again under Charles, he was an outsider looking in, driven to desperate attempts to write himself into favor through embarrassingly obvious self-portrayals that gave the lie to his favorite public pose of stoic indifference to the court.

If there were space in this essay to take on Jonson's portrayal of the court and courtiers in his lyric poetry, this perception of melancholy symmetry would be disrupted, for Jonson's literary production as a whole was far less centered on the court than were the entertainments explicitly designed for court consumption. In Jonson's *Epigrams*, for example, which he called "the ripest of my studies," published in his 1616 *Works* but mostly composed by 1612, Jonson mentioned the court only in connection with its vices, which he satirized with a corrosive directness that would not have been possible in his antimasques. The court in the *Epigrams* is pathetically reduced to a "Something that Walks Somewhere," a Lord dead in life and buried in its own "flesh and blood" (*Epig.* 11); a "Court-Worm" swathed in silk and as feeble as the small and lowly namesake that spun the substance with which he covers himself (*Epig.* 15); a spiteful "Courtling" who damns Jonson's work with a fashionable faintness of approbation, or sets himself up as a negative critic in order to gain a reputation for wit (*Epig.* 52 and 72); or a "Fine Lady Would-Be" who has secretly aborted her own child to avoid missing even a few months of the partying at court (*Epig.* 62).

Why is so little note taken in the *Epigrams* of positive forces at court? Jonson mentions King James I and his project for Great Britain in several handsome tributes, and he writes in praise of high government officials like Robert, Earl of Salisbury, James' principal Secretary of State and made Lord Treasurer in 1608; Thomas Egerton, Lord Chancellor; and Thomas, Earl of Suffolk, Lord Chamberlain 1603–14 and Lord Treasurer 1614–19. But never does he explicitly link such figures with the court; only in two cases is the grandee's title mentioned in the poem, and then part of his name is effaced (*Epig.* 64 to Cecil and *Epig.* 74 on Egerton). With lesser court officials the poet's reticence is even more pronounced, particularly if considered by the standards of the usual court panegyric of the time. Jonson's touching poem on Margaret Radcliffe (*Epig.* 40) does not mention her place at the time of her premature death as Queen Elizabeth's favorite Maid of Honor. Lucy, Countess of Bedford, is the recipient of several poems, none of which so much as hint at her high positions at the courts of both Queen Elizabeth and King James. Jonson's poems to Henry Goodyere praise him for his hawking and his choice of friends and books, without any mention of his position from 1605 on as a Gentleman of the Privy Chamber. The courtiers in the *Epigrams* are indistinguishable from the other luminaries in that they are praised for traits of character they hold outside of and in spite of their high office. Like Crites in *Cynthia's Revels*, they are valuable examples for the less centered creatures about court because whatever their official title and degree of responsibility, they remain true to an internalized stoic code of virtue. They are "never moved nor stirred at anything," and are hence most worthy of trust, whether by a mere subject like Jonson or by a Queen or King. And to the extent that they failed to live up to the poet's characterization of them, Jonson could claim that his goal was, as in the entertainments explicitly designed for the court, reform:

> I have too oft preferr'd
> Men past their terms, and praised some names too much,
> But 'twas with purpose to have made them such.
>
> ("An Epistle to Master John Selden" 20–2)

NOTES

1 *The Complete Plays of Ben Jonson*, ed. G. A. Wilkes (Oxford: Oxford University Press, 1981), II, xi.
2 Cited by Stephen W. May in *The Elizabethan Courtier Poets: The Poems and Their Contexts* (Columbia and London: University of Missouri Press, 1991), 20, from Public Record Office State Papers 12/274/86, March 29, 1600.
3 Ben Jonson's *Part of the King's Entertainment in passing to his Coronation* on 15 March 1604, his *Panegyre* on the King's opening of Parliament four days later, and the *Entertainment of the Queen and Prince at Althorp* in 1603 were originally published together (HS 7:67).
4 David Riggs, *Ben Jonson: A Life* (Cambridge, MA: Harvard University Press, 1989), 118.

4

R. V. YOUNG

Ben Jonson and learning

With the exception of John Milton, there is no English poet more learned than Ben Jonson, and none who makes learning such an integral part of his literary work. Jonson thought of poetry and drama as scholarly as well as imaginative enterprises, a conviction attested by his remark in the dedication to the Earl of Pembroke that the *Epigrams* were "the ripest of my studies."[1] The humanist educational and compositional ideal of imitation of the classics is exemplified by no one more thoroughly and successfully than by Jonson. He not only exhibits a remarkable familiarity with a wide range of Greek and Roman literature; he also converts ancient models into the very substance of his texts in a way that results in independent, coherent works of his own without erasing the visible features of the sources. Yet Jonson is not merely a literary antiquarian – the Renaissance counterpart to a modern writer who produces scrupulously accurate historical novels. Throughout his career and across the broad spectrum of genres that he attempted, Jonson manifests an extraordinary responsiveness to the political, social, and artistic issues of his age. He always writes with an awareness of his place among the other English poets of his own and the preceding generation, and of the intellectual context created both by British and continental scholars. Most remarkable, Jonson's formidable learning is embodied in plays and poems that, at their best, command a vigorous vernacular style and sure sense of the realities of everyday life. In the work of Ben Jonson, learning, which in some authors is mere pedantry, energizes a powerful artistic grasp of the world.

Jonson's intimate awareness of lower-class life on the London streets was largely the result of misfortune. The death of his father, a clergyman of the Church of England, before Jonson's birth left him and his mother in poverty, and she remarried a bricklayer. The poet, however unwillingly, seems to have plied his stepfather's trade from time to time into the late 1590s – a phase of his life that his literary enemies would never allow him to forget. Combined with his stint as a common soldier in the wars against the Spanish in the Low Countries and his entry into the theatrical world as an ordinary actor, Jonson's experience as an artisan who earned a living with his hands would have provided him with vivid experience of the lives of ordinary men and women. His formal learning and knowledge of the higher reaches of society he acquired as a result of good fortune. Someone – perhaps a patron of his father – made it possible for the intellectually promising stepson of a bricklayer to attend Westminster School, where he attracted the attention of the gifted scholar and educator, William Camden. The level of scholarly sophistication that the poet attained without ever attending a university is a tribute both to the general curriculum of Elizabethan schools and to Camden's individual dedication and skill. Jonson never forgot what he owed his scholarly mentor and remembered him gratefully in his poetry as "Camden, most reverend head, to whom I owe / All that I am in arts, all that I know" (*Epig.* 14.1–2).

To be sure, the education that the poet received at Westminster, though very solid, was hardly unique or even extraordinary for Tudor England. What sets Jonson apart is the way that he maintained a rigorous scholarly regimen throughout his life. Recently, Jonson's heavily annotated copy of the 1617 Folio of Spenser's *Works* has once again come to light. Sir Kenelm Digby, who was among the earliest important commentators on Spenser, as Jonson's literary executor and editor, almost certainly had possession of Jonson's copy of Spenser at some time. A careful examination of Jonson's marginal comments on the work of his fellow poet has thus led Riddell and Stewart to surmise that "Jonson has played a far more important role in the development of Spenser criticism than many of us have been taught to believe."[2] Similarly, Jonson is known to have owned the eight-volume 1623 edition of the *Opera* of the important Flemish humanist, Justus Lipsius (1547–1606), and to have carefully annotated many of his works. Jonson's tragedy *Sejanus* reveals the influence of the philological expertise of Lipsius' edition of the Roman historian Tacitus, and the penciled-in comments in Jonson's copy of *Lipsius' Six Books of Politics or Civil Doctrine* show the poet as a careful student of Renaissance political theory.[3] The dates of these marked-up editions, 1617 and 1623, demonstrate, if nothing else, that Jonson was reading books of poetry and learning in a scrupulously scholarly fashion well into middle age.

The most striking example of his lifelong scholarly preoccupations is *Timber, or Discoveries*, Jonson's elaborate commonplace book first published in the posthumous folio edition of the *Works* by Sir Kenelm Digby. Since a fire in Jonson's lodgings in November, 1623, seems to have destroyed most of his books and papers, including earlier commonplace books, the surviving text of *Discoveries* was apparently written after that date – indeed, some entries can be dated as late as 1630 and 1633.[4] There has been speculation that parts of *Discoveries* may have been prepared as lecture notes, since Jonson's scholarship gained contemporaneous recognition not only in an honorary degree awarded by Oxford University in 1619, but also in his holding a deputy professorship of rhetoric at Gresham College, London, sometime between 1619 and 1627. Although this theory remains problematic, there is no question that the collection is the work of an inveterate student and furnishes a superb example of that characteristic sub-genre of Renaissance humanism, the commonplace book.

A certain disappointment with Jonson's *Discoveries* can be explained as a failure fully to understand the nature and purpose of such a compilation. The more carefully it is investigated, the more apparent it becomes that even the most vigorous and distinctive entries – those that seem to disclose most vividly "the real Ben Jonson" – are copied or closely paraphrased from another, usually a classical, author. But Romantic self-expression is no part of Jonson's conception of a poet; he is not interested in unveiling to his readers the inmost workings of his soul. A commonplace book, as the term *commonplace* insists, is meant to be a collection of conventional wisdom, gathered and arranged to serve the poet's invention, which for a classically trained mind like Jonson's would retain the sense of "finding" or "discovery" from the Latin *inventio*, rather than "made up" or "imagined" as the term suggests to modern ears. Such a mind would likewise regard radical originality in morals, politics, or literature (the chief preoccupations of *Discoveries*) with grave suspicion. In broad outline at least, political prudence, moral probity, and poetic excellence were established categories; and innovation for its own sake would lead to anarchy, corruption, and barbarism. Naturally, changing historical circumstances, the growth of knowledge, and the unique talents of individuals would require adaptation and reinvigoration of traditional wisdom and established forms; but for Jonson such new developments would involve the augmentation and modification of received convention, not revolutionary change.

Hence in *Discoveries* Jonson writes, "The first [quality of epistolary style] is brevity. For they must not be treatises or discourses (your letters) except it be to learned men. And even among them there is a kind of thrift and saving of words."[5] Plainly Jonson had access to John Hoskyns' *Directions for Speech and Style*: "The first is *Brevity*, for letters must not be treatises, or discoursings, except it be amonge learned men & eaven amongst them, there is a kinde of thrift or saving or words."[6] Hoskyns has been influenced in turn by Justus Lipsius' *Principles of Letter-Writing* (1591), which maintains that brevity is the most important stylistic virtue of a letter, "For if too long (I agree with Demetrius), it assumes the name 'book' and loses that of 'letter.'"[7] Lipsius is citing the ancient Greek text *On Style* by an obscure Hellenistic writer called Demetrius, and *Principles of Letter-Writing* as a whole could be regarded as a compendium of classical stylistic advice with particular emphasis on the Roman writers Seneca and Cicero. To seek originality in Jonson's *Discoveries* or to be shocked by its "plagiarism" of numerous other writers, Jonson's contemporaries as well as ancients, is a futile exercise. The commonplace book provides, however, an invaluable revelation of how Jonson gathered and deployed the learned resources that constitute the foundation of his works of poetry and drama.

A good example of Jonson's quickly maturing use of learning comes in his first great dramatic success, *Every Man in his Humour*, initially staged in 1598. His only earlier play that has survived, *The Case Is Altered* – a play that Jonson never attempted to acknowledge or preserve – adapts plot elements from two plays by Plautus, *Captivi* and *Aulularia*; but it ends with the recovery of lost children, the revelation of mistaken identities, and the betrothal of lovers in the fashion of romance. *Every Man in his Humour* takes no particular classical work for its model, but its ironic tone and curt, colloquial style are far more compatible with the spirit of classical comedy. The specific allusions to and borrowings from classical sources is managed with admirable adroitness. Knowell's soliloquy in the Moorfields at the opening of the fifth scene of Act II is a remarkable pastiche of ideas and phrases from Juvenal, Quintilian, and Horace, with just a touch of Ovid, all blended into a vigorous blank verse:

> Note, what we fathers do! Look, how we live!
> What mistresses we keep! At what expense,
> In our sons' eyes! Where they may handle our gifts,
> Hear our lascivious courtships, see our dalliance,
> Taste of the same provoking meats with us,
> To ruin of our states! $(32–7)^8$

Jonson draws freely on a variety of Roman writers to arrive at this distillation of classical moralizing, yet it is fitted to the character and the circumstances of his play and embodied in his own crisp colloquial English.

Of course *Every Man in his Humour* is most famous as the epitome of the "humors comedy" – a dramatization of the way that individuals are inclined to behave in a compulsive, mechanical fashion according to the bias of their physiological constitution. Although the humoral explanation of human nature and conduct has its roots in the ancient medical theory descended from both Hippocrates and Galen, and developed throughout the Middle Ages, it seems to have been a subject of widespread interest in the sixteenth and earlier seventeenth centuries. A number of books dealing with various aspects of humoral physiology appeared during this era, of which Robert Burton's *Anatomy of Melancholy* (1621) is the most famous. Jonson wrote commendatory sonnets for *Melancholike Humours* (1600) by Nicholas Breton and for *The Passions of the Mind in Generall* (1601) by Thomas Wright – the Jesuit who converted the poet to Catholicism while he was in prison for the murder of the actor Gabriel Spencer. But for all Jonson's apparent interest in humoral theory, the term "humor" is, often as not, a synonym for "mood" or "passing fancy." Knowell claims simply to have outgrown the same frivolous "humor" that now possesses his son:

> Myself was once a student; and, indeed,
> Fed with the selfsame humour he is now,
> Dreaming on naught but idle poetry,
> That fruitless and unprofitable art,
> Good unto none, but least to the professors,
> Which then, I thought the mistress of all knowledge:
> But since, time, and truth have waked my judgment,
> And reason taught me better to distinguish
> The vain from useful learnings. (1.1.15–23)

A humor can also mean an affectation. When the son, Edward Knowell, sets about to gull his country cousin, Stephen, the latter resolves to be "more proud, and melancholy, and gentlemanlike" (1.3.104–5). "It will do well," Edward says in an aside, "for a suburb-humour" (1.3.107–8). Perhaps Kitely's choleric jealousy – "His jealousy is the poison he has taken" (4.8.37), says Wellbred, with disdain for his brother-in-law's suspicions – is the best example of a humor in the strict medical sense.

Every Man in his Humour thus lays down a pattern for Jonson's finest and most characteristic comedies. They are inevitably learned in the mode of Renaissance humanism: not only are there plentiful allusions to works of ancient Greek and Roman literature; these plays also are conceived according to the classical norms of comic drama. Jonson is attentive to the unities; his dialogue is written in a crisp, colloquial middle style, rather than grandly or lyrically; and his comic characters generally meet Aristotle's criterion by being, in some sense or other, "worse than are found in the world."[9] To the refinement of this learned perspective, Jonson adds the vitality that comes of his familiarity with the daily lives and language of a broad cross-section of the men and women of Elizabethan/Jacobean England, and a focus on some feature or preoccupation of the life of that era. The humoral psychology of *Every Man in his Humour* finds a more precise object in Morose's misogyny and pathological aversion to noise in *Epicœne, or The Silent Woman*. *The Alchemist* replaces the theme of the humors with the pseudo-science of turning base metals to gold and seeking the elixir of life, as its title indicates, and *Bartholomew Fair*, in the figure of Zeal-of-the-Land Busy, skewers the Puritans' increasingly vociferous – and, in Jonson's view, hypocritical – attack on the traditional customs and pleasures of English life. One of his "dotages," *The Magnetic Lady, or the Humours Reconciled*, expressly recalls the humors comedy of thirty years before, but also makes loose metaphorical usage of developing conceptions of magnetism. In tone, structure, and satirical vigor, Jonson probably comes closer to the classic comedy of Aristophanes than any other English playwright; however, Jonson knew that a genuine classicist adapts ancient literary practice to his own era. Hence his comedies are grounded as firmly in the streets of Renaissance London as those of Aristophanes were in the agora of ancient Athens.

The harshly satiric morality of *Volpone* provides the most thorough example of Jonson's deployment of learning in comic drama, revealing both the virtues and the problematic aspects of his procedures. The play was acted not only in London, but also at the Universities of Oxford and Cambridge; and in the Folio printing the play is dedicated "To the Most Noble and Most Equal Sisters the Two Famous Universities for Their Love and Acceptance Shown to His Poem in the Presentation." Jonson's designation of his play as a "poem" anticipates the defense of his comic drama as a learned work of literary art in the epistle to the Universities that precedes the dramatic text. He is careful to distinguish his work from the "stage-poetry" of the day in which "nothing but ribaldry, profanation, blasphemy, all licence of offence to God and man is practised." By contrast, Jonson proclaims "the impossibility of any man's being the good Poet, without first being a good man," and delivers a lofty image of the poet's rôle and status in the face of his detractors:

> He that is said to be able to inform young men to all good disciplines, inflame grown men to all great virtues, keep old men in their best and supreme state, or as they decline to childhood, recover them to their first strength; that comes forth the interpreter and arbiter of nature, a teacher of things divine, no less than human, a master in manners; and can alone (or with a few) effect the business of mankind: this, I take him, is no subject for pride and ignorance to exercise their railing rhetoric upon. (*Five Plays*, ed. Wilkes, 223)

Moreover, Jonson defends the classical pedigree of his particularly acerbic brand of comedy, insisting that he has "some lines of example, drawn even in the ancients themselves, the goings-out of whose comedies are not always joyful, but oft times, the bawds, the servants, the rivals, yea, and the masters are mulcted: and fitly, it being the office of a comic Poet, to imitate justice, and instruct to life, as well as purity of language, or stir up gentle affections" (226). He thus equips his play with a theoretical rationale for the ferocity of its conclusion and emphasizes the moral "profit" in his Horatian promise "To mix profit with your pleasure" ("Prologue," l. 8).

Although *Volpone* is chiefly classical in its overall tone and structure, it also includes numerous allusions to Greco-Roman mythology as well as a scattering of borrowings from Roman sources like the satires of Juvenal and the comedies of Plautus. Moreover, it boasts an exemplary instance of humanist imitation, which is also one of Jonson's most dazzling lyrics, skillfully fitted into a dramatic context. The avaricious and shameless Corvino, having left his young wife Celia alone with the supposedly decrepit and bedridden Volpone to "comfort" him in his mortal illness, the latter leaps up and recommends his carnal advances with a song:

> Come, my Celia, let us prove,
> While we can, the sports of love;
> Time will not be ours forever,
> He, at length, our good will sever;
> Spend not then his gifts in vain.
> Suns that set may rise again:
> But if once we lose this light,
> 'Tis with us perpetual night. (3.7.165–72)

Through these first eight lines Jonson's "Song" is a close yet graceful paraphrase of lines from Catullus 5 (*Vivamus, mea Lesbia, atque amemus*):

> Let us live, my Lesbia, and let us love
> and the whispers of the more strait-laced old men –
> let us value them all at a single pennyworth.
> Suns are able to set and rise again;
> For us, when this brief light has once set,
> There is one long night for sleeping.

This outburst of defiant youthful passion against the severity of age is followed by Catullus' famous exhortation to countless kisses, lest a determinate number leave the lovers vulnerable to an invidious curse. Volpone's song, however, urges upon the innocent Celia the ease with which adultery can be concealed:

> Why should we defer our joys?
> Fame and rumour are but toys.
> Cannot we delude the eyes
> Of a few poor household-spies?
> Or his easier ears beguile,
> Thus removed by our wile?
> 'Tis no sin love's fruits to steal;
> But the sweet thefts to reveal:
> To be taken, to be seen,
> These have crimes accounted been. (173–82)

An awareness that Jonson begins by imitating one of the most impassioned Latin love lyrics and then turns it toward Volpone's callous and furtive lechery enhances the irony of the dramatic scene. Both the adaptation of the imitated lines to a different context and the reader's or audience's awareness of the source contribute to the overall significance of the song. As Katharine Eisaman Maus points out, the significance of "the lyrics to Celia . . . depends . . . upon the context in which they are articulated and the occasion they commemorate. Thus they acquire a radically different import when that context is altered. 'Come, my Celia', which seems well-meaning enough in *The Forest*, becomes sinister on Volpone's lips."[10] Jonson's ironic handling of Catullus' fine lyric in *Volpone* epitomizes the contrast between his and Shakespeare's comedy, which ordinarily closes with a sense of buoyant jubilation. What Jonson provides by way of compensation is the intensity of acerbic satire. Both his comic virtues and limitations grow out of his learned adherence to the unyielding firmness of classical decorum.

Jonson's surviving tragedies, with their sources in Roman history, are even more committed to the rigor of unsentimental classicism. Here, however, the poet's prodigious learning is less successfully wedded to an effective dramatic vision than in his best comedies. *Sejanus His Fall* seems to be too scrupulously faithful to the tone and outlook, as well as the narrative, of its principal source, the *Annals* of Tacitus. As Maus observes, "Tacitus . . . separates entirely the rewards of fortune from the rewards of virtue. Success fails to correlate with goodness, and the outcome of events thus becomes morally irrelevant."[11] Jonson follows the historian so closely that he falls under the admonition of Sir Philip Sidney: "But the history, being captived to the truth of a foolish world, is many times a terror from well-doing, and an encouragement to unbridled wickedness."[12] Of course the dramatic problem is not just the grim pessimism of *Sejanus*: *King Lear* is hardly a model of poetic justice. As Maus adds, tragedy, as well as comedy, "demands that its audience recognize the appropriateness of the characters' fates. Their fortunes must matter to them and to us."[13] Jonson binds himself so tightly to the facts of the past that he fails to create a fiction that comes alive in the present. In Sidney's terms, he works too much like "the meaner sort of painters, who counterfeit only such faces as are set before them," rather than the sort who "painteth not Lucretia whom he never saw, but painteth the outward beauty of such a virtue."[14] *Sejanus* is less deficient in morality than in dramatic power. *Catiline* evinces many of the same problems and additionally, as Anne Barton observes, tends to slide into comedy.[15] It seems that Jonson's minute knowledge of the period and events that he wishes to treat, including a good many frivolous details, overwhelms the grave simplicity necessary for tragedy.

In a somewhat different fashion, Jonson's great learning and his singleminded commitment to poetic purposiveness render his long involvement with the production of royal masques even more problematic. To be sure, the rich mythological substance of Jonson's masques, enhanced by his extraordinary gifts as a lyricist, resulted in texts that are far more satisfying to a modern reader than those of any other masque-writer save Milton's *Comus*. But even during Jonson's period of royal favor while James I was on the throne, there was an inherent incompatibility between his sophisticated literary aspirations and the essentially visual orientation of the masque genre, with its tendency toward lavish spectacle. "We may appreciate some of the purely practical difficulties of the poet," writes Stephen Orgel, "by considering that the text of [*The Masque of*] *Blacknesse* comprises eleven pages (the length is about average), but that a masque often took three hours to perform."[16] Orgel also notices that the Platonism of some masques, manifest in characters who are absolute embodiments of good and evil like the queens and hags in *The Masque of Queens*, disables drama, because antithetical principles cannot interact, even in conflict.[17] Thus Jonson's learning and philosophical orientation are again an obstacle to the creation of a genre that was financially important to him. When Charles I, who was both less bookish than his father and less amused by the often crude humor of the antimasque, ascended the throne, Jonson's days as the chief author of royal masques were clearly numbered. Charles and his display-loving French Queen, Henrietta Maria, were bound to prefer Inigo Jones's luxuriant costumes and the marvelous "special effects" of his stage machinery to the more subtle delights of Jonson's learned verse. In fairness to Jones and his royal patrons, however, his artistic gifts and their tastes were more in keeping with the real artistic potential of the masque.

It is in Jonson's nondramatic verse that his gifts as a poet and scholar converge most fruitfully; hence it is no wonder that he regarded his *Epigrams*, the collection most closely modelled on a distinctive classical genre, as "the ripest of my studies." The chief influence is Martial, and Jonson is extremely deft at keeping the Roman epigrammatist before the attention of the reader, while establishing his own distinctive voice and ethos. "To My Mere English Censurer" proudly proclaims that the poet has restored "the old way and the true" to the epigram (*Epig.* 18.2); that is, he has captured in English the style and wit of Martial, unlike the wooden versifying of the *Epigrams* (c. 1590) of Sir John Davies (1569–1626) and the *Epigrams in the Oldest Cut and Newest Fashion* (1599) of John Weaver (1576–1632).[18] In the preceding epigram Jonson has submitted his own work "To the Learned Critic," with the implication that literary judgment requires learning not available to the Latinless reader. Similarly, Jonson sends his epigrams to be assessed by John Donne "That so alone canst judge, so alone dost make" (*Epig.* 96.3). The approval of one intelligent reader educated in timeless, classical standards is more valuable than any amount of vulgar praise.

At the same time, Jonson puts a certain moral distance between himself and Martial with the remark that closes the introductory dedication to the Earl of Pembroke that "in my theatre, Cato, if he lived, might enter without scandal."[19] In the preface to the first book of his *Epigrams*, Martial had written that Cato ought not to enter his "theatre," and if he did, he would have to watch the show.[20] Martial is referring to an incident when Cato of Utica (95–46 BC), an exemplar of Stoic virtue, attended the games of Flora, and the usual dance of naked girls was suspended in deference to his moral sensibility. Jonson is thus at pains to differentiate himself from the licentious side of Roman literature, and his handling of his classical sources always involves some kind of modification that emphasizes his status as a Christian Englishman.

This ability to adapt a classical form to Christian purposes is an essential feature of the most poignant epigrams in Jonson's collection, the epitaphs on his own son and daughter. "On My First Son" (*Epig.* 45) offers as its last line a translation of the last line of Martial's epitaph on a favorite slave boy. "To extravagant things life is short and old age rare," the Roman poet writes. "Whatever you love, hope that it not please too much" (*Epigrammaton Libri* 6.29.7–8). In Martial's pagan world, the gods are jealous and cruel, death a lapse into nothingness: human delight in love is a hollow cry in the face of meaningless oblivion. Jonson, however, while translating this last line literally, transposes it into a Christian context that alters its meaning:

> Oh, could I lose all father now! For why
> Will man lament the state he should envy?
> To have so soon 'scaped world's and flesh's rage,
> And, if no other misery, yet age?
> Rest in soft peace, and, asked, say here doth lie
> Ben Jonson his best piece of poetry;
> For whose sake, henceforth, all his vows be such,
> As what he loves may never like too much. (ll. 5–12)

In its original context Martial's line evokes Epicurean resignation before the bleak inevitability of fate. In Jonson's epitaph the line highlights the tension between proclivity toward pagan despair that afflicts man in his natural, fallen state and the hope of redemption, implied by the notion that the deceased boy ought to be envied.

Jonson's epitaph on his daughter who died in infancy similarly closes with an echo of a Martial epitaph on Erotion: "May no coarse turf cover her delicate bones nor be you, Earth, heavy to her: she was not so to you" (*Epigrammaton Liber* 5.34.9–10). Again, Jonson introduces the theme of Christian hope into the Roman poet's context of pagan pathos:

> At six months' end she parted hence
> With safety of her innocence;
> Whose soul heaven's Queen (whose name she bears)
> In comfort of her mother's tears,
> Hath placed amongst her virgin train;
> Where, while that severed doth remain,
> This grave partakes the fleshly birth;
> Which cover lightly, gentle earth. (22.5–12)

52

Here the Christian assurance is generally asserted much more confidently than in the epitaph upon his son. The last line, however, with its reminiscence of Martial's urbane despair, reminds us that assurance of the girl's salvation does not altogether mitigate for mortal men and women the sorrow for that "fleshly birth" laid in the cold ground. What is remarkable in these funerary epigrams is how Jonson's learned mastery of the classical tradition is the vehicle for revealing – very discreetly – the tenderness and anxiety of the man beneath the magisterial calm of the classicist.

The titles of two other collections of Jonson's nondramatic verse, *The Forest* and *The Underwood*, also reflect Jonson's knowledge of classical literary practice. In his preface "To the Reader" of *The Underwood*, Jonson explains these titles himself:

> With the same leave, the ancients called that kind of body *silva*, or ''γλη, in which there were works of diverse nature and matter congested, as the multitude call timber-trees, promiscuously growing, a wood or forest; so am I bold to entitle these lesser poems of later growth by this of *Underwood*, out of the analogy they hold to *The Forest* in my former book, and no otherwise.[21]

The obvious classical model for Jonson was the *Silvae* of Statius (c. AD 45–96), who was also the author of an epic poem, the *Thebaid*; and as a critical concept, *silvae* was discussed in the *Institutio oratorio* of Quintilian (c. AD 35– after 95) and in the *Attic Nights* of Aulus Gellius (c. AD 130–c. 180). Jonson's use of this somewhat arcane term is itself a demonstration of the breadth and detail of his classical erudition, and the strikingly literal English words he uses to translate *silvae* show the power of his imagination in appropriating the classical heritage to his own purposes. The individual poems in both *The Forest* and *The Underwood* are typically pervaded by allusions to Greco-Roman literature and mythology and frequently deploy stylistic devices of classical rhetoric. Moreover, many of these poems imitate particular classical genres such as the verse epistle and the ode, as well as the epigram.

A notable example in *The Underwood* is Jonson's emulation of the formal Pindaric ode, "To the Immortal Memory and Friendship of That Noble Pair, Sir Lucius Cary and Sir H. Morison." Availing himself, again, of stolid English terms, Jonson translates the conventional elements of the Greek ode – *strophe, antistrophe, epode* – literally as "turn," "counterturn," and "stand"; and he sets about to naturalize, for the first time in English, this most exotic and sophisticated of classical forms in a late Renaissance setting. In 1629 Sir Lucius Cary, one of the young "Sons of Ben," had lost his dearest friend, Sir Henry Morison, probably to smallpox. Jonson bases his consolation on the ancient philosophical conception of friendship – with broadly Platonic, Aristotelian, and Stoic roots – as the fruit of shared virtue, as a spiritual reality transcending material circumstance and mortality. The ode becomes an occasion to celebrate the interior integrity of life as opposed to any worldly or merely physical possession or attainment:

> It is not growing like a tree
> In bulk, doth make man better be;
> Or standing long an oak, three hundred year,
> To fall a log at last, dry, bald, and sere:
> A lily of the day
> Is fairer far, in May,
> Although it fall and die that night;
> It was the plant and flower of light.
> In small proportions we just beauty see,
> And in short measures life may perfect be. (65–74)

Since the Renaissance regarded the Pindaric ode as an irregular, impassioned form, Jonson decks his poem with startling conceits and prosodic devices: the infant of Saguntum who goes back into the womb to die in order to avoid Hannibal's sack of the town is made a symbol of the perfect epitome of a human life; "Ben" is the last word of the last line of a Counter-Turn and "Jonson" the first word of the first line of the following "Stand." "Twilight" is broken between two lines and the first syllable ("twi-") rhymed with "Harry." The poet thus endeavors to meld an arresting panoply of classical literary ornaments into an expression of deeply felt ancient wisdom. As Richard S. Peterson remarks, "In the ode Jonson characteristically combines patterns of classical thought and traditional associations in such a way that their full potential interconnectedness is brought out in a new and original whole."[22]

Jonson's role in the continuity of the classical humanist tradition is likewise manifest in the most famous poem of *The Forest*, "To Penshurst." He borrows from several classical sources, most obviously the *Epigrams* of Martial, but more important is the influence of a general Roman love of agrarian life best expressed in Virgil's *Georgics* and numerous poems of Horace. Jonson transforms these materials in a way that gives rise to the tradition of the country house poem that extends over the next century and a half and engages such writers as Robert Herrick (1591–1674), Thomas Carew (1594/95–1639), Andrew Marvell (1621–78), John Dryden (1631–1700), and Alexander Pope (1688–1744).[23] In some of the novels of Anthony Trollope (1815–82) and in Evelyn Waugh's *Brideshead Revisited* (1945) the same nostalgic attitude toward the life of the great country house persists in the fiction of the nineteenth and twentieth centuries. "To Penshurst" thus keeps the classical vision alive not only by adapting it to its own era, but also by establishing a sub-genre for development by subsequent English writers.

The theme of the poem is that rural life provides the optimal combination of nature and civilization: the landscape of the estate and the architecture of the great house itself become emblems of a way of life that is innocent and satisfying. The poem's structure is topographical: after a brief introduction that contrasts the old, relatively modest house at Penshurst with the ostentatious Renaissance palaces that were springing up around the English countryside, Jonson begins with the natural bounties of the manor's woodlands, river, and ponds, which provide timber, game, and fish. He then moves to the riches of the estate's orchards and gardens, describes the house itself, and concludes with the manner of life within. The entire scene is replete with meaning and memory, for instance an oak planted to mark the birth of Sir Philip Sidney: "That taller tree, which of a nut was set / At his great birth, where all the muses met" (13–14). A man does not plant a tree when a son is born unless he expects his family to live on the same property for a long time. A prelapsarian harmony between man and nature is signified by the hyperbolic descriptions of creatures that offer themselves for human nourishment: "The painted partridge lies in every field, / And for thy mess is willing to be killed" (29–30). As there is harmony between man and nature at Penshurst, there is likewise harmony among men symbolized by the construction of the house out of indigenous materials (rather than imported Italian marble):

> And though thy walls be of the country stone,
> They're reared with no man's ruin, no man's groan;
> There's none that dwell about them wish them down,
> But all come in, the farmer and the clown,
> And no one empty-handed, to salute
> Thy lord and lady, though they have no suit.   (45–50)

What holds it all together, both the material benefits and the peacefulness, is the virtue of the proprietors, Sir Robert and Lady Sidney, who are moral and religious and who strive to impart these characteristics to their children (ll. 90–98). Like their house, the Sidneys are genuine denizens of the land where they live:

> Now, Penshurst, they that will proportion thee
> With other edifices, when they see
> Those proud, ambitious heaps, and nothing else,
> May say, their lords have built, but thy lord dwells.   (99–102)

After we allow for the fact that Jonson is flattering a patron, after we allow for the fact that it was a time of grave financial difficulty for much of the landed aristocracy, and that he was making a virtue of necessity in praising the Sidneys for living at home on their rural estate when they could hardly afford to do otherwise – allowing for all this, "To Penshurst" remains a noble expression of the traditional conception of a community founded on the moral and spiritual integrity of its leading members. The poet was able to perceive the value of Penshurst and what it stood for because of his native intelligence and imagination, but it was his learning – especially his intimate knowledge of the classics – that furnished him with language and literary conventions sufficient to embody his vision. As much as any English poet, Ben Jonson used his prodigious learning to create a literary context for his own most original insights.

NOTES

1 *Ben Jonson,* ed. Ian Donaldson (Oxford and New York: Oxford University Press, 1985), 221. Jonson's nondramatic poetry and prose are quoted throughout from this *Oxford Authors* edition unless otherwise specified. Line or page numbers are henceforth supplied parenthetically in the text.

2 James Riddell and Stanley Stewart, *Jonson's Spenser: Evidence and Historical Criticism* (Pittsburgh: Duquesne University Press, 1995), 11.

3 See Robert C. Evans, *Jonson, Lipsius and the Politics of Renaissance Stoicism* (Durango, CO: Longwood Academic, 1992).

4 See the Commentary in Donaldson, ed., *Ben Jonson,* 735.

5 Ibid., 578.

6 Louise Brown Osborn, *The Life, Letters, and Writings of John Hoskyns, 1566–1638* (1930; rpt. Hamden, CT: Archon Books, 1973), 118–19.

7 Justus Lipsius, *Principles of Letter-Writing: A Bilingual Text of Justi Lipsi Epistolica Institutio,* ed. and trans. R. V. Young and M. Thomas Hester (Carbondale and Edwardsville: Southern Illinois University Press, 1996), 25.

8 Ben Jonson, *Five Plays,* ed. G.A. Wilkes (Oxford and New York: Oxford University Press, 1988). Jonson's plays are quoted from this edition unless otherwise specified.

9 Aristotle, *Poetics* 1449a, in *Classical Literary Criticism,* ed. D. A. Russell and M. Winterbottom (Oxford and New York: Oxford University Press, 1989), 56.

10 Katharine Elsaman Maus, *Ben Jonson and the Roman Frame of Mind* (Princeton, NJ: Princeton University Press, 1984), 104.

11 Ibid., 37.

12 Sir Philip Sidney, *Defence of Poetry,* ed. J. A. van Dorsten (Oxford: Oxford University Press, 1966), 37–8.

13 *Ben Jonson and the Roman Frame of Mind,* 37–8.

14 Sidney, *Defence of Poetry,* 26.

15 Anne Barton, *Ben Jonson, Dramatist* (Cambridge: Cambridge University Press, 1984), 154–69.

16 Stephen Orgel, *The Jonsonian Masque* (Cambridge, MA: Harvard University Press, 1965), 113.

17 Ibid., 138–9.

18 See the Commentary in Donaldson, ed., *Ben Jonson,* 649.

19 Ibid., 222.

20 M. Valerii Martialis, *Epigrammaton Libri,* ed. Walther Gilbert (Lipsiae: Teubner, 1886), I. pref.

21 Donaldson, ed., *Ben Jonson,* 307.

22 Richard S. Peterson, *Imitation and Praise in the Poems of Ben Jonson* (New Haven and London: Yale University Press, 1981), 197.

23 See G. R. Hibbard, "The Country House Poem of the Seventeenth Century," *Journal of the Warburg and Courtauld Institutes* 19 (1956), 159–74; and William Alexander McClung, *The Country House in English Renaissance Literature* (Berkeley, Los Angeles, London: University of California Press, 1977).

5

RICHARD DUTTON

Jonson's satiric styles

Well I will scourge those apes;
And to these courteous eyes oppose a mirror,
As large as is the stage whereon we act:
Where they shall see the time's deformity
Anatomized in every nerve, and sinew,
With constant courage and contempt of fear.

(*Every Man out of his Humour,* Grex
after the Second Sounding, 117–22)[1]

On June 1, 1599 Archbishop Whitgift and Bishop Bancroft denounced and proscribed a range of recent works by, among others, Thomas Nashe, Gabriel
Harvey, John Marston, Joseph Hall and Thomas Middleton. Many of these
described themselves as "snarling" or "biting" satires, and the Bishops' ban specifically required "That no Satires or Epigrams be printed hereafter."[2] Yet later
that year Ben Jonson produced *Every Man out of his Humour* and called it a
"comicall satyre": the label figures prominently in the entry of the play in the
Stationers' Register (April 8, 1600) and on the title page of the quarto printed
shortly afterwards, the first of his plays in print. It is a gesture typical of the
young Jonson, who seems to challenge authority by openly writing in a mode
that had been proscribed.[3]

Actually, the motives behind the Bishops' ban remain something of a mystery:
whether it was a response to the dubious moral tone, indeed sheer obscenity of
some of these works, or more generally to the political tensions as Elizabeth's
reign drew to an uncertain close, is unclear.[4] But its effects were localized, and
Jonson may not have been all that daring in so advertising his play – it was certainly not so daring that his play could not be performed at court at Christmas
1599. What is clear is that "satire" was very much an issue at the time, a self-conscious literary mode pursued by young and ambitious men, mostly connected
with the Inns of Court, who wanted to make their mark as much as anything
else. And that it could, on occasion, ruffle important feathers. So Jonson may

have been exploiting a dangerous vogue when he translated (as Marston also did) some of the features of proscribed verse satire to the medium of drama. But he was also inviting the spotlight on himself and his own literary ambitions.

Yet Jonson's commitment to "satire" (as he was to redefine it and make it his own) long outlasted the vogue moment in which he announced his presence, and in various ways informed his whole career. His works were never exactly proscribed, like those of 1599, but no other dramatist of the period ruffled as many feathers as he did. The OED defines satire as "A poem . . . in which prevailing vices or follies are held up to ridicule," and this undoubtedly comprehends most of Jonson's comic drama, significant parts of his tragedies, some of his antimasques, and a good deal of his nondramatic verse (especially in the *Epigrams*). What we may call a satiric impulse commonly lies behind Jonson's writing, informing the aggressive, mocking, superior and malevolent tones that are characteristic of so much of it. It also lies behind the suggestion inescapably present in virtually everything he wrote that however fantastic, improbable, grotesque, or historically distant his subject-matter might be, it all "oppose[s] a mirror" to the realities of his own time. Yet when we consider precisely how and why that is so, it is quickly apparent that the issue is neither as simple nor as straightforward as we may suppose. Jonson did, at least at times, think of himself as a satirist, often invoking classical precedent for writing in that mode. But he was not consistent about this, for reasons that are deeply inflected in the insecurity of his own position as an author.

Who was a man with no university education, a former bricklayer and traveling player, to be holding the prevailing follies and vices of his age up to ridicule? Was it not indeed likely that his own presumption deserved ridicule in itself? Contemporaries were not slow to tell him that it did. And even when Jonson outfaced such objections, there remained the problems common to all satirists: why should anyone attend to what he had to say (especially those he was satirizing)? What gives his writing authority? Is ridicule an end in itself, or should it be a means to an end (such as moral correction)? There are also issues of taste and principle: where does ridicule shade into personal abuse, and abuse into criminal libel? Can we be sure that the satirist is not at least partly in love with the vices and follies he invests so much in denouncing? Jonson's shifting critical positions suggest a degree of unease, indeed of tension about these matters, which become more disturbingly immediate in the live medium of theatre than they are in cold print. This is partly because all satirists ride a fine line with their audiences, who are (at least in part) implicitly guilty of the very vice and folly they collaboratively ridicule. In the heat of the theatre the terms of this collaboration are particularly difficult to negotiate, fraught with quasi-democratic misunderstanding, and subject to change without notice. What kind of compliment is Jonson paying his audience when he announces: "Our scene is London, 'cause we would make known / No country's mirth is better than our own" and promises "natural follies, but so shown, / As even the doers may see, and yet not own" (Prologue to *Alch.*, 5–6, 23–4)?

We may start with the three plays that Jonson explicitly dubbed "comicall satyres," *Every Man out of his Humour, Cynthia's Revels* and *Poetaster*. Actually, only the first of these was so dubbed from the beginning. The other two initially had no generic designation in their early quartos (1601 and 1602 respectively). It was not until the 1616 Folio of Jonson's *Works* that all three were so distinguished as a self-contained group from the "comedies" in that volume, *Every Man In His Humour, Volpone, Epicœne* and *The Alchemist*. The spelling, "satyre," suggests that Jonson (at least for these purposes) shared in the common Renaissance misapprehension that satire derived from the classical Greek "satyr," the half-man, half-beast companions of Bacchus, creatures whose language was supposed to be abusive or obscene. When Jonson himself brought such creatures on stage, in the antimasque to *Oberon* (1611), they are never more than mischievously suggestive. But that in itself is probably a knowing joke from a (by then) house-trained satirist, to be appreciated as such by his royal patrons: in the presence of royalty, even satyrs cannot be entirely themselves.

More typical of the unrestrained "satyrist" is Asper, the central voice in *Every Man out of his Humour*, who presents himself as a latter-day Juvenal, brushing off the alarm of his more cautious companions, Cordatus and Mitis:

> I'll strip the ragged follies of the time
> Naked, as at their birth . . .
>   . . . and with a whip of steel,
> Print wounding lashes in their iron ribs.
>   (Grex after the Second Sounding, 17–20)

In a *furor poeticus* he claims the stage as a corrective mirror in which he wields the beadle's whip, the surgeon's knife or the doctor's purgative, his punishment/medicine at least as repulsive as what it cures. Juvenal had been the key model behind much of the satire singled out by the bishops' ban. The *saeva indignatio* (savage wrath) of his verse affected a splenetic and at times obscene rage, all but out of control, which partly befitted the half-bestial nature of the satyr/satirist but was also implicitly the only appropriate response to the decadence of the world he addressed.[5]

Another thread linking the "comicall satyres" is suggested when Cordatus, in *Every Man out of his Humour*, describes that play as "strange, and of a particular kind by itself, somewhat like *Vetus Comœdia* [Greek Old Comedy]" (Grex after the Second Sounding, 228–9). Jonson draws the analogy again when he defends *Poetaster* from its detractors by invoking the most admired exponent of

Old Comedy, Aristophanes, and again following Renaissance precedent in linking him with Juvenalian satire:

> If all the salt in the Old Comedy
> Should be so censured, or the sharper wit
> Of the bold satire termed scolding rage,
> What age could then compare with those, for buffoons?
> What should be said of Aristophanes?
> Persius? or Juvenal? whose names we now
> So glorify in schools, at least pretend it?   (To the Reader, 184–90)[6]

Actually, none of these plays *is formally* very much like Aristophanic Old Comedy, which was to leave much clearer marks on *Volpone* and *The Alchemist*.[7] The real issue here is the degree of license available to the satirist in castigating his targets, especially those who were identifiable individuals. Aristophanes and Juvenal had enjoyed considerable liberty in these matters, and were now regarded as classics: Jonson asks for the same freedom. The whole apparatus of choruses, inductions and apologias with which Jonson invests these plays may smack to us of scholarly pedantry, but in fact they are marks of tension, of a *lack* of given authority, both at the level of artistic experiment and at the level of voicing what some might think ought not to be voiced.

The ambivalence of Asper as a "satyrist" is acknowledged in the "role" he adopts in the action proper of the play: Macilente (Envy) is motivated by nothing more altruistic than envy in his excoriation of the self-seeking folly and vice he encounters, subsumed in the play by another vogue term, "humor." Asper defines its specific Jonsonian sense, which is only a *metaphoric* application of the old medical notion of an imbalance of the bodily fluids. He talks rather of a condition which may truly be seen as a defect of character:

> As when some one peculiar quality
> Doth so possess a man that it doth draw
> All his affects, his spirits, and his powers,
> In their confluctions, all to run one way;
> This may be truly said to be a humour.
>
> (Grex after the Second Sounding, 105–9)

It is a self-centered, psycho-social condition, driven by an urban world of competition in money-making, status, fashion, sex and wit (the abiding concerns of the early modern gentry and the middling sort of people with whom they vied for power and prestige). As Don E. Wayne observes, dramatic characterization based on such an approach to human nature "amounts to a rudimentary social psychology, a technical apparatus for diagnosing the changes that affected English society in the Renaissance; and as such it involves an anticipatory awareness of the phenomenon of alienation in both the Marxian and existentialist senses of the term."[8] This remains central to Jonsonian characterization, and so to the satiric strategies of the drama which anatomize it, throughout his career, long after the experiments of the "humor" plays and "comicall satyres."

In *Every Man out of his Humour* itself, Macilente is the defining humor of all those exhibited in the play, not their antithesis. All those who stir his envy live in the condition of wanting to be, or pretending to be, something they are not – such as Puntarvolo, the vain-glorious knight, wrapped in self-congratulatory singularity; and Brisk, the "affecting courtier," whose manly bravado is never convincing, despite the near-adulterous admiration it arouses in Deliro's wife, Fallace, and the pathetic emulation it receives from Fungoso. Deliro's doting subjection to his own wife, Sordido's "wretched" dedication to exploiting the ill-luck of others, and Sogliardo's determination to become a gentleman, oblivious to the derision he incurs, are all forms of delusive obsession, so intense as to challenge their fundamental status as human beings. And so on. The striking exception to the pattern is Carlo Buffone, the one character whom Macilente does not envy: "I envy not this Buffon, for indeed / Neither his fortunes nor his parts deserve it: / But I do hate him . . ." (1.2.198–200). Their mutual hatred in fact points to their complementarity: Buffone "with absurd similes will transform any person into deformity" (Characters, 23). That is, his foul-mouthed name-calling mimics the role of the "satyr," though without the spleen, not so much transforming people as insisting upon the realities which their delusions resist.

Yet despite the verbal and competitive energy vested in Macilente and Buffone, the play remains essentially static, a thematic elaboration on the prose "characters" with which Jonson prefaces the printed text rather than a dynamic exploration of them. Although, as I have tried to show, there is a good deal of parallelism in the arrangement of the characters, such that their follies reflect on each other with a complex and deliberate variety (the admiration and lust which Brisk inspires, for example, and his own preening affectation, are all put into perspective by the easy wit with which his mistress, Saviolina, cuts him down to size), there is little in the way of plot or development. The play, and its satire, in effect end because Macilente runs out of people to envy and so loses his own humor, reverting to Asper.

Cynthia's Revels is similarly episodic, a pageant of follies and vices thematically linked by the symbol of the court as "The Fountain of Self-Love." Indeed, Jonson comically defuses any expectation of suspense or complex action by having one of the boy actors recite the plot (against the protests of his fellows) in the Induction. But the Asper/Macilente "satyrist" has disappeared altogether, to be replaced by Criticus (Crites in the Folio version), whom the god Mercury hails as a "creature of a most perfect and divine temper," asserting "I could leave my place in heaven to live among mortals, so I were sure to be no other than he" (2.3.109, 130–1). The biting satirist has given way to an improbably unruffled observer of the narcissistic court of Gargaphy, a poet/critic who laughs off plots to defame him: "Do, good detraction, do, and I the while / Shall shake thy spite off with a careless smile" (3.3.1–2). Safe in such self-belief he fashions a disdainful, but essentially detached critique of the world around him, as when he takes a scene of virtual soliloquy to describe to Arete (Virtue) "The strangest pageant, fashioned like a court" (3.4.4).

The role of Criticus is, however, complemented by that of the gods, Mercury and Cupid, who constantly mock the self-absorption of those like Amorphus and Asotus, Hedon and Anaides, who look for advancement at court. And if Criticus is in some ways too godlike, the gods are (in the manner of Lucianic satire) to a degree too human. We are reminded of Mercury's reputation as a thief, while Cupid is "giddy Cupid, Venus' frantic son" (5.6.54), who proves unwelcome at the court of Cynthia – the mythic "Queen and huntress, chaste and fair" – once his role in Criticus' masque has been revealed. At such moments, as Janet Clare has argued, the satiric treatment of classical mythology intersects with the play's treatment of the mythology of Elizabeth, the Virgin Queen (long identified with Cynthia/Diana), subjecting it to the same skepticism.[9] And once this equates Gargaphy with England we can see that this pointedly old-fashioned play (it evokes the plays of John Lyly from the 1580s) is more topically barbed than we might have appreciated.

Jonson had originally meant *Every Man out of his Humour* to end with Macilente losing his envy at the appearance of an actor dressed as Queen Elizabeth (an effect he was able to keep, without the actor, at its court performance). An illusion of absolute royal authority was meant to drive the envy out of him, and also resolve the residual ambiguities in Jonson's "satyric" strategy. But, as he fumed in the quarto text, "many seem'd not to rellish it; and therefore 'twas since alter'd" (HS, 3:602) – to the version I have described. *Cynthia's Revels* makes much more of that royal authority by making Cynthia/Elizabeth the nub of the piece, an unimpeachable fount of honor, justice, and patronage. She devolves to Arete and Criticus her own authority to punish the follies and vices revealed in the masque, which she had first commissioned from her critic-poet – a satirist's dream: "We give the charge; impose what pains you please: / The incurable cut off, the rest reform" (5.9.96–7).

It is difficult to determine at this cultural remove what difference it made to the tone of this play and its satiric aspirations that it was written for boy players, the Children of Queen Elizabeth's Chapel. To what extent was their aping of the adult world self-deflating, perhaps making the boy-Criticus a less priggish and self-congratulatory figure than he seems on the printed page? The unruliness of the children in the Induction may lead us to suppose that Jonson aimed to exploit some such effect. Conversely, what does the track record of this company tell us? Soon after this they became notorious for staging anti-court satires, targeting everyone from King James down. Jonson's own *Eastward Ho!* (with Chapman and Marston) is a prime example, a work which nearly led to the judicial mutilation of its authors.[10] *Cynthia's Revels* breathes not a breath of criticism of Cynthia/Elizabeth, in the way that the later play would brazenly comment on King James' selling of knighthoods ("I ken the man weel, hee's one of my thirty pound knights": 4.1.155–6). Yet if we stand back from the details of the text we see that the Virgin Queen presides over a court of fawning self-seekers, while Arete/Virtue is "scarce able to buy herself a gown" (Induction, 76–7) and Criticus receives credit for his service but little in the way of status or material reward. So at some level the play satirizes not only self-seeking courtiers, but also the court which allows them to flourish while neglecting more deserving servants – a sly ridiculing of social and political *structures,* as well as the individuals who inhabit them, which was to figure in many of Jonson's best plays. *Cynthia's Revels* was performed at court in 1600/1, but it would not be surprising if Thomas Dekker's suggestion that it was "misliked" were correct.[11]

All of these issues reassemble, in different forms, in *Poetaster.* But the distance Jonson has traveled in his satiric strategy is marked by his introduction of the Roman poet-critic Horace into the play. He is no snarling "satyrist" but a man of culture, moderation and good sense, who claims to write "sharp, yet modest rhymes / That spare men's persons, and but tax their crimes" (3.5.133–4) – a formula Jonson reiterated in "To the Reader." His "Author" says: "My books have still been taught / To spare the persons, and to speak the vices" (83–4). Horace in the play is the long-suffering subject of misunderstanding, suspicion and deliberate misconstruction, whose patient adherence to the civilizing ideals of poetry throws into stark relief the licentiousness, plagiarism, blasphemy and mendacity of the poetasters around him. The tone is set at his introduction (3.1.) in a scene which is essentially a dramatization of Horace's own *Satires* I.ix. He is trying to compose an ode to his great patron, Mæcenas, but is beset by the would-be poet, Crispinus, who simply will not leave him alone and prattles on in a way that reveals all his affectations and misapprehensions about poetry. This sets up a pattern of sympathies, and a comic dynamic, which makes Horace's "purging" of Crispinus (and Demetrius) a fitting climax of the play. Forcing them to vomit forth their affected language is paradoxically a vindication of all Horace represents.

But poetry in the play is always a metaphor for wider service of the state, so that the satire on poetasters compounds that of self-serving actors (Histrio, Æsop), soldiers (Tucca) and politicians (Lupus). Lawyers also come in for their fair share of ridicule, though this is largely conveyed through the conversation in which Ovid Senior urges his son to pursue the law (a profession apparently requiring no effort, learning or scruples) instead of poetry, rather than through a particular character. This appears more fully in the 1616 Folio (1.2.86–121) than it does in the 1601 quarto, as does the satire against the actors, and may originally have been suppressed. The willful misrepresentation of Horace's poetry as seditious libel by the spy, Asinius Lupus (the asinine wolf), parallels in more sober tones Crispinus' misplaced attentions. It fails largely because the emperor, Augustus, a genuine lover of poetry and its "useful light" (4.6.35), has implicit faith in Horace, recognizing that he has virtue despite his poverty: "Thanks, Horace, for thy free and wholesome sharpness: / Which pleaseth Cæsar more than servile fawns" (5.1.94–5). In the closing scenes of the play, where Augustus is surrounded by an array of fine poets, Tibullus, Gallus and Virgil, as well as Horace, we see acted out a perfect marriage between poetry and the state: the emperor and his counselors bring together insight and justice, reflection and action.

In the course of this it becomes clear that satire has it place, but is not the last word, which is reserved for Virgil, "Rome's honour" (5.1.69). His presence is particularly important for placing in perspective Augustus' banishment of Ovid and imprisonment of his own daughter, Julia, for their blasphemous imitation of the gods. He condemns Ovid's perverted use of his poetic inspiration as a betrayal of divine gifts. Horace intercedes on Ovid's behalf, calling on him to let "royal bounty . . . mediate," but Augustus insisted that "There is no bounty to be showed to such / As have no real goodness" (4.6.60–2). Virgil's reading from the *Aeneid* (in which the passion of Aeneas and Dido distracts him from his mission and her from her duty, defiling both their reputations) endorses Augustus' action, underlining the deep seriousness of the issues. It also implicitly defines the limits of Horace's "free and wholesome sharpness." Satire can cope with the affectations of a Crispinus or Demetrius, the bragging of a Tucca, the perverse scheming of a Lupus. But it is inadequate to address the highest mysteries of state and of the human heart, which are here shown to be the proper preserve of epic.

Although Jonson carefully varied his satiric strategies in these three plays, his rivals mocked them all as variations on the same theme, pretentious self-promotions. Dekker pointed the finger in *Satiromastix:* "you must be called Asper, and Criticus, and Horace" (1.2.376). And just as the satirist-figures are all flattering versions of himself, so his satires are scurrilous lampoons of known individuals. Ironically, this seems to be more the case the more he trumpets his Horatian determination "To spare the persons and to speak the vices." Demetrius in *Poetaster* is probably a lampoon of Dekker himself, while Crispinus is even more surely one (on linguistic evidence) of Marston. Beyond the in-fighting of the dramatists and actors, which we may partly ascribe to commercial rivalry (this play was Jonson's last shot in the so-called War of the Theatres), it is apparent that others also took offense – notably lawyers and soldiers. As Tom Cain has argued, Jonson's own claims not to have been "particular" ring quite hollow on examination, and he stirred up a hornets' nest in satirizing constituencies that had been associated with the recently fallen Earl of Essex.[12]

Much later in his career, in *Discoveries* (pub. 1640), Jonson criticized Old Comedy for making the creation of laughter an end in itself, thereby losing touch with the moral and artistic ends of comedy. And lampoons appealed only to the quirky lowest common denominators of popular taste:

> And therefore it was clear that all insolent and obscene speeches, jest[s] upon the best men, injuries to particular persons, perverse and sinister sayings – and the rather unexpected – in the Old Comedy did move laughter, especially where it did imitate any dishonesty, and scurrility came forth in the place of wit; which who understands the nature and genius of laughter cannot but perfectly know.
>
> Of which Aristophanes affords an ample harvest, having not only outgone Plautus or any other in that kind, but expressed all the moods and figures of what is ridiculous, oddly. In short, as vinegar is not accounted good until the wine is corrupted, so jests that are true and natural seldom raise laughter with the beast, the multitude. They love nothing that is right and proper. The farther it runs from reason or possibility with them, the better it is. What could have made them laugh, like to see Socrates presented – that example of all good life, honesty, and virtue – to have him hoisted up with a pulley, and there play the philosopher in a basket. . . . This was theatrical wit, right stage-jesting, and relishing a playhouse invented for scorn and laughter . . . This is truly leaping from the stage to the tumbril again, reducing all wit to the original dung-cart. (2677–700)[13]

He well knew that his own Old Comedy experiments had been accused of exactly the same vices, especially insolence and obscenity, the derision of known (and virtuous) individuals, and perverse novelty. Jonson might consistently claim that he depicted the species, not the individual, and that he wrote with a moral agenda, not just to please "the beast, the multitude." But it is in the very nature of satire that it muddies all such distinctions, and leaves the author vulnerable to a range of charges, especially arrogance and hypocrisy.

After *Poetaster* Jonson sought to deflect such charges by adopting very different satiric strategies. The beast fable of *Volpone,* the alchemical "commonwealth" of *The Alchemist,* the fair of *Bartholomew Fair,* are all metaphors of a rapacious world in which human aspiration is perverted by sub-human appetite. The poets are no longer an idealized Criticus or Horace, but Volpone or Subtle, inventing new worlds not to reform mankind but to exploit it. Or Littlewit, indulging his own vanity by peddling his bathetic puppet-play. Scathing, skeptical and virtuous voices are not absent, but they are weakly ineffective like Bonario and Celia, deeply suspect like Surly, ridiculously self-important like Overdo, or hypocritical like Zeal-of-the-Land Busy. We even get bizarre moments when it suits the agenda of vice to preach with the angels, as when Subtle reproves the erring Epicure Mammon: "Error? / Guilt, guilt, my son; give it the right name" (4.5.38–9). It is a predatory world of cozeners (deceivers) and gulls (dupes) – and, as the setting becomes an ever more particularized London (which begins in *Epicœne)*, it becomes apparent that the wiliest of the cozeners is the dramatist himself, and that the gulls who really matter are in the audience.

We see this new satiric strategy deployed most deftly, and with layer upon layer of irony, in one last play which Jonson interestingly associated with "*comedia vetus,*" but here English Old Comedy, rather than Greek (*Conv. Dr.* 351). This is the neglected masterpiece, *The Devil is an Ass.* The central on-stage gull is Fabian Fitzdotterel, who is ludicrously determined to "see 'The Devil is an Ass,' today" (1.4.21), which immediately undermines any comfortable demarcations between the play and its audience. But Jonson compounds the joke as he explores Fitzdotterel's motives for wanting to see this particular play, which are of a piece with the qualities which make him such a ready dupe for Merecraft, Engine and their "projections." Firstly, he is an avid attender of new plays because this is now the fashionable thing for gallants to do, especially at indoor theatres like the Blackfriars where they can pay extra to sit on the stage itself and show off their fine clothing – becoming as much objects of attention as the actors. He has already hired a suit for the occasion (and Engine has made a tidy profit by passing off something second-hand as new), but wants Wittipol's cloak to complete the outfit. He wants it so desperately that he is prepared to allow Wittipol a "conversation" with his wife, suppressing for once his morbid fear of being cuckolded.

Fitzdotterel's other motive for wanting to see *this* play is that he has an obsession with devils, so much so that he has been employing necromancers to conjure one (actual people, like Simon Forman, are named), though without success. The joke is that his entire view of devils has been formed by watching plays – so much so that when Pug, a real one, presents himself to him, Fitzdotterel refuses to accept him for what he is because he does not have the cloven heels which the devils wore in the old Elizabethan morality plays. The basic conceit of Jonson's play is simply that Jacobean London has become so sophisticated and ingenious in its vices that it goes far beyond anything hell and Satan can offer: all of Pug's efforts to encourage sin fail pathetically. But this is self-referentially developed through the idea of devilry as something theatrically defined.

The play Fitzdotterel is determined to see initially evokes the morality plays of fifty years before, like *The Nice Wanton* and *King Darius,* in which Iniquity (whom Pug is anxious to have with him) had played the Vice. Jonson depicts Iniquity as stuck in a time-warp, only able to talk in cumbersome old verse, like fourteeners; but he later signals his own ingenuity by inverting the traditional formula in which the devil carries the Vice off on his back. Yet *The Devil is an Ass* also alludes to the more sophisticated 1580s/1590s generation of plays in which devils are conjured (like Greene's *Friar Bacon and Friar Bungay,* and

Marlowe's *Dr Faustus),* and to yet more recent works which had already begun to parody those conventions, such as The *Merry Devil of Edmonton* (c. 1602), *If This Be Not a Good Play, the Devil Is In It* (1611; both mentioned in the Prologue) and Haughton's *Grim the Collier of Croydon* (1600), which Jonson follows quite closely in some respects.[14] It is a history in brief of the Renaissance stage, and Fitzdotterel would doubtless be happy with any of these. But Jonson is determined to provide him – and other members of the audience – with something different again.

This is signaled in the Prologue, which was specifically written for the play's performance at the Blackfriars. The indoor theatres had no tradition of devil plays which, with their horseplay and fireworks, were associated with the roomier open air amphitheatres. Their stock-in-trade was satirical comedy and courtly tragicomedy. So there is an extra edge to the Prologue's grousing about the Fitzdotterel-like gallants on the stage: they are making a stage already rather small for this kind of play far too cramped.[15] But after an initial scene in hell (and apart from Pug's final translation back there, leaving a stink of brimstone) very little of the play proves to be about devils at all – at least, not supernatural ones. Fitzdotterel finds his real devils in the projector, Merecraft, with his sometimes unreliable allies, Engine, Everill, Trains and Gilthead – so that it is entirely appropriate that, after being bewitched by one far-fetched scheme after another (such as reclaiming acres of "Drowned-land" and thereby gaining a dukedom, or making a fortune from leather made of dog-skins) he spends most of the final scene in a counterfeit fit of diabolic possession, foaming at the mouth with soap.

But Jonson springs a greater surprise on his audience by devoting a good deal of the play to a love plot, of a kind that has no generic association with any form of devil play or indeed with the satiric drama with which Jonson was now firmly associated. This looks as much forward to the sentimental romances of Caroline drama and the Restoration as the devil play looks back to the Tudor interlude. Wittipol's relationship with Frances Fitzdotterel, passionate but chaste, is like nothing Jonson had essayed before. She is beautiful, intelligent, desirable and utterly wasted on her jealous husband; he is ardent, witty, resourceful, but respectful. And in the moment Fitzdotterel strikes her, after Wittipol has lavished on her some of the finest love poetry in the language, Jonson presents his audience (tantalizing them about moral values, as he had previously about theatrical tastes) with as strong a case for adultery as one can imagine. But both are too honorable for that, and Wittipol proves his love rather by an ironic subterfuge in which, cross-dressed as a Spanish lady, he contrives to seduce Fitzdotterel into enfeoffing his lands upon Manley. (The cross-dressing involves the play's crowning piece of metatheatrical bravura, when Merecraft argues that Wittipol is less fitted for the role than his own candidate, the actor Dick Robinson: but the real Dick Robinson was actually playing Wittipol.)[16] By the enfeoffment, Fitzdotterel surrenders legal and financial control of his estates, as a man might do who anticipates death. But this is not a Merecraft-style fraud: Wittipol trusts his friend, Manley, to use this power to ensure that Fitzdotterel will henceforth treat his wife properly. In an age when a woman could not hope to have such power over her husband's property, it is as near as the play could come (short of Fitzdotterel dying – which, like Morose in *Epicœne,* there is some hope may happen shortly) to freeing her. The virtuous triangle of love and trust between Wittipol, Manley and Frances Fitzdotterel is in diametric opposition to the "diabolic" scheming and self-interest elsewhere in the play.

The play thus teases the audience on a number of levels about their taste in the theatre for what is old or familiar, predictable or illicit. It asks them about their own motives for being there. As Anne Barton observes: "There is no trace in this comedy of the old hectoring, moralistic approach to the spectators or readers which had marked a number of his Elizabethan plays. Instead, he contents himself with a series of subtle demonstrations that our judgement too is fallible, and the ethical and intellectual superiority of the onlookers to the characters on stage is by no means certain."[17] Yet at another level there is reason to suppose that the play's satire bit just as hard as that of the old plays had. Jonson told Drummond that it was a "play of his upon which he was accused" and "Parergwz is discoursed of the Duke of Drown-land. The king desired him to conceal it" (350, 354–5). We know nothing else about the accusation, though the latter passage apparently means that the king asked Jonson to suppress its incidental theme of Fitzdotterel being promised the Dukedom of Drowned Land.

The play, for all its metatheatrical fantasy, is sharply attuned to contentious contemporary issues. Merecraft and Everill's "projections" (a difference here from the schemes peddled by Volpone and Subtle) all depend for their credibility on securing legal monopolies, which required royal patents – and these were a major source of friction between James and his parliaments at the time. Moreover, as Helen Ostovitch has argued, Frances Fitzdotterel's situation seems to touch on those of a number of distressed aristocratic women, including notably Frances Howard and Mary Wroth.[18] And several of the individual characters might well be lampoons; the case for Sir Paul Eitherside, for example, "representing" Sir Edward Coke has been made more than once.[19] There were any number of counts on which he might well have been "accused." Jonson may have adopted a less hectoring tone, but the satirist in him had lost none of his bite.

But it is a measure of the distance he had come since the "comicall satyres" that he acknowledges – however obliquely and ironically – that he is himself an element in the folly and vice that the play ridicules. Fitzdotterel and his counterparts in the real Blackfriars audience may have dubious motives for going to see *The Devil is an Ass,* but the reality is that Jonson and his play are part of the market economy which drives them. Jonson may demonstrate the aesthetic and intellectual superiority of his own wares over what the commercial theatre usually has to offer, and over the limitations of his audience's tastes and expectations. But he can never totally efface his own implication within them. He may continue to look for true "understanders" among his readers, as he will look for the royal sanction of his work to lift it above the sordid entanglements of satire. But he cannot ignore the reality that when he "oppose[s] a mirror" to his age, the first face he sees in it is his own. Since he cannot, however, he makes a virtue of necessity and turns that face (and his spreading paunch) into a point of entry to his poems and plays – the undecorous poet at decorous Penshurst where "no man tells my cups," whom the Stage-keeper fears may be behind the arras at *Bartholomew Fair,* or Mirth describes "rolling himself up and down like a tun" behind the scenes of *The Staple of News* (Induction, 56). It is all so disarmingly genial and familiar that it would be churlish to refuse the old satirist's offer "To feast you often, and invite new guests" (*Alch.,* 5.5.165). But if Jonson amiably shows us himself in the mirror, he still insists that we see ourselves there too.

NOTES

1 All references to Jonson's plays are to *The Complete Plays of Ben Jonson,* ed. G. A. Wilkes, 4 vols. (Oxford: The Clarendon Press, 1981–2). The Grex is a chorus of Cordatus and Mitis, who are present throughout the play. "Soundings" were fanfares announcing that a performance was about to start, and the Grex after the second of these (1: 285–93) acts as an induction to the play. References within the text are to line-numbering.

2 Edward Arber, ed., *A Transcript of the Register of the Company of Stationers of London 1554–1640,* 5 vols. (London: Privately Printed, 1875–94), 3:677. Hall's satires, although called in, were not actually burned.

3 See O. J. Campbell, *Comicall Satyre and Shakespeare's "Troilus and Cressida"* (San Marino: Huntington Library, 1938).

4 See Cyndia Susan Clegg, *Press Censorship in Elizabethan England* (Cambridge: Cambridge University Press, 1997), 198–217.

5 See Alvin Kernan, *The Cankered Muse: Satire of the English Renaissance* (New Haven and London: Yale University Press, 1959), 64–80, 156–91.

6 "To the Reader" is printed after the play (2: 221–8). References in the text are to line-numbering.

7 See Anne Barton, *Ben Jonson, Dramatist* (Cambridge: Cambridge University Press, 1984), 113–4.

8 Don E. Wayne, "Drama and Society in the Age of Jonson: An Alternative View," *Renaissance Drama* 13 (1982), 105. See also Lawrence Danson, "Jonsonian Comedy and the Discovery of the Social Self," *PMLA* 99 (1984), 179–83.

9 See Janet Clare, "Jonson's 'Comical Satires' and the Art of Courtly Compliment," in *Refashioning Ben Jonson: Gender, Politics and the Jonsonian Canon,* edited by Julie Sanders with Kate Chedgzoy and Sue Wiseman (Basingstoke and London: Macmillan, 1998), 28–47. Clare points out that some of the most pointed elements of the critique

of Elizabeth's court were either removed from the quarto text, or discreetly not included until the 1616 Folio.

10 See Richard Dutton, *Mastering the Revels: The Regulation and Censorship of English Renaissance Drama* (Basingstoke and London: Macmillan, 1991), 171–9.

11 *Satiromastix*, in *The Dramatic Works of Thomas Dekker,* ed. Fredson Bowers (Cambridge: Cambridge University Press, 1953–61), 1: 5.3.324.

12 See Tom Cain, Introduction to the Revels edition of *Poetaster* (Manchester: Manchester University Press, 1995), esp. 30–6, 40–9; also "'Satyres, That Girde and Fart at the Time': *Poetaster* and the Essex Rebellion," in *Refashioning Ben Jonson,* 48–70.

13 Quotations from *Discoveries* are from the edition by Ian Donaldson in *Ben Jonson: The Oxford Authors* (521–94); those from *Conversations with William Drummond of Hawthornden* are from the edition in the same volume (595–611). References in the text to both works are to line-numbering.

14 See Robert N. Watson, *Ben Jonson's Parodic Strategy: Literary Imperialism in the Comedies* (Cambridge, MA: Harvard University Press, 1987), 178–80.

15 James Shirley, in the prologue to *The Doubtful Heir* (1641), claimed that the Globe stage was "vast" compared with that of the Blackfriars.

16 See Barton, *Ben Jonson, Dramatist,* 227–8. The joke was retained and updated in the 1995 production of the play at The Swan; see Peter Happe, "Staging *The Devil is an Ass* in 1995," *The Ben Jonson Journal* 2 (1995), 239–46.

17 Barton, *Ben Jonson, Dramatist,* 227.

18 Helen Ostovich, "Hell for Lovers: Shades of Adultery in *The Devil is an Ass*" in *Refashioning Ben Jonson,* 155–82.

19 See, for example, Robert C. Evans, *Jonson and the Contexts of His Time* (Lewisburg: Bucknell University Press, 1994), 77–86, and David Lindley, *The Trials of Frances Howard: Fact and Fiction at the Court of King James* (London and New York: Routledge, 1994), 145–93.

6

DAVID BEVINGTON

The major comedies

Ben Jonson wrote *Volpone* for the King's Men in 1605–6. This premier acting company had been given the accolade of that title, the King's Men, when James I came to the English throne in 1603. Its roster included Richard Burbage and William Shakespeare, both of whom, along with Augustine Phillips, Henry Condell, Will Sly, Will Kemp, John Heminges, Thomas Pope, Christopher Beeston, and John Duke, are listed in the Jonson Folio of 1616 as having acted in Jonson's *Every Man in his Humour* in 1598.[1] They then constituted the Lord Chamberlain's Men, and for some years had been the premier acting company of England (in fierce competition with the Admiral's Men, headed by Edward Alleyn). In 1599, the Lord Chamberlain's Men had moved into their new theatre, the Globe, on the south side of the Thames across from London in Southwark. Jonson's *Every Man out of his Humour* was one of their new plays in this location, along with Shakespeare's *Julius Cæsar* and *Henry V*. Jonson's *Sejanus* was acted here in 1603, *Volpone* in 1605–6 (featuring Burbage, Condell, Heminges, Sly, and two newcomers, John Lowin and Alexander Cooke), *The Alchemist* in 1610, and *Catiline* in 1611. The King's Men presented Jonson's *The Staple of News* in 1626 at their second Globe Theatre, the first having burned down in 1613.

Jonson thus wrote plays for Shakespeare's acting company. Yet he also wrote for the private acting companies and under aristocratic auspices during these years. *Cynthia's Revels* and *Poetaster* were acted by the Children of the Chapel Royal at the second Blackfriars Theatre in 1600–1; *Epicœne* was acted by the same company, now renamed the Children of the Queen's Revels (also known as the Blackfriars or Whitefriars Children), at Whitefriars in 1609. *Bartholomew Fair* was staged by Lady Elizabeth's Servants at the Hope Theatre in 1614, a company that had recently united with the Children of the Queen's Revels. The Queen's Revels company was patronized by Queen Anne; Lady Elizabeth, the daughter of Queen Anne and King James I, was herself Queen of Bohemia after her marriage in 1613. Jonson wrote masques and royal entertainments as well, for performance at court or in aristocratic venues: *The Entertainment of the*

Queen and Prince at Althorp in 1603, part of *The Coronation Triumph* for the coronation of King James in March of 1604, *The Masque of Blackness* in 1605, *Hymenæi* in 1606, *The Haddington Masque* and *The Masque of Beauty* in 1608, *Oberon* in 1611, and still more.

Jonson's divided career between public and private theatre, and his keen sense of rivalry with Shakespeare as the leading dramatist for the Lord Chamberlain's and then King's Men, are on display in *Volpone*. The play is a brilliant satire, of greed, of hypocrisy, of affected mannerisms. So, to be sure, are *Every Man In* and *Every Man Out*, acted by the same company in 1598–9. Yet satire was also a speciality of the boys' companies that had reopened in 1599 after nearly a decade of enforced inactivity; in fact, they had been closed around 1591 for their satirical bent. Jonson's own inclination seems to have been toward the kind of theatre that sophisticated spectators could expect to find in so-called "private" houses like Blackfriars. Featuring performances indoors, in the evening, and a limited audience capacity, these theatres attracted elite spectators willing to pay higher prices for plays that catered to the elite.[2] The differences between the public and private theatres must not be overemphasized, to be sure, and Jonson's own capacity for writing in both theatrical worlds is well attested to.[3] Still, the rivalry between the two was real enough and could erupt at times into open hostility.[4] Jonson's straddling both worlds provides a source of ambiguity and conflict in many of the plays he wrote.

The Prologue to *Volpone* is, like many of Jonson's prologues and inductions, a manifesto, a statement of artistic purpose. His stance is neoclassical; his tone is defensive, outspoken, even arrogant. Paraphrasing Horace's famous dictum that art should be both pleasing and useful, able to delight and instruct, Jonson insists that "In all his poems still hath been this measure: / To mix profit with your pleasure" (7–8).[5] The choice of the word "poems" for his writings, including his plays, suggests that he thinks of them as part of a great literary tradition, capable of bestowing immortality on their author. Jonson is proudly conscious of his place in a classical tradition, observing (in his own fashion) the rules of classical decorum: "The laws of time, place, persons he observeth; / From no needful rule he swerveth" (31–2).[6] That is, Jonson commits himself to limiting his dramatic action to a period of roughly twenty-four hours and to a single location (Venice), so that the spectators' credulity will not be stretched by having to imagine that the stage represents several distinct places, or that a character is supposed to age before the spectators' eyes from a young to an old person. Jonson refuses to obligate himself to unnecessary rules, but he cherishes the ideas of five-act structure and unities of time and place that are the hallmark of classical composition. Jonson thus fashions himself as a learned poet in the best tradition of Plautus, Terence, and Ariosto. Jonson was openly proud of his command of Latin and Greek, and was quite prepared to be critical of those (like Shakespeare) who were not so well versed as he in ancient languages and literatures.[7] He dedicated *Volpone* "to the most noble and most equal sisters, the two famous universities" of Oxford and Cambridge, as a token of his partnership in learning with those institutions.

Jonson speaks of himself, in his Prologue to *Volpone*, as surrounded by enemies. Some accuse him by crying hoarsely: "All he writes is railing," that is, he can write nothing but satire. These same carping critics "flout" him for taking "a year" to write each play (10–12), thus accusing him of being too labored. Jonson replies testily that he wrote *Volpone* in only five weeks. Later, he will take Shakespeare to task for being too facile a writer. Clearly he is sensitive to the charge that his writing smells of the lamp and the study, in contrast to Shakespeare's more "natural" flow of language.[8]

Jonson is no less proud and touchy in his defiance of the "rout" of undiscerning theatre-goers who call for slapstick effects like the breaking of eggs and employment of "quaking custards" (20–1) – the equivalent of a pie thrown in somebody's face to get a quick laugh. Jonson will have none of this gratuitous, crowd-pleasing horseplay. All his jests will "fit his fable" (28), that is, be integral to the plot and dramatic composition. His play will offer "quick [i.e. lively] comedy refined," such as "best critics have designed" (29–30). It will be satirical but not vituperative or sadistic: his ink will contain no "gall or copperas" (i.e. rancor and vitriol). Jonson is here answering a common accusation, that satire is nothing but libel and personal abuse under the guise of moral instruction. He will, however, rub "a little salt" on his hearer's cheeks in order to bring laughter and to cure affectation, as with rubbing salt in a wound (33–6).

Jonson's tone is so insistently hostile to the values of public entertainment, and so scornful in defense of the classical and elitist tradition, that we can understand why he found himself facing a chorus of nay-sayers. Yet *Volpone* did appear on the public stage. It is a satire. Volpone and his servant Mosca are expert at fleecing those who deserve to be fleeced. Posing as an old man on the verge of death without natural heirs, Volpone uses his great wealth (cunningly obtained by his con games of the past) to entice a series of would-be inheritors into presenting him with huge gifts as a way of seeking to be the sole benefactors of Volpone's last will and testament. Significantly, they are all prosperous members of what we would call the middle class. Voltore, the advocate or lawyer, brings a massive engraved piece of plate (precious metal) as his offering. Corbaccio, an old and deaf gentleman, consents to disinherit his son, Bonario, in favor of Volpone, in the hope that Volpone will reciprocate by making Corbaccio his heir and then die first. The merchant Corvino proffers the most astonishing gift of all: his attractive young wife Celia, whom he will order to climb into bed with Volpone and comfort his dying moments so that her husband will be named heir. Mosca's bland assurance that Volpone is past love-making hardly justifies the way in which Corvino is proposing to use his wife as chattels, over her vehement protests.

These three craven worldlings clearly deserve what they get. Their names – Voltore the vulture, Corbaccio the crow, Corvino the raven – all point to their being carrion birds, disgusting in their alacrity to feed on decaying human flesh. No sympathy need be lost on them. The satirical comedy invites derisive laughter at their hypocrisies and at those of the learned and business professions generally. Mosca marvels sardonically at lawyers who can plead either side of a law case with equal ease, and who can turn with "quick agility," re-turn, "make knots and then undo them, / Give forkéd counsel, take provoking gold / On either hand," etc. (1.3.52–60). Doctors, similarly, are worse than the diseases they treat; their fees are intolerable, and "they kill / With as much license as a judge" (1.4.20–33). Even those who pretend to be learned do not escape laughter: "Hood an ass with reverend purple, / So you can hide his two ambitious ears, / And he shall pass for a cathedral doctor" (1.2.111–13).

No less amusing are the ways in which these gulls are tricked into betraying their hypocrisies. Corvino, persuaded by Mosca that the bed-ridden Volpone is comatose, takes delight (egged on by Mosca) in bellowing into Volpone's presumably deaf ear a series of hyperbolical invectives: "His nose is like a common sewer, still running" (1.5.65), and so on. Corvino is especially funny as a satirical butt because two "humors," or obsessions, are in conflict within him: his greedy desire for wealth and his insane jealousy of his young wife. We laugh to see him struggle with the suggestion that he prostitute his wife to Volpone in return for a promise of wealth, especially when the desire for wealth wins out. Corbaccio is similarly a comic figure because his greed succeeds in overcoming the paternal feelings that must prompt him, however ineffectually, to pass his property on to his son. As Volpone triumphantly comments, "What a rare punishment / Is avarice to itself!" (1.4.142–3).

These devices of trickery are brilliant in their variety and in cleverness of execution. Part of our admiration goes to Jonson, the inventive playwright, who knows how to plot such a richly complicated narrative; part of it is directed to Volpone and Mosca, the architects and executors of this ingenious chicanery. Yet their names are a warning: Volpone is the fox and Mosca is the fly (meaning a flying insect, not just a house-fly). Can such personifications of craftiness and parasitism be admirable? Jonsonian satire proceeds by a set of discernible rules that provide a basis for making such judgments.[9] Volpone and Mosca are partly admirable at first because they are clever and self-knowing, unlike their victims, in whom an insufficient knowledge of self is overwhelmed by "humorous" obsession. Volpone and Mosca laugh at human folly and point out for us its absurdities. At first, they also proceed by carefully defined rules as to whom they will victimize. As Mosca observes, they do not attack widows or orphans

(1.1.49–50). They gull those who deserve gulling. No less importantly, the sport and cleverness of their devices seem to mean more to them than the actual financial gain. Volpone insists, "I glory / More in the cunning purchase of my wealth / Than in the glad possession" (30–2). So long as they observe these rules, Volpone and Mosca, however self-indulgent they may be, and however ruthless in their cunning, are true satirists doing what satire is supposed to do: expose folly and make the victim suffer.

The punishment is supposed to fit the offense: this is another capital rule of comical satire. And, for a time in the play, it does. What more fitting comic punishment could one devise for a madly jealous and greedy merchant than to inveigle him into ushering his young wife into another man's bed? What better sentence could one pass on a grasping old gentleman than to induce him to disinherit his own son?

The trouble begins for Volpone when he starts to break these rules and allows his own obsessions to overwhelm his delight in the "sport" of satirical plotting. The moment can be clearly defined: it is when he attempts to seduce Celia. She is innocent and virtuous, and horrified at her husband's insistence that she bed down with the presumably dying Volpone. When Volpone turns out to be very much alive and ready for action, she is not inclined to join in his game. However much she deplores her husband's treatment of her, she sees Volpone's attempts on her as rape, and of course she is right. Similarly, the young Bonario emerges as an innocent victim of Volpone's manipulations. However amusing and fitting it may be to trick an old tightwad into disinheriting his son, the son stands to lose everything, and has done no wrong. Appropriately, Jonson casts Bonario as Celia's deliverer from attempted rape.

At this point, then, Volpone's attempts have gone beyond the proper bounds of satire. What he now undertakes is illegal and reprehensible. If satire is supposed, in Jonson's own words, to "sport with human follies, not with crimes,"[10] how is satire to handle Volpone's criminal behavior? The problem is especially acute in a play written for a public theatre, away from the elite confines of the "private" stage where satire generally reigns supreme and is sole arbiter of human folly. In a play for public audiences, criminal behavior requires the intervention of the law. Thus it is that Volpone is brought to trial before the avocatori, or magistrates, of Venice. His lustfulness has made him careless and vulnerable to Mosca, who, under cover of the guise of loyal and inventive servant, has had his own designs on Volpone's wealth. Mosca, a descendant of the clever servant of Roman and neoclassical drama, is ultimately more clever and self-knowing than his master, and so he gains the upper hand.

When the case is thrown into court, it occasions more delicious satire at the expense of the learned and legal professions; the avocatori are no less venal than anyone else and are quite prepared to marry their daughters to Mosca, now that

76

he is no longer a servant but evidently a rich and powerful man (5.12.50–1). This is a good joke on the law itself. At the same time, it raises a big problem for the ending of the play. These corrupt justices must pass sentence on Volpone, and they do so, not lightly: he is to be whipped. Cornered, he turns on Mosca, exposing him to the court as a knave and Voltore and the rest as fools. Because Mosca stands convicted of being "chiefest minister" of all the plotting, and, much worse, a parvenu of "no birth or blood" who has had the gall to dress himself in the "habit of a gentleman," he is sentenced to be whipped and then to live "perpetual prisoner in our galleys" (106–14). Bonario greets this conclusion with a pious exclamation that "Heaven could not long let such gross crimes be hid" (98), and the avocatori speak sanctimoniously of crime and due punishment (146–8), but what are we to think of such a travesty of justice in which the magistrates are no better than the felons they thus condemn? Jonson's presentation of the role of law in dealing with human corruption is deeply ambivalent at best. Satire is ideally a better instrument, more honest and efficient and self-knowing, but then Volpone's and Mosca's crimes, in this public arena, have been allowed to go beyond the point where satire is appropriate and sufficient.

A function of the subplot of *Volpone*, in these terms, is to demonstrate by contrast how satire is truly supposed to work. The plot of Sir Politic Would-Be, his wife, and Peregrine is only tangentially connected to the main plot of the play; Jonson, in a neoclassical vein, elaborates his plotting with more amplitude than he could have found precedent for in his ancient Roman sources. Here, in the subplot, folly reigns supreme and is dealt with by the perfect satirical persona, Peregrine. His name is that of another bird, the falcon, but, unlike the revolting carrion birds (Voltore, Corbaccio, and Corvino) that seek to feed on decaying flesh, Peregrine is a raptor – swift, bold, beautiful in execution. Sir Politic and his wife, correspondingly, are suitable gulls for a perfect plot of folly meeting deserved exposure. Sir Pol's name reminds us of the parrot, mindlessly repeating what others have said. He is also associated with the tortoise. Sir Pol is a traveler in Venice, a fatuous English knight who prides himself on being the complete cosmopolitan but who in fact is Jonson's anticipation of "the ugly American," cameras slung over both shoulders, absurdly dressed, and provincially impervious to all the nuances of local language and culture.

Sir Pol does not have a camera, of course, but he does have all sorts of absurd ideas, such as his plan of using the reek of onions to disinfect ships suspected of carrying the plague (4.1.100–25). His wife is a gossipmonger who yearns in vain to be fashionably dressed and received in the best society; she is idiotically enamored of all things Italian. Both she and her husband are amusing in their conflicting attitudes about sexuality: they are fascinated and repelled by the notorious courtesans of Venice and inclined to be prudish in their attitudes, and yet Lady Pol (for all her mistaken jealousy of her husband) flirts outrageously with

Volpone. Peregrine takes delight in baiting them and drawing them out, especially Sir Pol. Peregrine does so for his own amusement and because such folly deserves to be exposed. He has no economic motive, and never lapses, as Volpone does, into uncontrolled obsession.

Peregrine is thus the perfect satirical instrument. His final exposure of Sir Pol is a deft demonstration of how the satirist works. He frightens the susceptible Sir Pol into thinking that he is being spied on by the Venetian state, thereby encouraging Sir Pol to take shelter in one of his ridiculous contrivances, a tortoise shell. Then, in the presence of witnesses, Peregrine simply exposes Sir Pol for the fool that he is: "*They pull off the shell and discover him*" (5.4.35–73). The animal symbolism is transparent: the slow-moving, ungainly Sir Pol has been swooped upon by his deadly but brilliant foe, the falcon, and subjected to a punishment that fits his folly. The law is neither needed nor used; this is the kind of comic situation for which satire is best fitted. In *Volpone*, however, the chief dramatic purpose of this neat and perfectly resolved subplot may well be to delineate by contrast what remains so complex and unresolved in the punishment of Volpone and Mosca. Satire on the public stage is a contested genre, and its rules of engagement are compromised by the demands of public justice.

With *Epicœne, or The Silent Woman*, acted by the Queen's Revels company of boy actors at Whitefriars in 1609, Jonson is more in his element as a satirist. The play's chief butt of humor, Morose, is guilty of no crime more serious than his wish to marry an obediently chaste young wife and at the same time enjoy perfect quiet. These hopes are absurdly in conflict with one another, given the antifeminist premise of the play that all women, and especially wives, employ their tongues as potent weapons with which to control men. Among the other figures of ridicule are Captain Tom Otter, the uxorious husband of a domineering wife who "takes herself asunder still when she goes to bed, into some twenty boxes, and about the next day noon is put together again, like a great German clock" (4.2.87–9); Sir John Daw, a foolish knight and dabbler in poetry – the sort of "poetaster" that Jonson had lambasted in his satirical comedy of that name written for the Chapel children; and Sir Amorous La Foole, Daw's companion in silliness.

The wits of the play, meantime, are Sir Dauphine Eugenie, Morose's nephew, and his friends Ned Clerimont and Truewit. They are young, gentlemanly, disengaged, and sardonically amused by folly. They take pleasure in displaying to one another, and to us as audience, the "humors" of the gulls. They administer comeuppances that are comically appropriate and entirely within the purview of satire, needing no social institutions like the law. The demarcation between wit and folly seems at all times perfectly clear.

Epicœne is a cruel play, but then satire is designedly cruel. It sees its mission of stripping away veneers of social pretension, self-importance, and hypocrisy as an unsentimental business requiring swift dispatch. The wits are accordingly not what one would call warm-hearted young men. They laugh among themselves at women's cosmetics and wigs and false teeth, at horse-racing and laying wagers, at men with "gray heads and weak hams, moist eyes and shrunk members" who nonetheless visit their ladies at night with rich gifts (1.1.13–43). They have heard of a new "foundation" in town, of ladies that call themselves the "collegiates," who live apart from their husbands and who "cry down, or up, what they like or dislike . . . with most masculine, or rather hermaphroditical authority" (70–7). Rather than rail shrilly at such inversions of the presumed norm of male ascendancy over the female, the wits amusedly devise ways to use Lady Haughty and Lady Centaur, of the "college," in their schemes of exposure and ridicule.

Dauphine hopes to inherit from his uncle Morose, but is aware that he is unlikely to succeed as things stand, because of Morose's miserliness, his dislike of Dauphine's witty company, and his fear of the satirical threat that the young men pose to his dignity (1.2.8–10). This slender plot situation, derived from comparable situations in Plautus and Terence in which resourceful young men and their clever servants must outwit older figures of authority who stand in the way of their happiness, sets in motion in *Epicœne* a plot of outmaneuvering and revenge against Morose. Dauphine and his friends are justified, in the ethos of satirical comedy, by their cleverness and by the churlish miserliness of the old man.

Then, too, the punishment must fit the crime. What better way to punish a man who can "endure no noise" and yet "will venture on a wife" (1.2.19–20) than to fill his house with unbearable cacophony and inveigle him into marrying a person who appears to be a tractable and silent young woman but who in fact is a boy playing the part that the wits direct him to play? This is precisely what Dauphine and his friends set about to do. Along the way, they take occasion to collect specimens, as it were, of human folly, whose ridiculousness they can anatomize and whom they can then employ in the business of filling Morose's house with the sounds of unwelcome revelry.

In order for this satirical punishment to seem just, Morose must be set up as truly deserving of what he gets. Jonson does not disappoint. Morose is a wonderful caricature of fussy self-importance and male anxiety about women. He employs mutes to serve him. He orders thick quilts on his doors, and oiled hinges. He cringes at Truewit's outspoken lecture on the follies of marriage in an age when chaste wives are scarcely to be found and when there are instead "so many masques, plays, Puritan preachings, mad folks, and other strange sights to be seen daily" that a man might have to hearken back to the days of Edward the Confessor in hopes of finding a "dull, frosty wench" (2.2.30–6). Morose is taken in entirely by Epicœne, the boy engaged by Dauphine (2.4.35–40) to pose as the silent wife; her almost inaudible voice and her deferring to him on every point enchant him and, at the same time, offer him the seeming opportunity of being "revenged" on his "insolent kinsman" Dauphine and "his plots to fright me out of marrying" (2.5.96–7).

Any grasping old miser who is this intent on putting down youth deserves what he gets, in the code that governs this play. Morose's craving for a young and silent wife betrays a male insecurity no less worthy of reprisal: his Epicœne will turn out to be endlessly talkative, brazenly managerial, and an apt pupil of the "college" of castrating ladies. Morose will be "tormented" with a noisy houseful of guests, suffering his "purgatory." So loud are "the spitting, the coughing, the laughter, the sneezing, the farting, dancing, noise of the music, and her [Epicœne's] masculine and loud commanding" that he is driven to take refuge in the top of his house, cowering on a crossbeam of the roof (4.1.1–22). As if that were not enough, Epicœne will turn out to be a boy.

Daw and La Foole are also taken in by Epicœne and the wits. As would-be courtiers and men about town, Daw and La Foole must of course offer their devotions to a lady of quality. Both are socially pretentious, eager to shine in courtly society. Daw invites guests to his suppers "out of his window as they ride by in coaches" (1.3.33). Daw's poetry, part of his attempt to be fashionable, jingles awkwardly and is cribbed out of other writers. "How it chimes, and cries tink in the close, divinely!" mocks Clerimont. He and Dauphine ironically compare Daw's verse to Seneca or Plutarch. Daw is not savvy enough to know that Seneca and Plutarch are scarcely models for the writing of amorous verse; he hates the whole lot, including Aristotle, Plato, Thucydides, Livy, Tacitus. "What a sack full of their names he has got!" (2.3.39–65), wonders Clerimont.

How can one who thus slights "all the old poets" justify being a poet himself (95–6)? Daw's insistence that his poems are entirely his "own imaginations" (42–3), when in fact they are absurdly imitative and trite, makes him an appropriate target of satirical laughter. Dauphine and Clerimont are Jonson's vehicles for satire; we cannot doubt the dramatist's endorsement of their critical stance and his deploring of Daw. The proper comeuppance for Daw, and La Foole, is to be exposed as poseurs, Daw as a poetaster and both as ladies' men. Brought in as witnesses to a divorce trial instigated against Epicœne by her now hysterical husband, Daw and La Foole confess to having had sexual relations with the bride (5.4.99–100) only to be confronted with the play's great *coup de théâtre*: Epicœne is a boy. They thus are forced to confront both their hypocrisy and their apparent lack of proper masculinity.

Jonson's comic denouement is brilliantly aware of its own theatricality. Epicœne turns out to be a boy. But of course! The audience in a Jacobean private theatre has known all along that Epicœne is played by a boy actor, as indeed so are the rest of the characters. Presumably the audience has accepted that fiction as part of the semiotics of this particular kind of theatre, in which boys play women, old men, and young wits – roles in which boy actors can excel. By literalizing a convention of theatrical presentation, Jonson calls attention to the illusory nature of theatre and perhaps of sexuality as well. Gender is a construction, and a very unstable one in this play for most of the characters. The very name, "Epicœne" or "Epicene," meaning "partaking of the characteristics of both sexes," revels in this instability.

Concurrently, the revelation of Epicœne's ambivalent sexuality resolves the plot of the play, by giving Dauphine a means of bludgeoning his churlish uncle into naming Dauphine as his heir in return for being given the perfect reason for annulment of his unhappy marriage – an impediment *in primo gradu* (5.4.187), of the highest order, since marriage to a young male is legally impossible. The delight with which Jonson laughs at his own device suggests the comfort and ease with which he constructs this "comedy of affliction," this "device of vexation" (2.6.20–36) in the compatible surroundings of a sophisticated theatre.

In *The Alchemist* (1610), Jonson returns to the public stage and to the King's Men. No less significantly, he revisits the problem of folly vs. crime that had presented such an interesting puzzle in *Volpone*, and with results that are, one imagines, more congenial to the artist. *The Alchemist* is, to a remarkable degree, a replay of *Volpone*. Two con artists, Subtle and Face, in collusion now with a third if subordinate partner, Doll Common, bilk a series of gulls with their razzle-dazzle. Once again the servant, Face, is the more resourceful of the two. Their victims run the gamut of affectation, hypocrisy, and greed. Satirical exposure and loss of hoped-for gain are the weapons used to teach the gulls a lesson. Celia and Bonario, the innocent victims of *Volpone*, are transmuted into Dame Pliant and Pertinax Surly, with structural functions like those of their counterparts in *Volpone* but with significantly different motivations. Once again, the chief manipulators, Subtle and Face, turn on one another and end up in trouble, despite the brilliance of their evasions. The law, however, proves to be superbly irrelevant in *The Alchemist*. The final presiding genius is Lovewit, whose function as arbitrator and judge replaces that of the corrupt avocatori in *Volpone*. All is finally contained within the precincts of Lovewit's house, the perfect venue for a satirical action.

The con game this time is alchemy. Jonson shows himself to be immensely learned in lore about this fascinating pseudo-science. As Chaucer in his "Canon Yeoman's Tale" and others had plentifully shown, alchemy was often a scam, a way of entrapping gullible suckers eager to make a quick profit. The idea of a "philosopher's stone" that could transmute all metals into gold proved to be an especially enticing trap for the unwary.

Jonson uses the device to put on display the infinitely varied cravings of humankind among the various classes of English society. Young Abel Drugger is setting up a small tobacco shop in London and would like to learn, by the "necromancy" or magic of alchemy, where to place his shelves, boxes, and pots in hopes of attracting customers (1.3.7–13). As a member of the Grocers' Guild, he represents the bourgeois world of mercantile London. Dapper, a lawyer's clerk, hopes to obtain by alchemical means a "familiar" or familiar spirit that can advise him on his gambling when he undertakes to "rifle" (i.e. raffle, roll the dice) and bet on the horses (1.1.190–3). Epicure Mammon is a knight who longs for unparalleled luxuries, including "a list of wives and concubines / Equal with Solomon," oval rooms filled with naughty pictures exceeding the indecencies of Aretino, mirrors cut at angles to reflect his own naked figure in multiple perspective, dishes studded with rare jewels, and a bill of fare made up of exotic items like "The swelling unctuous paps / Of a fat pregnant sow." Even his footboy will dine on pheasant (2.2.35–84). Tribulation Wholesome and Ananias are pastor and deacon of a reform Protestant church in Amsterdam, determined to find wealth for the "Brethren" and "Elders" of their austere faith and thereby deliver the *coup de grâce* to bishops and other heretical representatives of "antichristian hierarchy" in the Roman and English churches (2.5.64–83).

With a resourcefulness that makes for delightful theatre, Subtle and Face (and Jonson) find satirical punishments that are admirably suited to the follies of these various specimens of human perversity. The superstitious Drugger is given a set of instructions for orienting his tobacco shop that sound impressive and will accomplish nothing. Dapper is introduced to the Queen of Fairy, alias Doll Common, as his familiar, and is obliged to await her in "privy lodgings" (i.e. a privy), gagged with a dead mouse from the Fairy Queen's own private trencher or plate and a piece of gingerbread (3.4.66–79). Mammon is given an object lesson in covetousness by being told that any impure thought will undo his quest for the philosopher's stone and that he must accordingly dedicate his promised wealth to charitable causes ("Founding of colleges and grammar schools, / Marrying young virgins, building hospitals, / And now and then a church," 2.2.49–52); then, when his alchemical project is about to reach its climax, it apparently explodes because he succumbs to lust in the presence of the delectable Doll Common posing as "a poor baron's daughter" (4.1.43, 4.5.57–62). (Mammon also casts an amorous eye on Face at 2.3.326–7; he is ready for sexual and other sybaritic pleasures in any way, shape, or form.) Tribulation Wholesome and Ananias are punished for railing against plays and for the hypocrisy of coveting the worldly wealth and power they profess to despise by having their investment in an alchemical bubble simply disappear.

Subtle and Face operate by the same rules of satirical exposure that governed the machinations of Volpone and Mosca. Subtle and Face are con men, unscrupulous, devious, and loyal to no one except themselves – or so it seems until the very end. They are also endlessly clever, and motivated as much perhaps by delight in their manipulative skill as by the profit it brings them. Their adeptness at handling several con operations simultaneously makes for fine theatre, as they seek means to keep their various victims from meeting one another. As in *Volpone*, this bravura improvisation builds toward a climax, is constantly threatened with disaster, and finally unravels, thereby giving a perfect classical structure to the play as it moves from protasis (exposition), epitasis (the main action), and catastasis (the height of the action) toward catastrophe and denouement. We excuse much of the knavery of Subtle and Face because they are witty and self-knowing and because, like Volpone and Mosca, they are doing the work of the satirist by exposing and punishing folly. That object lesson is reiterated again and again. "O, my voluptuous mind!" cries Mammon, "I am justly punished"; to which Subtle adds, with delicious sanctimoniousness, "O, the cursed fruits of vice and lust!" (4.5.74–7). Subtle and Face know how to laugh at themselves as well as at their victims.

Subtle and Face are also involved in criminal behavior, to be sure. Setting themselves up in a London house left vacant by its master during the hot and plague-threatened months of summer, they operate a racket that the legal authorities, if they knew, would hasten to shut down. In fact, Subtle and Face nearly meet their match in Pertinax Surly, the counterpart of Bonario in *Volpone*. As a friend of Mammon's who comes with him to the house, Surly is skeptical in a way that Mammon is not. Announcing at the start that he "is somewhat costive of belief / Toward your *stone*" and that he "would not be gulled," Surly sees through all the hocus-pocus of pretended miracles and is not taken in by Subtle's brilliant exposition on the theory and practice of alchemy (2.3.25–176). What's more, he is alarmed to discover in the house a seemingly innocent victim, one Dame Pliant, young and wealthy widowed sister of a country squire named Kastril, who has come to town to learn the ways of a sophisticated London gallant. Surly to the rescue!

Surly would appear at first, then, to be an upright citizen bent on not being hoodwinked and on exposing a con operation for what it really is. In this guise he begins to look like the satirist's spokesman operating from a moral vantage superior to that of Subtle and Face. Yet Surly's name hints at a disagreeable nature that is hardly consistent with the role of rescuer, and Dame Pliant too is named in such a way as to suggest that she is no Celia after all. The compromising situation in which she finds herself, being used as a female bait to entrap Surly (now disguised as a Spanish Don visiting what he takes to be a house of prostitution), does not appear to distress her, and she ultimately comes to no harm. Surly, meantime, is shown to be motivated by self-interested concerns: a longing to revenge himself on Face for aspiring to the widow, and a coveting of Dame Pliant and her wealth for himself. Surly, in other words, turns out to be yet one more "humors" character in this zoo of satirical types, deserving to be fleeced just like the rest. As "Monsieur Caution, that will not be gulled" (2.4.15), Surly invites comic retribution no less than those who are more gullible.

Lovewit's role as master of the house is crucial to a resolution in which the law and its cumbersomely corrupt ways will have no part. When, at the end, the bilked victims are hammering at the door of Lovewit's house, demanding that the officers of the law provide them with restitution, Lovewit coolly reappears to reclaim his house and blandly joins in a conspiracy with Jeremy, his loyal servant (a.k.a. Face), to deny that any of the actions alleged to have occurred there ever in fact took place. Subtle and Doll meantime have escaped out the back way, leaving behind their ill-gotten gains and having to content themselves with avoiding arrest. Dame Pliant and her wealth go to Lovewit, now that Surly has been driven into retreat and Face (Jeremy) has relinquished his claim in favor of that of his master. All the profits of the alchemical con game also go to Lovewit. He is one who, as his name implies, knows how to "love a teeming wit as I love my nourishment" (5.1.16). He admires Face's "devices" for their sheer cleverness, and forgives the servant for using his house as the center of a vice ring – as well he might, since Lovewit stands to gain mightily. Lovewit's motivation is not the wealth itself, even though, like a perfect gentleman he knows how to live comfortably without the obscene extravagances coveted by Mammon.

Lovewit thus encapsulates the spirit of comedy in *The Alchemist* and its stunningly amoral (though not immoral) ending. He presides genially over the defeat of all unwarranted aspirations and rewards wit for its own sake. As an "indulgent master" who has always been inclined to "affect mirth and wit" (5.3.77–80), he is vastly amused by what he has seen and passes judgment in terms that we are invited to share. That judgment is most harsh on the "brethren" of the Dutch church, for they are the most fanatical and socially disruptive of the many fools who populate this play. Jonson will give no quarter to the Puritans and their extremism.

By the same token, Lovewit's house becomes an apt embodiment of the theatrical space that Jonson seeks to create for his satirical comedy. The play's very title, *The Alchemist*, suggests the nature of a dramatic action: lively, illusory, full of trickery, and at last evanescent. As the play's "Argument" or plot summary puts it, the show will continue, with its company of "coz'ners," "Till it and they and all the fume are gone" (The Argument, 6, 12). Playwriting is like alchemy: the dramatist conspires with an acting company to manufacture an exotic dream, for which the spectators must pay good money only to discover at the end that the whole thing has disappeared.[11]

Yet the wry joke should not conceal Jonson's pride of accomplishment. As his Prologue boasts, his aim has been to people the stage with "manners, now called humors," and to direct his spectators' attention to their own imperfect world: "Our scene is London, cause we would make known / No country's mirth is better than our own." No climate does better at breeding "your whore, / Bawd, squire, impostor," and many persons more, all in need of the "wholesome remedies" that satire, with its "fair correctives," can offer more effectively than any other kind of human endeavor (Prologue, 5–18). Only a learned humanist and satirist like Jonson can hope to construct such a "feast of laughter at our follies" (1.1.166). The success of *The Alchemist* suggests that Jonson feels thoroughly at home in the theatrical world he has discovered with the help of his alchemical metaphor. It is a world where the satirist reigns supreme, unchallenged by any authority figures of law and order.

In *Bartholomew Fair* (1614), Justice Adam Overdo is the embodiment of the law. He is also one of Jonson's most hilariously amusing types of folly. As magistrate in charge of overseeing the affairs of a district called Pie-Corner, he holds jurisdiction over the notorious Bartholomew Fair, set up in West Smithfield outside of London and deriving its name from the Feast of St. Bartholomew on August 24 when the fair was annually held. There, disguised in "the habit of a fool" (2.1.9), Overdo spies disapprovingly on every sort of vice and dissipation known to the human condition. The fair has its booths and stalls, of course, notably those of Lanthorn Leatherhead, the toyman and hobby-horse seller; Joan Trash, the gingerbread-woman; and Ursula, the pig-woman, who deals in roast pig, draughts of ale, tobacco, and, it appears, sexual assignations. These booths are present on stage in Act 2 and subsequently; the stage becomes, in effect, Bartholomew Fair. As such, it is an emblem for Jonsonian theatre, much in the same way that alchemy is. The emphasis is still on theatre as con-game, but it is also, in *Bartholomew Fair*, more cheerfully inclusive of the whole complex range of human folly and aspiration. This play is less of a satire than its predecessors, and more of a celebration of *la comédie humaine*.

Justice Overdo, stern-faced representative of law and order, finds much to worry about at the fair. Frequenting the various booths and byways are Nightingale, a ballad-singer; Ezekiel Edgworth, a cutpurse; Dan Jordan Knockem, a horse-corser or dealer in horses; Val Cutting, a loud-mouthed swaggering bully; Captain Whit, a bawd or pimp; Mooncalf, tapster to Ursula; a "punk" or "mistress o' the game" called Alice; and, inquiring zanily into all that goes on, the mad Troubleall. The fair is a place of petty crime where the unwary stand an excellent chance of being fleeced, but it also bustles with vitality. Ursula, a kind of female Falstaff, "all fire and fat," so gross that she "water[s] the ground in knots, as I go, like a great garden pot" (2.2.50–2), and whose booth is emblematic of the flames of hellfire, is perhaps its most vivid embodiment. The fair is thus a kind of Saturnalia, an occasion of profane release and celebration and occasional riot. It is a theatre of the world in which the norms of everyday life are inverted and exploded.

Those who visit the fair do so for a medley of reasons. John Littlewit is a proctor (legal agent or attorney) with a penchant for scribbling bad verse, whose wife, Win-the-fight (*née* Winifred) Littlewit, and her widowed mother, Dame Purecraft, have become devout Puritans. The reverend elder whom they so admire is Zeal-of-the-land Busy, once a baker but now an inveterate foe of "bridales, maypoles, morrices, and such profane feasts and meetings." He is, in the opinion of at least one sophisticated observer, "a notable hypocritical vermin," one who is "ever in seditious motion and reproving for vainglory; of a most lunatic conscience and spleen." He "affects the violence of singularity in all he does," "derides all antiquity," and "defies any other learning than inspiration" – that is to say, the word of God as set down in Holy Scripture (1.3.120–42). Busy is, like Wholesome in *The Alchemist*, an unsparing caricature of the Puritan hypocrite; and here he takes on the particular role of being the enemy of theatre.

Yet he and the Littlewit family come to the fair. Littlewit unashamedly longs to "eat of a pig," and his wife, for all her religiosity, is no less eager: "I'll not make me unready for it. I can be hypocrite enough, though I were never so strait-laced" (1.5.151–8). She at least understands her hypocrisy, and longs for release. Dame Purecraft consents to go with pretended reluctance, provided "it can be any way made or found lawful" (1.6.29–30). Busy, pompous hypocrite that he is, needs to find a specious rationalization, pronouncing that "we may be religious in the midst of the profane so it be eaten with a reformed mouth, with sobriety and humbleness, not gorged in with gluttony or greediness." Thus even he finds a way to visit the "tents of the wicked" in Sodom and Gomorrah, in the home of "idolatry" (54–71).

One of Littlewit's legal clients, Bartholomew Cokes, is also drawn to the fair. A foolish young gentleman whose money has enabled him to be contracted in marriage to the attractive and intelligent Grace Wellborn, ward to Justice Overdo, Cokes has a child's curiosity about everything and a child's lack of restraint. He is repeatedly victimized at the fair by his inability to understand how he is being taken to the cleaners by its various con artists. His name, "Bartholomew," recalls the fate of the saint who was flayed alive. Cokes is the despair of his officious guardian and nanny, Humphrey Waspe, but in fact Cokes is not seriously wronged by his mishaps; the fair is an education for him in the facts of life, and he has money he can afford to lose.

Cokes is not even bothered by losing Grace Wellborn, whom he never deserves and whom he does not know how to love with any kind of mature, reciprocating affection. She is sought after by the better-educated and more urbane Tom Quarlous and Winwife, while Winwife is also a suitor for the hand of the widowed Dame Purecraft and hence a rival of Busy. These three, Grace and the two wits, occupy the needed point of view of cultural sophistication in Jonsonian comedy; they take on the roles of commentators and clever undoers of human folly previously exercised by Volpone, Mosca, and Peregrine in *Volpone*,

Dauphine and his young friends in *Epicœne*, and Subtle, Face, and Lovewit in *The Alchemist*. Like many of those satirical personages, Quarlous and Winwife are not especially likeable, and certainly not idealistic; their approach to marriage is calculating and materialistic. At the same time, they enjoy their sport, and invite laughter at human ridiculousness. They inventively employ the demimonde figures of the fair like Nightingale and Edgworth in their plots to outwit authority figures. Grace, cool and unemotional like them, is glad to be freed of her obligation to marry Cokes. She resembles to an extent Celia in *Volpone* and Dame Pliant in *The Alchemist* in that she is the woman in distress rescued from her plight, but she is also sardonic and resourceful in a way that makes her a fit companion for Winwife and Quarlous. Together, these three represent for us the point of view of the detached, amused, intelligent observer and critic.

Justice Overdo and the madman Troubleall serve as viewpoint characters in quite a different, but no less important, fashion. They are complementary to one another: Overdo disguises himself as a fool, while Troubleall acts out in fantasy the idea of authority. Overdo is also a kind of comic King Lear, if such a thing is possible, a figure of authority who becomes so caught up in the Saturnalian world of the fair that he ends up in the stocks, humbled, ruined, and forced to confront his own presumed former wisdom as a kind of madness. Jonson thus plays beautifully with the devastating paradoxes of *King Lear*, in which true sanity comes only to those who have gone insane and true vision only to those who have lost their worldly sight. Overdo needs to be humbled and reviled in order to be disabused of his own sense of self-importance. To his immense credit, he learns the lesson, and gains a kind of humanity that Lear also finds in his madness. If humanity and compassion can be discovered only through being thrown down, then Overdo's humiliation is a paradoxical blessing. He is finally wise enough to recognize it as such, and to see the fair as emblematic of a topsy-turvy world in which such a precious lesson is to be learned.

Troubleall is the inverse figure, a madman whose wisdom is discoverable only in one who is so mad. Having been put out of his place by Overdo in the previous year, he has gone mad and now refuses to do anything, not even "make his water or shift his shirt," without Justice Overdo's warrant (4.1.49–57). The wonderfully searching question posed by Troubleall at every turning of the plot – "Have you a warrant?", "Where's your warrant?", "Have you any warrant for this?" (4.1.102, 4.2.2, 4.3.70, etc.) – proves time and again to be the truly incisive question. He has no understanding of what his own question means, and yet it awakens in its hearers a voice of conscience. What is one's authority for doing anything, for proceeding against some other person, for seeking selfish gain, for wishing to marry? How can we justify what we do? Troubleall unknowingly puts all his hearers on the spot. He becomes a catalyst in the plot as well, for his utterly unhinged judgments are permitted to decide (for example) whom Grace

Wellborn will marry. Troubleall is the conscience both of the fair and of the play that takes its name from the fair. As such, he is another kind of zany authorial persona, a splendid joke on the idea of play construction in which the outcome is finally dependent on the whim of a madman.

Jonson's last loving glance at theatre in *Bartholomew Fair* is the puppet-show staged by Lanthorn Leatherhead and scripted by that aspiring and talentless playwright, John Littlewit. His play about Damon and Pythias is an irrepressible spoof, a collection of inanities worthy of comparison with, and no doubt indebted to, Shakespeare's "Pyramus and Thisbe" in *A Midsummer Night's Dream*. Jonson shows by contrast what it is to distinguish a great play (*Bartholomew Fair*) from a piece of fluff. At the same time, "Damon and Pythias" mounts Jonson's final and brilliant attack on the Puritans. Zeal-of-the-land Busy cannot tell that it is a bad play; he knows only that it is a play, and that plays are the work of the devil. Theatre revels in illusion and falsehood, and (like Bartholomew Fair) attracts riff-raff and the criminal element. Its subject matter is irredeemably profane. Leatherhead seems to confirm this charge in his catalogue of the various "motions" that he has presented at the fair: "Jerusalem was a stately thing, and so was Nineveh, and the City of Norwich, and Sodom and Gomorrah, with the rising o' the prentices, and pulling down the bawdy-houses there, upon Shrove Tuesday" (5.1.8–11).

Busy's outrage takes the form of an acrid debate with one of the "actors," i.e. one of the puppets, about the infamous immorality of the stage. His trump card is to cite the "abomination" that "the male among you putteth on the apparel of the female, and the female of the male." But to this allegation of the evils of cross-dressing, that *bête noire* of Puritan moralists, the puppet representing Dionysius has his ready answer: he pulls up his garment and reveals that gender lines have not been transgressed at all! A puppet has no gender (5.5.91–9). Busy, refuted at last, becomes a convert and allows the play to go on with himself as a beholder. The fair has worked its magic; all are transformed, all come to accept the messy complexity of life and of the dramatic art that must seek to represent that complexity. Jonson's last great comedy is also his most accepting and generous. The satire is tempered by humanity.

NOTES

1 This list of actors appears at the end of the Folio version of *Every Man in his Humour*, published in 1616.
2 See Alfred Harbage, *Shakespeare and the Rival Traditions* (New York: Barnes and Noble, 1968).
3 Significant qualifications to some of Harbage's claims are put forth in Ann Jennalie Cook's *The Privileged Playgoers of Shakespeare's London, 1576–1642* (Princeton: Princeton University Press, 1981).

4 See, for example, Hamlet's disquisition on the child actors, the "little eyases," that "cry out on the top of question," so much so that the adult players, the "tragedians of the city," are forced to travel in the provinces (*Hamlet*, 2.2.326–62). Shakespeare citations are from David Bevington, ed., *The Complete Works of Shakespeare*, 4th edn. updated (New York: Longman, 1997). See also Josiah H. Penniman, *The War of the Theatres* (Boston: Ginn & Company, 1897); R. A. Small, *The Stage-Quarrel between Ben Jonson and the So-called Poetasters* (Breslau, 1899); and Robert B. Sharpe, *The Real War of the Theatres: Shakespeare's Fellows in Rivalry with the Admiral's Men, 1594–1603* (Boston: D. C. Heath, 1935), whose sometimes extravagant claims for a "War of the Theatres" have been put in a more moderate perspective by John J. Enck, "The Peace of the Poetomachia," *PMLA*, 77 (1962), 386–96, among others.

5 Jonson quotations (lightly modernized) are from the Revels editions of *Volpone* (ed. R. B. Parker, Manchester: Manchester University Press, revised edn., 1999), *The Alchemist* (ed. F. H. Mares, London: Methuen, 1967), and *Bartholomew Fair* (ed. E. A. Horsman, London: Methuen, 1960). For *Epicœne*, not in the Revels plays, quotations are from the edition of L. A. Beaurline (Lincoln: University of Nebraska Press, 1966).

6 As Brian Parker observes in his Revels edition of *Volpone*, Jonson replaces the more traditional unity of action with a unity of "persons," allowing him the multiplicity of plot that one sees in many of his plays.

7 Jonson's swipe at Shakespeare for having "small Latin and less Greek" appears in his commendatory poem, "To the memory of my beloved, the author, Mr. William Shakespeare," in *Mr. William Shakespeare's Comedies, Histories, and Tragedies* (London, 1623), the so-called First Folio.

8 Jonson's complaint that Shakespeare had "never blotted out line . . . would he had blotted a thousand" appears in his *Timber: or, Discoveries* (F2 of 1641), reprinted in E. K. Chambers, *William Shakespeare: A Study of Facts and Problems*, 2 vols. (Oxford: Clarendon, 1930), 2.210.

9 Gabriele Bernhard Jackson, *Vision and Judgment in Ben Jonson's Drama* (New Haven: Yale University Press, 1968).

10 *Every Man in his Humour*, Folio version (1616), Prologue, 24.

11 Michael Flachmann, "Ben Jonson and the Alchemy of Satire," *SEL*, 17 (1977), 259–80.

7

RICHARD HARP

Jonson's late plays

John Dryden made what has been for centuries the definitive critical judgment on Ben Jonson's late plays, describing them as his "dotages." Fortunately, the past few decades have seen a critical re-evaluation of these plays which has in important ways contradicted this opinion and concentrated on the merit of dramas which reiterate the important ideas of Jonson's life's work while embodying them in, for him, new dramatic modes, including the romantic drama which he had once despised. Whatever these plays were, as Martin Butler says, "they certainly were not 'dotages.'"[1]

The Staple of News, the earliest of the dramas to be considered here, was performed in 1626 by the King's Men, first at court and then on the public stage; it was printed in 1631. It was Jonson's first play since *The Devil Is An Ass* in 1616, although he had been busy during these ten years in the production of thirteen masques. It was also his first play after the coronation of King Charles I, with whom he was not to have the close relationship that he had enjoyed with Charles' father, James. The play opens when Pennyboy Junior is informed by an old beggar, Pennyboy Canter, that his father has died and left him a fortune of £60,000. This is in fact a ruse, as Pennyboy Canter is the father in disguise and he wishes to see how his son will make use of his sudden wealth. The results are not surprising, as Junior follows the familiar pattern of the New Testament parable of the Prodigal Son, wasting his wealth on clothes, luxurious living at the Apollo tavern, and buying news bulletins at London's most fashionable institution, the Staple of News. "Staple" is a word deriving from sixteenth-century commercial practice, denoting a monopoly, and the news "staple" employs emissaries to circulate around town to procure the latest gossip to sell to customers. Jonson is here satirizing journalism's chaotic beginnings where citizens will pay to hear any rumors, the more outrageous the better, as well as using classical sources such as Aristophanes' play *Plutus* and the *Timon* of the Hellenistic writer Lucian, which had personified wealth.[2]

For Pennyboy Junior uses his new wealth to court the play's "heroine," Lady

Pecunia, whose name means "money," and he can think of no better entertainment for her than to bring her to the Staple for the latest foreign reports (the government maintained a tight control on domestic news). These include rumors that the "Hollanders" have "an invisible eel / To swim the haven at Dunkirk and sink all / The shipping there" (3.2.76–8)[3] and that an "alewife" has found the secret of perpetual motion "in Saint Katherine's [tavern], / At the sign o' the Dancing Bears" (ll. 105–7). Much of what Jonson satirizes has at least some basis in contemporary gossip, but the transparent foolishness of such "news" is of course lost on those with the pressing need for novel ways to spend their newly acquired money. "News" is here merely what is new and its relation to truth is beside the point, a particularly gross example of moral disorder for Jonson whose devotion to honesty was proverbial. In addition, Jonson had little use for reports, accurate or not, of merely contemporary affairs, preferring to search for universal and durable truths rather than to be titillated by curiosities of passing events. In this play Jonson has institutionalized and put on the public stage the foolish individual vagaries of a Sir Politic Would-Be from *Volpone* and the news-junkies of his 1621 court masque *News from the New World Discovered in the Moon* and has shown an entire society given over to rumor-mongering. The chief clerk, or "Register," with the eye of experience, speaks for the dramatist about the Staple's true meaning:

> 'Tis the house of fame, sir,
> Where both the curious and the negligent,
> The scrupulous and careless, wild and staid,
> The idle and laborious; all do meet
> To taste the cornucopiae of her rumors,
> Which she, the mother of sport, pleaseth to scatter
> Among the vulgar.   (3.2.115–21)

Jonson's talent for allegory is most conspicuous in his masques, but it is apparent in this play as well. Lady Pecunia is the object of male desire (her full name is "Aurelia Clara Pecunia," "Golden Bright Money"), and one of the simple members of the play's audience, whose comments on the events Jonson inserts between the acts, objects, "What have Aurelia, Clara, Pecunia to do with any person? Do they any more but express the property of money, which is the daughter of earth, and drawn out of the mines?" (2. Intermean. 22–5). But this is an inattentive spectator. Pecunia is not merely a passive embodiment of wealth, as was the heap of gold which Volpone worshiped each morning when he arose from bed. She is kept under a tyrannical watch by Pennyboy Senior, Pennyboy Junior's uncle, a miser, so that he may have her all to himself, and her predicament is therefore like that of Celia in *Volpone* and Mistress Fitzdottrel in *The*

Devil Is An Ass, other distressed women kept under house arrest by their husband/guardians. She is liberated by Pennyboy Junior when he comes to court her, and her guardian's initial approval of this backfires on him when she rejoices in her liberty and lavishes herself upon any number of (foolish) devotees whom she encounters at the Staple and in the Apollo tavern. She is, that is to say, not merely "money" but also a woman who desires, like the Wife of Bath, to "go abroad." To Pennyboy Senior's boast that he is her "martyr" (2.1.10) because he has, in popular opinion, made himself a "sordid rascal" by eating only moldy pie crusts rather than normal food (2.1.15–19), Pecunia replies: "Why do you so, my guardian? I not bid you. / Cannot my grace be gotten, and held too, / Without your self-tormentings and your watches. . ." (2.1.21–3).

Which is not to say, of course, that she is exactly a heroine. She is bold to Pennyboy Junior upon first meeting him, offering her lips rather than her hand to him to be kissed (as did the disguised Doll Common to Mammon in *The Alchemist*) and she is more than willing to be courted by everyone in the Staple or the tavern. But Jonson's point in this play is that money is not in itself good or evil; such judgments depend, rather, upon the use to which it is put, and Pecunia's womanliness as well as her abstract nature of "money" helps to reveal what is wrong with the miserliness of Pennyboy Senior. Her complaint about him, for example, is exactly the same as that of Pennyboy Canter, the disguised beggar and the play's moral center, who says to his usurious brother: "you are near as wretched as myself. / You dare not use your money, and I have none" (2.5.19). Jonson's point about money, that it is to be used and enjoyed, not hoarded, is neatly encapsulated at the very end of the play when, upon his betrothal to Pecunia, Pennyboy Junior wishes the audience may, "as I, enjoy Pecunia" (5.6.59). When Pecunia herself advises the spectators that in regard to wealth they should live by the golden mean, being neither prodigal nor covetous (5.6.65), she reveals as part of her nature a kind of biblical conjunction of wealth and wisdom as found in King Solomon.

Pennyboy Junior wastes his inheritance under the eyes of his disguised father by wearing elaborate new finery, buying a clerk's place at the Staple for his barber, Tom, and entertaining Pecunia at the Tavern. Interspersed with this "activity" he wastes time with some minor characters, including a doctor, a sea captain, and Madrigal, a "poetaster" or self-deluded poet, who practice the art of "jeering," making insulting comments, as Madrigal says, at "all kind of persons . . . of any rank or quality, / And if we cannot jeer them, we jeer ourselves" (4.1.7–9). In Act 4 Pennyboy Canter administers to the jeerers a dose of their own medicine, persuasively telling them that they were as much "canters," i.e., whiners, as they accused him of. After quitting his charade, he tells his son that its purpose was to see "how you would use / Pecunia when you had her," and that he will now "take home the lady to my charge" (4.4.119–21), a further sign

92

that it is not money itself which causes vice in the play but rather the use that is made of it. The final act is negligible, notable mainly for the announcement that the Staple had blown up when those who worked there heard that "th'Infanta [i.e., Pecunia] was got from them" (5.1.42). There is also some perfunctory detective work done by Pennyboy Junior which foils the lawyer Picklock's scheme to rob his father and which has the effect of restoring the prodigal to his father's good graces.

A principal criticism of this play has been, in David Kay's words, "its divided focus on wealth and on news."[4] There is certainly validity to this, as the play loses steam with the announcement of the Staple's demise at the beginning of Act 5. Still, there is coherence in *The Staple*. Both news and money demand by their nature to be current – old "news" is of course no news at all and currency is the tangible sign of wealth – and Jonson admirably dramatizes this basic fact in the chaotic gossip of the Staple where novelty rather than truth is grotesquely pursued and in Pennyboy Junior's aimless and dissipated wanderings with Pecunia. And, he further shows, it is only the profligate spending of money that can sustain such an appetite for news; when the money is gone, the news enterprise fails. There is a certain prophetic insight to this.

The New Inn (acted 1629, published 1631) was a play of Jonson's that some of his contemporaries would have agreed with Dryden was indeed a product of his "dotages." It was not liked by its one and only contemporary audience, a fact we know emphatically because of the fury with which Jonson attacked what he thought their failure in taste. In an epilogue to the 1632 printed version of the play Jonson wrote an "Ode to Himself," prefaced by his explanation that it reflected "The just indignation the author took at the vulgar censure of his play by some malicious spectators," and which began

> Come, leave the loathed stage,
> And the more loathsome age,
> Where pride and impudence, in faction knit,
> Usurp the chair of wit.

His printed attack on the play's reception had actually begun in the title page to the 1631 edition, which reads in part: "THE NEW INNE . . . / As it was never acted, but most /negligently play'd, by some, / the Kings Servants. / And more squeamishly beheld, and censu-/red by other, the Kings subjects." There were a flurry of responses to this offensive of the poet; some of his friends, like Thomas Randolph, urged him not to follow through on his vow to leave the stage and to realize that to common understandings "'twere a sin / For them to like thine *Inn*: 'Twas made to entertain / Guests of a nobler strain" (25–8); others, like Thomas Carew, while defending his genius, called upon Ben to abate his "immodest rage" (24) and to realize that this play was not the equal of *The Alchemist*: his comic muse has "since decline[d] / From that her Zenith, & foretells a red/ And blushing Evening, when she goes to bed" (6–8). Then there were the replies that were not friendly at all, especially that of Owen Felltham, best known as a moral essayist, who parodied Jonson's ode with one of his own, beginning it by saying,

> Come leave this saucy way
> Of baiting those that pay
> Dear for the sight of your declining wit.

This is the kind of controversy, of course, that Jonson had been familiar with all his life.[5]

What is the truth of the matter? *The New Inn* does depart from Jonson's familiar pattern of a coherent comedic action integrated with sharp satire on the mores of the time. The play is divided between a basically serious main plot about love with a romantic denouement of fantastic familial reunions (the kind of conclusion Shakespeare had popularized and which Jonson had previously rejected) with a below stairs subplot about, basically, servants getting drunk. The two plots seldom intertwine. In the play's "Epilog" Jonson says he neglected the servants entirely in the fifth act for reasons of decorum – "better 'twas that they should sleep or spew / Than in the scene to offend or him or you" (17–18) – but there was in fact no way he could make them a reasonable part of the final crucial revelations. He may also have been particularly sensitive about this play because it was the first one performed after he had suffered a paralytic stroke in 1628, and he was determined that it should not be judged inferior. His epilogue implores his readers that if his "numbers, both of sense and wit" have miscarried, it should not be imputed to his mind: "That's yet unhurt, although set round with pain" (6–10).

When detached from the controversy surrounding its initial performance, however, the play has much of value. While the working out of the plot recalls Shakespeare's final romances, its full title, "The New Inn, or The Light Heart," recalls Shakespeare's earlier joyous comedies as well. The Host of the inn greets the servant of the lovelorn hero, Lovel, by saying that "if his worship think here to be melancholy / In spite of me or my wit, he is deceived" (1.1.7–8); he later tells Lovel himself:

> Be jovial first and drink, and dance, and drink!
> Your lodging here, and wi' your daily dumps,
> Is a mere libel gain my house and me.　　　　(1.2.14–16)

In response to Lovel's accusation that an innkeeper's was a "sordid" (112) occupation, the Host says that "in keeping this Light Heart/ . . . I imagine all the world's a play" where he can see "the variety and throng of humours/ And dispositions that come justling in/ And out. . ."(128, 134–6), thus adopting the character of a considerably merrier Jaques from *As You Like It* (2.7.139–42). And he further upbraids Lovel by saying, "Why, will you envy me my happiness?/ Because you are sad and lumpish?" (37–8), which is another Shakespearean echo, this time of Sir Toby Belch in *Twelfth Night* (2.3.105–6). The Host may be Jonson's self-portrait and if so, we find for once the merriment that Jonson knew in his own life at the Mermaid and Apollo taverns reflected in his plays.

The romantic plot is developed with ingenious complication, thematically enriched by two long speeches by Lovel – and in a modern revival by the Royal Shakespeare Company in 1987, proving dramatically effective as well. Lovel is enamored of Lady Frampul, also staying at The Light Heart, but is unable to pursue her because he is guardian to Lord Beaufort who is also in love with her. While calling her a "noble lady," he also considers her flighty, "of so bent a phant'sie/ As she thinks nought a happiness but to have/ A multitude of servants" (1.5.50–3). One of those servants is her maid Prudence, whose interaction with her mistress and the other gentry signals Jonson's unusually close attention in this play to feminist issues[6] – and belies his presumed misogyny. "Pru" is called upon to govern a Court of Love, a gathering with historical analogs "in which noble men and women assembled to hear 'questions' of love," and which also reflects Jonson's concern with the neo-Platonism in vogue at the court of Charles and his queen, Henrietta Maria.[7] Pru's authority is accepted by all and they reenact a chaste Saturnalia in which a servant rules her betters. She allows Lovel to make two addresses to Lady Frampul on the subjects of love and valor in the hope that he will impress her with his sincerity and eloquence. His reward is to receive a kiss at the end of each speech but he is then to make no further suits to her. Following the Host's advice that it is "Better be happy for a part of time, / Than not the whole; and a short part, than never" (2.6.254–5), Lovel accepts these conditions.

Lovel's speeches draw upon Platonic notions of love, defined as "the most noble, pure affection / Of what is truly beautiful and fair / Desire of union with the thing beloved" (3.2.72–4), and upon Aristotle's definition of courage, "A certain mean 'twixt fear and confidence" (4.4.41), along with Seneca's advice not to respond angrily to ignorant criticism. Lady Frampul professes to be much moved by Lovel's words about love and asks, "What penance shall I do to be received / And reconciled to the church of Love?" (3.2.215–16), but Pru, showing what is her characteristic independence, is skeptical and replies, "Most Socratic lady, / Or, if you will, ironic!" (235–6). Lovel agrees and after receiving his kiss from her says, "Tut, she dissembles; all is personated, / And counterfeit comes from her" (258–9).

After Lovel's speech on valor is concluded, and he has claimed his second kiss, Lady Frampul declares she is even more in love and is vexed that Pru did not help her approach Lovel, but Pru again is doubtful: "I swear I thought you had dissembled, madam / And doubt you do so yet" (4.4.311–12). Pru's character is one that successfully combines a character's name, intellectual virtue, and social position, a conjunction Jonson frequently sought to make explicit in his masques and even in epigrams such as those to Lucy, Countess of Bedford (*Epig.* 76, 84). Both Pru's prudence and her experience as her lady's maid teach her not to take at face value Lady Frampul's affirmations.

Pru is one of the triumphs of the play. Her wit and independence are all her own and not part of her blood. When Lady Frampul furiously says that Pru should trust her sincerity toward Lovel because she has been given rich clothes, Pru tears off her gown and says, "I will not buy this play-boy's bravery / At such a price, to be upbraided for it / Thus every minute" (4.4.322–4). Here is a reversal of the Shakespearean pattern where the discarding of disguise means for the heroine a revealing of her noble nature and the consequent putting on of fashionable clothes. Pru, to the contrary, gives back her disguise of a rich gown to Lady Frampul to show a nature of spirited independence. She confirms this when she tells her lady, in the presence of the Host and his servant in Act 5, that she is a "fine, froward, frampul lady" who has "run mad with pride, wild with self-love" (2.29–30), and Lady Frampul finally demonstrates convincingly her sincerity by accepting this rebuke: "I prithee, Pru, abuse me enough, that's use me / As thou think't fit, any coarse way, to humble me" (42–3). Deepening the idea of Saturnalia, Christian wisdom made commonplace the notion that those "who would be master of all must be servant of all"; here Pru the servant asserts her mastery of the play's love story – for even the Host has given up his hopes of making a match between Lovel and Lady Frampul by the beginning of the last act ("all fails i' the plot," 5.1.27) – through educating her mistress in self-knowledge.

This enlarging of Lady Frampul's character is one important climax of the action. But the subsequent unveiling of hidden identities comes gratuitously – no preparation had been made for them – and undoubtedly contributed to the play's poor reception. The Host turns out to be Lord Frampul who had deserted his wife and small daughters to live a vagabond life with "savages" (5.4.99), some of whom he had brought to the Inn to be his servants, and he rejoices to learn that the boy and Irish nurse that he had given shelter to years before were in reality his other daughter, Lætitia, and his wife who had gone searching for him. That husband and wife should not recognize each other despite years of cohabitation is of course grossly improbable. Marriages are arranged between Lovel and Lady Frampul, and Beaufort and Lætitia. One fit of realism in these incredible reunions is the Host's observation about Pru, who stood "neglected, best deserving / Of all that are i' the house, or i' my Heart" (131). Finally, she is married to Latimer, a companion of Beaufort.[8]

Beginning with *The New Inn* Jonson's late plays have a quality of romance and retrospection that is new for him. In his next play, he makes this backward look more explicit; its title page reads, "The Magnetic Lady: or Humours Reconciled" (acted 1632; published 1640). This reference to his earlier humor plays, though, does not mean that he will merely repeat himself in the new drama. Rather, in the Induction of the play the Boy, an authorial spokesman, says that Jonson, "now near the close, or shutting up of his circle" – the impresa that Jonson chose for his work – has made Lady Lodestone a "center attractive, to draw thither a diversity of guests, all persons of different humours to make up his perimeter. And this he has called 'humours reconciled'" (Ind. 88–95). Here affectations will not only be exposed for the laughter of ridicule, as happened in the earlier comedies, but will in some ways be harmonized with one another. To at least one of his contemporaries, though, what was surprising about the play was that it was written at all; a letter dated September 20, 1632, says, "Ben Jonson, (who, I thought, had been dead) has written a play against next term called the Magnetic Lady."[9]

Jonson shows again in this play his ability to incorporate science into his drama, as he had in *The Alchemist*. Magnetism is the play's central metaphor. Besides Lady Lodestone as the hostess of the dinner which is the occasion for all the action, the characters include as principal protagonist Compass, "A scholar, mathematic," who says his wit is "magisterial" (1.1.13) if he can hold together all those of opposite humors and professions attending the dinner; Captain Ironside, Compass' best friend and "brother," who is in the end attracted, appropriately enough, and married to Lady Lodestone; and Placentia Steel, the marriageable woman who herself magnetizes a number of suitors in her direction. Even some of those characters with more typically Jonsonian comic names, such as Sir Diaphanous Silkworm, the foppish courtier, and Practice, the sharp lawyer, are incorporated into the metaphor; they are, says Compass, "the prime magnetic guests / Our Lady Lodestone so respects: the Artic and the Antartic" (1.6.2–3), the area of the earth's two magnetic poles.

There are any number of other satiric characters – the garrulous Polish, Placentia's gossip and a "she-Parasite" to Lady Lodestone; the "money bawd" Sir Moth Interest who has been the trustee of Placentia's dowry and looks to keep it for himself; the incompetent physician Doctor Rut, who cannot diagnose an advanced pregnancy nor then persuade the household that a birth has occurred when the child is secretly delivered; the "pragmatic," that is, busybody courtier Mr. Bias who trades on his contacts at court for influence and to aid his own courtship of Placentia. In order to help complete the circle of his own work Jonson has grafted this telling of a humor play onto his more recent interest in New Comedy's romantic love plots. This marriage is an uneasy one, as the action at times must be too compressed in order for the humors to be adequately displayed and ridiculed. Yet there is virtue in the method, too: the relentless satire

97

of the earlier plays is here softened by the intrigues of courtship and such venerable story complications as babies having been changed in their cradles, and by a satiric spokesman, Compass, who is personally involved in the love match as well as a critic of the foppishness or venality of the suitors.

To further complete his circle Jonson uses his skill as an epigram writer to introduce quickly some of his characters. Compass sums up Parson Palate in seventeen lines and when Ironside asks him, "Who made this epigram, you," replies, "No, a great clerk / As any is of his bulk, Ben Jonson, made it" (1.2.33–4). This serves to identify Compass with Jonson as well as to bring to the reader's mind the whole complex society that Jonson had earlier delineated in his Epigrams, the "ripest of my studies" (*Epig.,* Dedication to Pemboke, 4). Compass also provides similar descriptions for the physician Rut, the lawyer Practice, and the courtier Bias. The central event of the play, the dinner which Lady Lodestone serves her variegated company, recalls the delight Jonson had shown in such things in his epigram "Inviting a Friend to Supper," but here the dinner is a parody of the liberality and sincerity Jonson praised in that poem and his spokesman is the bluff military man Ironside, who chides Compass for inviting

> . . . your friend, and brother to a feast,
> Where all the guests are so mere heterogene,
> And strangers. . . (2.6.105–7)

The dinner, not shown on stage, is pivotal to the plot as Ironside there becomes enraged at the "perfumed braggart" Silkworm who must drink "his wine / With three parts water" and consequently breaks a glass in his face. The resulting uproar so upsets Placentia that she gives birth to the child that hardly anyone knew she was carrying and this rearranges all the plans of the suitors.

Jonson complicates the last half of the play with considerable action while still trying to allow his characters' humors to unfold naturally, and the result is somewhat chaotic and hard to follow. Sir Moth Interest is delighted that his niece's looseness will prevent her marriage and allow him to keep her dowry. The tables are then turned on him when Compass overhears Polish and Keep, Placentia's nurse, admit that they switched Placentia and Pleasance, Polish's daughter, as infants in their cradle so that Polish could eventually share in the wealth of Lady Lodestone. This delights Compass, who had shown a rather perfunctory love interest in Pleasance, and he then spirits her away to be married, the compliant Parson Palate performing the hasty service. Pleasance's other suitor, the lawyer Practice, is bribed by Compass as he gives him a civic office which he had just obtained, Ironside commenting, "To a lawyer . . . any half title, / Is better than a wife" (5.4.24–6). Compass remarks that he and Practice are thus "reconciled," but this and other such instances which fulfill the play's subtitle are not fully realized, as events are in too much of a rush. More revealing of the play's vein of sym-

98

pathetic comedy is Lady Lodestone's tolerant defense of the villainous Polish's loquaciousness, "You must give losers / Their leave to speak" (5.5.44–5), an even more understanding compassion than Lovewit's encouragement of his false servant Face that he loved a "teeming wit" (*Alch.* 5.1.16).

Jonson's final complete play is *A Tale of a Tub*, first performed in 1633 and published in the second Folio of his *Works* in 1640. Thought by Herford and Simpson to be an early play in Jonson's career and only revised in the 1630s, scholarly consensus now ascribes the play completely to his late works. Jonson was indeed forced to revise the play but this was because of Inigo Jones' objection to the depiction of him as the character Vitruvius Hoop (a milder version of this character, In-and-In Medlay, was substituted), not because he was trying to make an old play "modern." This may also be the reason the play was "not liked" at court.[10]

The *Tale* is a remarkable play in many ways and again shows Jonson's energy and dramatic inventiveness even while old and bedridden. It continues in certain ways the romantic vein of the late plays, as it is set in the remote Elizabethan past, or even perhaps in the time of Queen Mary, but the Middlesex villages which compose its setting are so completely realized by means of its characters' language and diversity that there is little anachronistic about it. Indeed, as Martin Butler has shown, Jonson's very fidelity to historical fact helps the play to comment constructively on matters of king, court, and commoners in the 1630s.[11]

The play's comedy effectively combines the villagers of Finsbury's devotion to the traditions of St. Valentine's Day, especially the drawing by lottery of one's mate, with the local gentry's desire to appropriate that mate for themselves. Audrey Turf, daughter of the local High Constable, has drawn John Clay, a local tile-maker, as her Valentine, but she is also desired, for reasons that seem purely arbitrary, by Squire Tub of Totten Court and by the area's magistrate, Justice Preamble, or "Bramble." In the end, neither cultural tradition nor *droit de seigneur* wins out, as Audrey is married to Pol-Marten, a servant to the Squire's mother, whom she raised to the status of a "gentleman." Jonson's considerable achievement is to give both village custom and the devious intrigues of gentility (and the servants whom they conscript to their cause) their due while believably resolving the conflicts between them.

The Turfs are especially anxious to marry Audrey to Clay because they were similarly betrothed on Valentine's Eve thirty years ago. Turf also learns, from the dubious chronicling of the local historian, Diogenes Scriben, that he is a descendant of the ancient Roman colonists, and he declares that "I had rather be / An ancient colon, (as they zay) a clown of Middlesex" than any knight or squire "or gentleman of any other county/ I' the Kingdom" (1.3.45–9). Thus, he does not favor Squire Tub as a husband for his daughter; he is indeed a "fine man, but he is too fine a man" (1.4.27). Turf's devotion to the land and custom is genuine but is also shaded by Jonson; thus, while Turf approves of the festivities surrounding the approaching wedding, he also wants the expense reduced by eliminating beef from the wedding supper and restricting the presence of musicians. Similarly, the villagers' enthusiasm for St. Valentine is real – even though they do not have the foggiest idea who he is. Clench, the farrier (blacksmith), says comically, "He was a deadly Zin, and dwelt at Highgate / As I have heard, but 't was avore my time" (1.2.8–9) and Turf thinks that the proper name of the festival is "Son Valentine's Day" (1.3.28). Jonson makes devotion to tradition both genuine and comic.

The gentry are more knowledgeable but in fact have much the same interest in the day as do the villagers. Lady Tub, the Squire's mother, knows that Valentine was a bishop who "Left us example to do deeds of charity" rather than to "look for lovers, / Or handsome images to please our senses" (1.7.8–9,14–15) but she then immediately asks her servant Wisp, "What man would satisfy thy present fancy" (l.20). The two women amuse themselves by taking, to his horror, Ball Puppy, Turf's servant, as their Valentine and propose to divide him in two to satisfy their mutual needs. And while Squire Tub and Justice Preamble do not draw Audrey as their Valentine, the intricacy of their plots to keep her away from Clay and her father and each other make their chances of success in love as problematic as if they were throwing darts blindfolded. As Canon Hugh, the local vicar (and assistant to Bramble's plot) accurately forecasts at the beginning of the play:

> I smile to think how like a lottery
> These weddings are. Clay hath her in possession;
> The Squire he hopes to circumvent the tile-kiln [Clay]:
> And now, if Justice Bramble do come off,
> 'Tis two to one but Tub may lose his bottom. (1.1.97–101)

In fact, the arbitrariness of the Valentine Day's custom seems a fitting image of the general arbitrariness of courtship in this play, an aspect of romance Jonson was never shy in noticing. Lovewit wins Dame Pliant in *The Alchemist* merely because he was more forward in proposing than was Surly, who had done her greater service; the eminently attractive and winning Grace Wellborn vows to marry the next man she meets in *Bartholomew Fair*; and Compass in *The Magnetic Lady* marries Dame Pleasance because of an overheard conversation and conducts, at best, an offhand courtship. At one point Puppy finds himself alone with Audrey and immediately proposes, and Pol-Marten takes advantage of a moment of similar isolation to make his successful proposal, conceiving it on the spur of the moment and saying, "Twere but a mad trick to make the essay"

(4.5.68). Only Squire Tub expresses romantic sentiments towards Audrey – "There is a pointed luster in her eye / Hath shot quite through me, and hath hit my heart" – but concludes this speech with perhaps his true motive (there being little about Audrey to substantiate this romantic vision): "I must love her, / The naked truth is: and I will go on, / Were it for nothing, but to cross my rivals" (2.4.88–9, 93–5).

The play illustrates with a vengeance, then, the proverb "Hanging and wiving go by destiny," or in the tinker To-Pan's version, "Wedding and hanging both go at a rate" (2.1.8), which serves to illustrate the basic humanity of high and low alike, a point underscored by the convivial dinner served by Squire Tub at the conclusion, where he vows to have "such a night / Shall make the name of Totten Court immortal" (5.6. 25–6) and where the "wise of Finsbury" are to be made especially welcome (56–7). In love social status does not guarantee success and, indeed, the machinations of Tub, Canon Hugh, and Preamble are as comically reprehensible as are the ludicrous attempts to do his duty that characterizes Turf's raising the "hue and cry" against his prospective son-in-law Clay because of a bogus robbery.

Jonson's final dramatic work is *The Sad Shepherd*, written at the end of his life and left uncompleted at his death in 1637. It is again a new departure for him, an adaptation of the folk material concerning Robin Hood and his band of merry men, which draws in addition on the pastoral traditions of Theocritus and Virgil, as well as Renaissance pastoral found in the work of Spenser's *Shepherd's Calendar* and in his third book of the *Færie Queen*. The action of the play takes place in Sherwood Forest, and the translation of pastoral material from open meadow to English woods is reminiscent of Shakespeare's *As You Like It*. Jonson finished about half the play and it contains some of his finest work. Robin Hood is a vigorous woodsman and a mature lover of Marian, and their dialog, says Anne Barton, "would be at home in Shakespearean comedy."[12] The "sad shepherd" is Æglamour who pines for Earine, a shepherdess he thinks drowned but who is in fact enchanted inside a tree by the witch of Papplewicke, Maudlin. One of the principal characters, the shepherd Alken, may again be a Jonsonian self-portrait (he had played a similarly named character in his lost pastoral play, *The May Lord*); Alken helps to track down Maudlin to her den in the forest and utters comments typical of Jonson when he says of the witch, "She may deceive the sense, but really / She cannot change her self" (2.6.124–5). The list of "Persons of the Play" contains one named Reuben and called "The Reconciler," a "devout hermit" who, although he does not appear in the existing fragment, would apparently resolve the play's conflicts. The excellence of the play's poetry, decorous and vigorous without sentimentality or affectation, and the freshness of the story, which employs the convention of a pastoral plot and characters while never being merely conventional in its development, is only a final refutation of the idea that Jonson's late plays were "dotages." Although his physical vitality was diminished during the last decade of his life, his dramatic accomplishments in this period exemplify Dylan Thomas' admonition that one should not "go gentle into that good night."

NOTES

1 Martin Butler, "Late Jonson" in *The Politics of Tragicomedy: Shakespeare and After,* eds. Gordon McMullan and Jonathan Hope (London: Routledge, 1992), 166.

2 Contemporary sources for the play include the late morality play *The Contention between Liberality and Prodigality,* published in 1602, and the anonymous 1604 play, *The London Prodigal.*

3 All quotations from the plays are taken from the edition of G. A. Wilkes, *The Complete Plays of Ben Jonson* (Oxford: Oxford University Press, 1981).

4 W. David Kay, *Ben Jonson: A Literary Life* (London: Macmillan, 1995), 166.

5 Jonson's poem and the replies to it can be found in the Revels edition of *The New Inn,* edited by Michael Hattaway (Manchester: Manchester University Press, 1984), 204–8.

6 See Helen Ostovich, "Mistress and Maid: Women's Friendship in *The New Inn,*" *Ben Jonson Journal,* 4 (1997), 1–26.

7 See Hattaway's introduction to *The New Inn,* p. 30.

8 In a benign interpretation of the improbabilities of this final act, Harriet Hawkins suggests that Jonson "probably intended the final set of recognitions" to be a surprise to the audience "dependent upon the powers of acting and costume which make it possible for an audience to accept an actor, or a character in a play, for what he is not." See her "The Idea of a Theatre in Jonson's *The New Inn,*" *Renaissance Drama,* 9 (1966), 225.

9 HS 2: 203.

10 HS 2: 275.

11 See Martin Butler, "Stuart Politics in Jonson's *Tale of a Tub,*" *Modern Language Review,* 85 (1990), 13–28.

12 Anne Barton, *Ben Jonson, Dramatist* (Cambridge: Cambridge University Press, 1984), 346. Anne Barton has done as much as anyone to reorient the interpretation of Jonson's late plays in a positive direction.

8

RUSS MCDONALD

Jonson and Shakespeare
and the rhythms of verse

John Dryden's confession that "I admire [Jonson], but I love Shakespeare" helped to establish the discourse for subsequent response to the two great figures of English Renaissance drama. The first assessment is intellectual, the second chiefly emotional, and for the next three centuries most readers and audiences endorsed these judgments and developed the critical conversation accordingly. Thus Jonson has usually been regarded as pedantic, classical, satiric, Shakespeare as natural, accessible, romantic. Actually the division began even earlier than Dryden, originating to some degree in Jonson's own stated and implicit articulation of the difference: he the scrupulous classicist, Poet, and disdainer of the "public riot," Shakespeare the crowd-pleasing professional and fluent writer who (unfortunately) never blotted a line. Later critics accepted the comparative description but inverted the evaluation, preferring the work and persona of the natural genius to those of his crabbed competitor. For most of the twentieth century, scholarship agreed to observe a rigid critical segregation: Shakespeareans rarely devoted much attention to Jonson, while most Jonsonians sought to remove their subject from the shadow of the master. It is heartening to observe that recent critical trends, particularly the interrogation of canonicity and renewed interest in historicism, have encouraged simultaneous consideration and helped to identify some theatrical and thematic intersections between the men and their work. We have begun to contemplate the significance of their theatrical association, to notice those instances where one seems to have been conscious of the other's work, and to recognize that each dramatic canon is less monolithic than the prevailing distinctions would suggest.[1] For the most part, however, the traditional categories have remained sturdily in place because they are helpful, grounded in certain indisputable differences.

My purpose in re-opening this topic is two-fold. First, I shall review the contemporary relations between the two playwrights mainly from Jonson's position. Although much of this material is familiar, it is vital that we examine it as dispassionately as possible, reconsidering their pronouncements and practices historically and reminding ourselves that Shakespeare and Jonson had not yet become the marmoreal opposites that literary history has created. If Shakespeare has tended to tyrannize modern criticism, it is also true that this sovereignty extends an early modern phenomenon: Jonson's incessant efforts at artistic self-justification are partly a reaction to the popular hegemony that Shakespeare had already begun to attain when the younger man turned to the stage. A fresh look at Jonson's view of his colleague will clarify the major differences between them while avoiding the prejudice and evaluative condescension that have afflicted much of the critical discourse to date. My second purpose is less familiar and more ambitious, an effort to add something new to our understanding of the artistic relation by investigating a feature of their work that has been truly neglected: prosody. Jonson's poetry sounds different from Shakespeare's. It sounds different because it is constructed differently, and these aural distinctions reinforce and amplify our understanding of the orthodox differences in purpose, method, and artistic temperament.

I

Jonson's identity as English literary arbiter (self-appointed) required that he define himself in relation to his contemporaries, and them in relation to himself. Consequently, many of his impressions, assessments, and reported accounts of Shakespeare and other writers have been preserved, some in William Drummond's 1619 memoir and some in Jonson's own writing. All these opinions must be read through the filter of Jonsonian self-regard, and virtually all are marked by a mixture of praise and blame, but it seems clear that Jonson felt sincere personal affection for Shakespeare. In *Discoveries*, a collection of commentary and reflections on literary and other matters, Jonson declares, "I lov'd the man, and do honour his memory (on this side Idolatry) as much as any. He was (indeed) honest, and of an open and free nature." Jonson frequently separates the personal from the poetic, and the crucial phrase in this passage is "the man." About the work, his attitude is more ambiguous.

The famous poem that prefaces the 1623 Folio and other proofs of respect and endearment cannot alter the artistic reservations that Jonson harbored and that, once he had found his artistic footing, he did not hesitate to proclaim.[2] The most memorable of these judgments, reported by Drummond, is that "Shakespeare wanted art." From about 1600 Shakespeare served Jonson as a synecdoche for all those dramatists who refused to subscribe to the Jonsonian artistic program.[3] The comical satires, beginning with *Every Man out of his Humour* (1599), represent a deliberate break with the kind of normative comedy in which Shakespeare specialized and which Jonson had himself attempted in *The Case Is Altered* (1597) and to a lesser extent in *Every Man in his Humour* (1598). In fact,

Every Man Out is a kind of manifesto, a massive and vehement effort to set himself apart from the comic style that Shakespeare, more than any of his contemporaries, represented. A gallery of satiric portraits designed to exhibit and ridicule the kinds of folly and self-delusion that never ceased to fascinate Jonson, the printed play ("as it was first composed") comes complete with prologues, introductory meta-dramatic sketches, authorial surrogates, critical interludes, and onstage commentators, all devised to expound and justify the author's original efforts at comic form. In the middle of the play, Mitis, one of the on-stage observers, turns to his fellow and expresses the wish "[t]hat the argument of his comedy might have been of some other nature, as of a duke to be in love with a countess, and that countess to be in love with the duke's son, and the son to love the lady's waiting maid: some such cross wooing, with a clown to their serving man; better than to be thus near and familiarly allied to the time" (3.6.169–74). Although the referent is not specific, most members of the Globe audience would have recognized the general target. Mitis' preference for romantic or intrigue comedy is the kind of taste that Jonson felt compelled throughout the remainder of his career to frustrate and thus to correct.

For more than a decade Jonsonian prologues and front men continue to hector audiences with similar declarations, some of them good humored, some cranky. His most frequent criticism concerns the means of representation, and such complaints are part of a larger dispute over the ends of drama. Jonson subscribed wholeheartedly to the Horatian principle that the twin functions of art are instruction and delight, and his manifest impatience with Shakespeare and others arises from their shirking of what he believed to be the poet's proper role. Sidney, in the *Apologie*, refers to poetry as "a medicine of cherries," and Jonson's viewpoint is mostly consistent with that therapeutic conception, although it took him several years and multiple attempts to find the proper balance between the drug and the flavoring. The asperities and assaults of *Every Man Out*, *Cynthia's Revels*, and *Poetaster*, for example, seem to have delighted almost nobody, and thus, as Jonson eventually acknowledged, their corrective function was necessarily blunted. But by 1605, when he began to write the comic masterpieces, Jonson had learned to promote his moral and ethical principles by means of an amusing story. The Prologue to *The Alchemist* promises "wholesome remedies" that are also "sweet," "fair correctives" that will cure "diseased" spirits. The medical discourse appears repeatedly in the prologues and theoretical pronouncements, reminding audiences that Jonson believed theatre to be ethically and socially efficacious.

Shakespeare left no explicit record of his opinion about Jonson and his work; indeed he left no extra-dramatic observations on any subject. However, certain details about their professional association indicate some regard on Shakespeare's part for the younger man's theatrical talents: the Lord Chamberlain's Men (after 1603, the King's Men), the company of which Shakespeare was a principal shareholder, produced six of Jonson's most important plays during Shakespeare's lifetime, and according to the Jonson Folio of 1616, Shakespeare acted in the original performances of both *Every Man In* and *Sejanus*. A legend traceable only as far back as Nicholas Rowe in 1709 – by which time the myth of Shakespearean generosity had taken root and flowered – claims that Shakespeare recommended *Every Man in his Humour* for performance by his company after it had been rejected, thus sponsoring Jonson's first theatrical hit. Colorful tales of "wit-combats" in taverns imply fraternity and good will. And a Stratford vicar (some fifty years after the supposed fact) reported a visit to Stratford in 1616 by Jonson and Michael Drayton at which Shakespeare drank too much ale, caught a fever, and shortly died. On the negative side, some nineteenth- and twentieth-century critics identified the vain and blustering Ajax in *Troilus and Cressida* as Shakespeare's unflattering portrait of Jonson, who was then engaged in a series of public quarrels with Dekker and Marston. The evidence, as these tales and speculations imply, is sparse.

The absence of prologues, inductions, and other extra-dramatic supplements from most of Shakespeare's plays says much about his representational bias. His usual method is to stage an imaginary world that he trusts to beguile the audience into belief and participation. That he forgoes such intermediaries and other bridging mechanisms to connect the audience with the play attests to what is often known as his mimetic approach to the theatre. This confidence in the power of theatrical mimesis indicates a commitment to fiction as an end in itself, a view that Jonson pointedly rejects. A source of Shakespeare's greater popularity with audiences over the past four centuries is his devotion to narrative and character as self-justifying; putting it another way, his interest is in the process and success of representation, not in its moral and social utility. This is not to characterize the most profound artist of the age as some kind of simpleton who was unaware of or unconcerned with the meanings his dramas might have generated. It is to say, rather, that he began with the dramatic story and the people who enact it, allowing ideas to proceed from his representation of humans in action. Jonson, on the other hand, seems to have begun with a topic or idea and then fashioned a dramatic action and actors to explore it, providing introducers and commentators and (in the printed texts) marginalia to guarantee that the audience doesn't miss the meaning. Representation, to him, is mainly an instrument. This distinction helps to explain the two attitudes toward sources. Shakespeare adapted the plots of others, ancient and modern European writers from Plutarch to Painter, whose stories had already proved their appeal. Jonson, on the other hand, made up most of his own plots to illustrate the behavior he wished to expose. Significantly, his debt to his predecessors mainly took the form of quotation: he appropriated the words of Juvenal, Horace, Lipsius and a host of others so as to clarify and emphasize the significance of an action.

For Jonson, the purpose of playing was and is to hold the mirror up to the crowd, to make the audience see itself, and once he matured artistically, he pursued that goal by means of a familiar setting. In much of his early work, contemporary English concerns – social pretension, literary vulgarity, self-regard of all kinds – are transposed into fictional or historic locations: a generalized Italy in *Every Man out of his Humour*, the mythical court of Gargaphie in *Cynthia's Revels*, Augustan Rome in *Poetaster*. The Roman political struggles of *Sejanus* must have reminded its audience of the misfortunes of the ambitious Earl of Essex, put to death for treason just two years before the play was performed. Jonson apparently begins to consider the benefits of familiar surroundings around 1605: *Eastward Ho!*, on which he collaborated with Marston and Chapman, depicts a gang of London merchants, apprentices, and social climbers; it is so topical – especially in its ridicule of the Scots who trouped to London to be knighted by the new king – that its authors were imprisoned and investigated for sedition. Even though *Volpone* takes place in Venice – with two imported English travelers who gabble about English gossip and fashion – the setting carries a powerful connotative charge: the Jacobeans conceived of Venice as the archetype of corruption, decadence, and greed. Beginning with *Epicœne* (1609), Jonson sets all his plays (except, of course, for *Catiline*) in England, usually in the heart of London. So insistently do his characters refer to the local topography – its theatres, streets, gates, churches, prisons, brothels, taverns, china shops, neighborhoods, fashionable meeting-places, local celebrities, even some famous racehorses of the day – that the audience could not fail to identify dramatic embodiments of their neighbors and themselves.

Nowhere does he exploit the London setting more brilliantly than in *The Alchemist*. It was staged in the autumn of 1610, exactly when the action takes place; the theatres had recently reopened after having been closed by plague, the same pestilence that has sent Lovewit into the country and made his house available for the con-game. That house is located in Blackfriars, the district that contained and gave its name to the theatre where the play was first performed. The customers who come to seek the help of Subtle represent a cross-section of English culture in 1610: the modest lawyer's clerk, the hopeful shopkeeper, the lubricious knight, the radical Puritans, the roaring boy, the rich widow, even a visiting "Spaniard." All hope to have their lives transformed by "the cunning man." The painstaking allusion to locations, persons, court cases, political and religious controversies, and other immediately recognizable topics is essential to Jonson's heuristic aim because it converts the theatre audience into clients of the alchemical con-game. Jonson has developed an elaborate symbology equating alchemy and theatre, while also distinguishing between them: those who seek to change nature, to convert base metals into gold, are exposed as self-deluding fools; the only real transformation occurs in the play itself. The genuine artist transmutes the people and places of the London underworld into a theatrical object that clarifies experience and forces the audience to see itself and its faults. The same immediacy governs the action of *Bartholomew Fair*, in which the audience members become fairgoers. We recognize ourselves as self-deceivers, Jonson as the real cunning man. All Jonson's plays – even the early, putatively Italian plays – are about London because Jonson is the consummate Londoner, and he repeatedly stages refracted versions of himself *in situ*. Perhaps the most pointed instance of this self-consciousness occurs in *The Devil is an Ass*, when one of the characters goes to the theatre to see a play called *The Devil is an Ass*.

Shakespeare, on the other hand, who always kept himself in the wings, never wrote a London comedy. Location is important in his plays, generalized though it might be: to take the obvious example, the green world of the romantic comedies is the source of restoration and clarification for the characters. It is very important in certain plays, such as *The Tempest* or *Antony and Cleopatra*. In fact, place might be seen as the main issue in the English histories, but their numerous specific references to persons and places are presented at a temporal remove. Once again, Shakespeare differs from Jonson in affording the audience greater liberty to imagine the world of the play. We might say that Shakespeare defends the power of theatrical illusion by stimulating and releasing the imagination of the audience in an unreal realm, whereas Jonson uses his London setting to ensure that his spectator's imagination is appropriately directed. Jonson's attempts to restrict imaginative response are a function of his obsession with the self-destructive power of the imaginative faculty, particularly the intimate connection between illusion and delusion. In this, as in most other respects, we see Shakespeare as more or less flexible, balanced, willing to consider alternative points of view. Jonson, by contrast, seems prescriptive and sure of his opinions.

II

These opposing attitudes are detectable even in the two verse styles. The poetic vehicle is the same: both writers employ blank verse, or unrhymed iambic pentameter, lines consisting of five pairs of syllables, one unstressed and one stressed. But each approaches the form so distinctively that the two poetic products sound vastly dissimilar. As a means of comparing the two bodies of work, such stylistic comparison is necessarily partial: Shakespeare mixed verse and prose throughout most of his plays, occasionally employing rhyme or tetrameter or other specialized poetic forms for specific theatrical purposes, while

Jonson wrote some comedies entirely in prose (*Epicœne*, *Bartholomew Fair*) and occasionally mixed verse and prose (*Every Man In*, the Comical Satires). But blank verse is Shakespeare's principal medium, and Jonson adopted it for several of his greatest works, notably *Sejanus*, *Volpone*, and *The Alchemist*.[4] To make oneself sensitive to these distinctive aural patterns is to recognize that they betoken larger differences – habits of thought, attitudes toward theatre, opposing views of the role of the artist. It is important to keep in mind that both careers are complex and various: Shakespeare's verse changes noticeably from the beginning of his career to the end, and Jonson's literary output includes – in addition to his verse plays – prose comedy, masques (mostly written in rhyme), and a vast amount of lyric poetry, much of it in rhymed couplets. Nevertheless, stylistic analysis of two distinct approaches to the same medium offers specific, material evidence for the orthodox but rarely studied differences between the two playwrights.

At the risk of crude generalization, it is fair to say that Shakespeare's verse is metrically balanced, whereas Jonson's is aggressively asymmetrical. Careful descriptions are necessary, of course, since terms such as "balance" and "asymmetry" are not normally associated with iambic pentameter, and since each poet adjusts his verse style according to character and story. Another major variable is the enormous change in the sound of Shakespeare's verse over the course of his twenty-year career: in the early plays he strictly observes the prevailing Elizabethan metrical conventions, writing mostly regular iambic verse in which the sentence or clause corresponds to the length of the line; as he gains experience with blank verse, he begins to vary the pattern, enjambing lines, introducing numerous midline pauses, and adding variations such as spondees and weak line endings. Such permutations notwithstanding, it is still possible to hear and to articulate the differences between Shakespeare's and Jonson's blank verse. To some extent this comparison merely amplifies Jonas Barish's classic discussion of contrasting prose styles, especially his description of Jonson's spiky irregularity versus Shakespeare's logical balance.[5] Barish's well-tested insights are helpful as a starting point: considering that Jonson and Shakespeare are, along with Marlowe, Webster, and perhaps Middleton, the greatest theatre poets of the greatest age of English drama, the structure and sound of their poetry deserve as much attention as their prose.

Shakespeare's blank verse is governed by a sense of equilibrium, a rhythmic poise that marks the poetic language of all his speakers. Even when characters speak the most tortured and irregular poetry, the unruliness of the rhythm declares itself as an aberration, a temporary and exceptional violation of the normally balanced blank verse. A major source of the foundational stability audible in his poetry is Shakespeare's instinctive devotion to antithetical structures.

> If I were to offer one single bit of advice to an actor new to Shakespeare's text, I suspect that the most useful thing I could say would be, "Look for the *antitheses* and play them"... Shakespeare was deeply imbued with the sense of it. He *thought* antithetically. [6]

So John Barton, the director and language specialist for the Royal Shakespeare Company, advises actors confronted with the initial difficulties of Shakespearean language. Barton illustrates the centrality of antithesis by referring to Sonnet 144 ("Two loves I have, of comfort and despair"), to Falstaff's balanced prose, and then to Hamlet's "To be or not to be," moving quickly beyond the first line to address the subsequent oppositions (suffer/take arms, misery/fear, life/death) that crowd the speech. In developing this perception, Barton concentrates on semantic contrariety, but awareness of such structures of meaning should alert us to the sonic equivalences in which antithetical ideas are conveyed to the mind through the ear.

When Shakespeare first began to write dramatic poetry, probably for his *Henry VI* plays at the beginning of the 1590s, blank verse was a relatively new medium, only about fifty years old (although Chaucer, of course, had written rhymed pentameter). The most salient feature of English dramatic verse at this time is the identity between the syntactic unit, usually the sentence but sometimes the clause or phrase, and the poetic line. In other words, the ten-syllable line was constructed to sound like a ten-syllable line.

> Why, love forswore me in my mother's womb;
> And for I should not deal in her soft laws,
> She did corrupt frail nature with some bribe,
> To shrink mine arm up like a wither'd shrub,
> To make an envious mountain on my back,
> Where sits deformity to mock my body;
>
> (*3 Henry VI*, 3.2.153–8)[7]

The aural effect of this regularity is inescapable: each line stands in equivalent balance to those that precede and follow it; the speaker proceeds through a series of ten-syllable units that announce themselves as such; the ear becomes accustomed to units of sound divided equivalently. One of the sources of this balance is John Lyly's euphuistic rhythms which, as Falstaff's great prose speeches attest, Shakespeare seems to have relished and absorbed. Even as he began to develop poetically, complicating the sound of his verse and attempting various technical innovations, Shakespeare retained his sense of metrical equipoise, chiefly by indulging the fondness for antithesis that Barton describes.

In *Richard II*, for example, the deposed king's bitter prophecy to Northumberland is structured upon a series of oppositions between Henry IV and his henchman.

> Thou shalt think,
> Though he divide the realm and give thee half,
> It is too little, helping him to all;
> He shall think that thou, which knowest the way
> To plant unrightful kings, wilt know again,
> Being ne'er so little urg'd, another way
> To pluck him headlong from the usurped throne.　　(5.1.59–65)

This passage is especially pertinent because its antitheses are not only semantic (in this case political) but also rhythmic. That several lines divide in half is only the most obvious property. Even more telling is the metrical equivalence in each part of the prediction's two halves, with phrases of roughly equal length given over to each of the competitors.

Thou shalt think	He shall think that thou
Though he divide the realm and give thee half	which knowest the way / To plant unrightful kings
It is too little	wilt know again
helping him to all	Being ne'er so little urg'd

This series of isomorphic phrases finishes with a coda, "another way / To pluck him headlong from the usurped throne," a phrase that sweeps across one line break and accelerates to the end of the next, "gathering head," as Richard says of the "foul corruption." The speech as a whole concludes with another set of oppositions – "The love of wicked men converts to fear, / That fear to hate, and hate turns one or both / To worthy danger and deserved death" – in which the poetic balance extends as far as consonantal repetition and the matched adjectives and nouns in the last line quoted.

Richard's prophecy illustrates Shakespeare's penchant for dividing a subject into opposites because the speech is about division: the metrical counterweights register the force of the contest between the usurper and his agents. Of course *Richard II* as a whole works by means of political and emotional equipoise, juxtaposing an ineffectual, poetic monarch with a practical usurper, and this opposition is reinforced by the visual imagery, particularly the figure of the two buckets. It is also worth emphasizing that the play's metrical balances – it is composed entirely in verse – create an aural frame designed to give physical support to the semantic oppositions.

Such regularity is perhaps to be expected from a young theatre poet who grew up reading Elizabethan poetry and who listened carefully to Marlowe's mighty line. But even Shakespeare's mature verse displays a commitment to antithetical structures. The difference is that the oppositions have been made to function *within* the lines rather than *on* the lines; the metrical balances still obtain. *Macbeth* is the touchstone for such sophisticated use of aural antithesis. Set against the rhymed tetrameter of the witches, what L. C. Knights described as their "sickening, see-saw rhythm," the language of Macbeth himself represents a subtler, more internalized form of antithetical verse.[8]

> This supernatural soliciting
> Cannot be ill; cannot be good. If ill,
> Why hath it given me earnest of success,
> Commencing in a truth? I am Thane of Cawdor.
> If good, why do I yield to that suggestion
> Whose horrid image doth unfix my hair
> And make my seated heart knock at my ribs,
> Against the use of nature? Present fears
> Are less than horrible imaginings:
> My thought, whose murther yet is but fantastical,
> Shakes so my single state of man that function
> Is smother'd in surmise, and nothing is
> But what is not. (1.3.130–42)

The rhythmic equivalents audible here differ conspicuously from those of Shakespeare's earlier style: the structure of the sentences is no longer strictly parisonic; lines are frequently enjambed and fractured with midline pauses; and the aural matching of phrases is sometimes approximate. But the auditory effect is antithetical, complementary, equivocal – like the language of the play as a whole.

Recognition of such characteristic aural equipoise, even in the late work, even in some of the most complex passages, makes it possible to abstract from these verbal habits some conclusions about the relation of sound to sense in Shakespearean drama generally. And for such conclusions *Macbeth*, again, is a useful starting point because its metrical symmetries physically manifest Shakespeare's concern with equivocation and other forms of double-talk. The see-saw rhythms function in concert with the serious puns and the other verbal amphibologies on which the action depends: "If it were done, when 'tis done," the quibble about Birnam Wood coming to Dunsinane, and the ambiguity of Macduff's birth. When Macbeth learns that his challenger was not "born of woman," he responds with an attack on the "juggling fiends" that "palter with us in a double sense, / That keep the word of promise to our ear, / And break it to our hope" (5.8.19–22). All these figures of equivocation are related to the overriding kind of doubleness that permeates *Macbeth*, Shakespeare's stimulation of ambiguous response. As with all the tragic figures, the spectator observes Macbeth's career with a mixture of blame and sympathy, and in each of the major tragedies Shakespeare adjusts the balance between judgment and commiseration, according to the particular experience of the protagonist. Hamlet usually evokes greater admiration than Coriolanus, but the audience feels emotionally divided toward both. Thus Shakespeare's pervasive binary rhythms are part of an enormous system of equivalence and duplication: puns, alliteration, rhyme, twins, scenic alternation between parallel plots, the blending of tones, the representation of both comic and tragic experience, investigation of the marginal territory between (or shared by) comedy and tragedy, the stimulation of pity and horror, ridicule and sympathy. All these bespeak an ingrained commitment to interpretive balance, what Norman Rabkin calls "complementarity."[9] It is a mode of vision that distinguishes Shakespeare from his great competitor.

"Complementarity" is not the first word that comes to mind in connection with Ben Jonson, who rarely seems interested in two sides of an action or character. His belief in correction, enlightenment, and exposure accounts for the single-minded energy of his comic masterpieces and the unbridled monstrosity of his tragic villains. This is not to say that he was blind to multiple points of view, or that his great dramatic characters – the comic titans such as Volpone and Sir Epicure Mammon – are merely one-sided caricatures. In the words of Aldous Huxley, Jonson "might have been a great romantic, one of the sublime inebriates."[10] But the conventional descriptions of Jonsonian comedy as satiric, acerbic, and anti-romantic are as familiar as they are because, although he modified his theatrical means until he finally succeeded at amusing his audiences, Jonson never abandoned the aim, expressed through his mouthpiece Asper to "strip the ragged follies of the time / Naked as at their birth" (*EMO* "After the second sounding," 17–18). As we might expect, this obsessive urge to expose pretension, greed, deception, and especially self-deception left its imprint on Jonson's verse. It is the one-sided complement to Shakespearean antithesis.

The poetic instrument that Jonson creates to excoriate folly in the comedies and crime in the tragedies is unbalanced, anti-symmetrical, and accumulative.

> SEJANUS   . . . Then there is one Cremutius
> Cordus, a writing fellow they have got
> To gather notes of the precedent times,
> And make them into annals – a most tart
> And bitter spirit, I hear, who under color
> Of praising those, doth tax the present state,
> Censures the men, the actions, leaves no trick,
> No practice unexamined, parallels
> The times, the governments, a professed champion
> For the old liberty –   (*Sej.* 1. 303–12)

From a rhythmic standpoint, this passage is difficult to classify. Although it consists of a single incomplete sentence, the longest uninterrupted segment is one-and-a-half lines long; mostly the phrases are staccato; virtually every line contains a midline pause, with some displaying multiple stops, and the pauses refuse to conform to a regular pattern. Sejanus' desire to persuade Tiberius of the danger Cordus embodies leads him to pile verb upon verb, direct object upon direct object, to add still another appositional phrase. It is helpful to read this passage in light of Jonas Barish's analysis of Jonsonian prose, specifically the playwright's adaptation of the "curt style":

> its characteristic device is the so-called "exploded" period, formed of independent members not linked by conjunctions but set apart by a vocal pattern of stress, pitch, and juncture rendered typographically by a colon or a semicolon, sometimes a comma. The members of the exploded period tend to brevity, also to inequality of length, variation in form, and unpredictability of order; hence they are likely to suggest the effect of live thinking rather than of logical premeditation. The "mere fact" or main idea of the period is apt to be exhausted in the first member; subsequent members explore the same idea imaginatively, through metaphor or aphorism or example, but not through ordered analysis.[11]

The pertinence of such a description to Sejanus' verse is immediately clear, and it is even more telling with the contrary example of Shakespearean metrical habits in mind.

Numerous other passages in the verse plays might be summoned to demonstrate the same additive habit, Jonson's desire to make an irrefutable case, to accumulate evidence, to exemplify ever more specifically. Sometimes the aggregative urge comes together with the satiric object, as in Mosca's praise of Volpone's contempt for ordinary greed:

> You shall ha' some will swallow
> A melting heir as glibly as your Dutch
> Will pills of butter, and ne'er purge for 't;
> Tear forth the fathers of poor families
> Out of their beds, and coffin them, alive,
> In some kind, clasping prison, where their bone
> May be forthcoming, when the flesh is rotten.
> But, your sweet nature doth abhor these courses;
> You loathe the widow's or the orphan's tears
> Should wash your pavements, or their piteous cries
> Ring in your roofs, and beat the air for vengeance –
>
> (*Volp.* 1.1.41–51)

In discussing Jonson's extravagant speakers – Volpone, Sir Epicure Mammon, Corvino, to name some of the most impressive – Peter Womack refers to their "indiscriminate supplementarity," their "indefinitely additive speech. . . . Like Mammon's mirrors, words are so arranged as to disperse and multiply the intention that seeks to command them."[12] Among the fools, this kind of supplementarity measures obsessive greed or jealousy or appetite, as in Mammon's voluptuous speeches: "Dishes of agate, set in gold, and studded / With emeralds, sapphires, hyacinths, and rubies." At times the satirists or con-men indulge in such list-making for the purposes of parody, as when Surly delivers a (literally) breathtaking seventeen-line recital of alchemical terms, ending with "worlds of other strange ingredients, / Would burst a man to name" (*Alch.* 2.3.182–98); or when Wittipol, dressed as the Spanish lady, enumerates through some forty lines (with only the briefest interruptions) the animal, vegetable, and mineral contents of "your Spanish fucuses" in *The Devil is an Ass* (4.4.17–56). But such outlandish inventories are not merely a conscious instrument of Jonsonian exposure. To some extent they represent the playwright's own compulsion to overwhelm his audience with illustration.

This kind of authorial supplementarity also produces the distinctive Jonsonian rhythms. Reiteration and amplitude make for an irregular, spasmodic-sounding verse line. The usual cautions about the uncertainty of Renaissance punctuation are for once unnecessary, not only because we know that Jonson supervised the printing of his texts, but also because he has clearly built the stops and hesitations into the verse.

> *Hos.* Fly, come you hither; no discovery
> Of what you see to your Colonel Toe, or Tip, here,
> But keep all close, though you stand i' the way o' preferment,
> Seek it from the road; no flattery for't:
> No lick-foot, pain of losing your proboscis:
> My lickerish Fly.
> *Tip.*　　　　What says old velvet-head?
> *Fly.* He will present me himself, sir, if you will not.
> *Tip.* Who? He present? What? Whom? An host? A groom?
> Divide the thanks with me? Share in my glories?
> Lay up. I say no more.　　　　　　　　　　(*NI*, 2.6.33–42)

Of course such jaggedness is functionally specific to the character, and Jonson was obviously capable of writing smooth iambic pentameter, as he does in some of the lyrics. But in the dramatic verse the rhythmic structure is determined by asymmetries, grammatical gaps, relative pronouns, appended clauses, and staccato phrases, and these are determined by the passionate outrage that Jonson feels toward the world he represents. The strength of his conviction exerts such pressure on the verse that he rarely develops rhythmic momentum or anything approaching a "poetic" tone. The nearest he comes to such lyricism, probably, would be Volpone's seductive plea to Celia, where the lyricism is heavily ironized. But rarely does he depict any situation where lyricism or regularity would be appropriate. The verse is unbalanced because the world is tilted.

Two additional measures of Jonson's poetic irregularity require notice, one impressionistic and the other statistical. The first is his taste for a figure not much remarked upon but particularly revealing of Jonson's emphatic style: the spondee.

> Can it call, whore? Cry bastard? Oh, then, kiss it,
> A witty child! Can't swear? The father's darling!
> Give it two plums.   (*EMI*, 2.5.21–3)

> *Sej.* 'Tis Agrippina?
> *Tib.*   She, and her proud race.   (*Sej.* 2.190)

> Hang him proud stag, with his broad velvet head.   (*Alch.* 1.2.61)

> He made me a Captain. I was a stark pimp,
> Just o' your standing, 'fore I met with him: (*Alch.* 3.4.44–5)

> she has sent you,
> From her own private trencher, a dead mouse   (*Alch.* 3.5.64–5)

It is easy to see why Jonson so frequently introduces the spondee: the distinctive foot adds emphasis by loading a supplementary beat onto an already irregular line. And as in several of these examples, the spondaic effect is often intensified by a preceding trochee. The figure is typical of a poetic style marked by shifts in direction, emotional flashes, surprising turns, short stops.

This non-scientific survey of Jonson's metrical bent is validated by statistics. Ants Oras' meticulous analysis of midline pauses in English Renaissance drama discloses that as major playwrights grew more comfortable with iambic pentameter as a dramatic medium, they became much more willing to pause in midline and even to stop repeatedly.[13] What is especially notable is that the normal position of the pause begins to move: whereas Elizabethan playwrights, like the lyric poets from whom they learned, tended to rest after the fourth or the sixth syllable, the Jacobeans used the stop much more liberally and were more inclined to halt the clause or the sentence near the end of the line. In other words, in plays written by major dramatists from about 1590 to about 1610, the position of the pause tends to migrate towards the end of the line. This historical development is conspicuous in the Shakespeare canon: in *Richard III*, exemplifying his early prosodic practice, only 12.7% of the poetic lines contain pauses after the seventh, eighth, or ninth syllable; in *Antony and Cleopatra*, by contrast, 31% of the lines require stops in those late positions.

Although Oras' set of numbers can seem formidable, they help to document what the ear senses. They reveal that Shakespeare employs the comma, the semicolon, the colon, and the period deliberately, often for a particular dramatic end such as pointing up a contrast, whereas Jonson stops promiscuously, sometimes two or three times in the course of a single line, occasionally even more. In absolute terms, the number of midline pauses in Jonson's verse plays is vastly greater than in Shakespeare's. *The Alchemist*, for example, contains over 5,000 stops in about 3,000 lines of verse, and while that total is the highest, each of Jonson's major verse plays contain over 4,000 pauses. For Shakespeare, on the other hand, the highest number of stops occurs in *Cymbeline*, about 3,100 stops in 2,600 lines of verse. And in most of the plays, even the late, prosodically complex romances, the numbers don't even approach the Jonsonian average. As for the location of stops, Jonson does not discriminate, stopping wherever it suits him, sometimes even after the first and before the last syllable in the line. It is similarly instructive to consider split lines, a line of verse divided among two or more speakers. Jonson frequently arrests a speech in midline and resumes it with another speaker. Shakespeare rarely does so in the 1590s: there are 33 split pentameters in *Richard II*, for example. In the second decade of his career, he is more likely to divide a line, an inclination consistent with his more flexible approach to prosody: *Antony and Cleopatra* contains 433 such instances. But this is moderate compared to Jonson, who is prodigal with such divisions: *Volpone* contains 768, *The Alchemist* 933, and *The Devil is an Ass* 669. Even *Sejanus*, which lacks the heteroglossic exuberance that helps to generate such numbers in the comedies, contains 498 instances of split lines. Critics have been reluctant to attend to Oras' daunting graphs and charts, but his analysis helps to document the textural differences between Shakespeare and Jonson that are immediately striking to an attentive listener.

Metrical study is scarcely the most glamorous of critical approaches, but its value is being reconsidered as a minor branch of historicism; it constitutes an effort to listen to the language of early modern drama as its original audiences would have heard it. And in the hands of its most talented practitioners, such analysis can augment and even alter the way we think about familiar texts.[14] We know that Shakespeare's way of looking at the world is complementary, and sensitivity to his rhythmic complements helps to reveal the extent of that habitual vision. Jonson repeatedly declares his belief in the therapeutic function of the stage, and the aggregative style of his verse represents the grammatical and rhythmic manifestations of that conviction. Likewise, his commitment to realism entails the urge to create something like realistic speech, "language such as men do use," and this desire accounts for the syntactical knots, appositives, hesitations, supplements, and modifications that crowd his verse. Admittedly men and women in Jacobean London were no more apt to talk like Sir Epicure Mammon than they were to talk like King Lear. In other words, Jonson's dramatic verse is just as artificial as Shakespeare's. Nevertheless, the poetic patterns he devises look and sound much less like patterns than do Shakespeare's. The sound of their verse suggests that, in this one sense at least, Jonson is more "natural" than his famously untutored rival. Awareness of these different aural textures offers insight into why Dryden admired one poet and loved the other, and why later readers have concurred in that assessment: Shakespeare's balances are more immediately appealing than Jonson's heaps. Although stylistic study mostly confirms our familiar construction of the differences between Shakespeare and Jonson, it is uncommonly useful in its capacity to make us understand why we think what we think.

NOTES

1 See Ian Donaldson, *Jonson's Magic Houses: Essays in Interpretation* (Oxford: Clarendon Press, 1997); Donaldson's *Jonson and Shakespeare* (Atlantic Highlands, NJ: Humanities Press, 1983); Anne Barton, *Ben Jonson, Dramatist* (Cambridge: Cambridge University Press, 1984); and Russ McDonald, *Shakespeare and Jonson / Jonson and Shakespeare* (Lincoln: University of Nebraska Press, 1988).

2 The specific complaints about Shakespeare's disregard for verisimilitude are widely available, perhaps most readily in the introductory chapter to my *Shakespeare and Jonson/Jonson and Shakespeare.*

3 See Richard Helgerson, *Self-Crowned Laureates* (Berkeley: University of California Press, 1983), 151ff.

4 These plays contain deviations from blank verse: the great scene in which Volpone disguises himself as a mountebank is a tour-de-force done in a con-man's prose. But essentially they are verse plays.

5 Jonas Barish, *Ben Jonson and the Language of Prose Comedy* (Cambridge, MA: Harvard University Press, 1960).

6 John Barton, *Playing Shakespeare* (London: Methuen, 1984), 55.

7 Quotations from Shakespeare are taken from *The Riverside Shakespeare*, ed. G. B. Evans (Boston: Houghton Mifflin, 1974).

8 L. C. Knights, "How many children had Lady Macbeth?" rpt. in *Explorations* (New York: New York University Press, 1947), 23.

9 Norman Rabkin, *Shakespeare and the Common Understanding* (New York: The Free Press, 1967), 22.

10 Aldous Huxley, "Ben Jonson," *London Mercury* 1 (1919): 187. Also see Robert Ornstein, "Shakespearian and Jonsonian Comedy," *Shakespeare Survey* 22 (1969): "Contemptuous as he was of romantic fabling, Jonson had . . . an instinct for romantic variety and multiplicity which, though severely disciplined in *Volpone* and *The Alchemist,* burst forth in the noisy carnivals of *Epicene* [sic] and *Bartholomew Fair*" (43).

11 Barish, *Language of Prose Comedy*, 50.

12 Peter Womack, *Ben Jonson* (Oxford: Basil Blackwell, 1986), 6.

13 Ants Oras, *Pause Patterns in Elizabethan and Jacobean Drama: An Experiment in Prosody* (Gainesville: University of Florida Press, 1960).

14 The best book on Shakespeare's verse is George T. Wright's *Shakespeare's Metrical Art* (Berkeley: University of California Press, 1988).

9

IAN DONALDSON

Jonson's poetry

1 Rare poems, rare friends: the *Epigrams*

In conversation with the Scottish poet William Drummond of Hawthornden over the winter of 1618–19, Ben Jonson gloomily predicted that the work of his friend John Donne, "for not being understood, would perish" (*Conv. Dr.* 158). Writing to William Herbert, Earl of Pembroke, just a couple of years earlier, however, Jonson had imagined his own poems being studied with attention by "posterity" – that ideal readership to which, on more than one occasion, he had confidently commended his work (*Epig.* Ded. 15). Neither of these predictions has proved to be exact. Donne's poetry, though relatively neglected throughout the eighteenth and nineteenth centuries, has scarcely perished; admired and mediated by Eliot, it spoke powerfully to modernist sensibilities and proponents of the new criticism, and is familiar today to readers throughout the English-speaking world. Jonson's poems, on the other hand, are less well known and perhaps (ironically) less well understood. It is not that they have lacked discerning admirers such as James Joyce, Marianne Moore, Yvor Winters, and Thom Gunn, but the band of witnesses has always been small in number. In *Epig.* 17, addressed "To the Learned Critic," Jonson declared that it was the opinion of the single judicious person that he esteemed, not that of a wider public: "And but a sprig of bays, given by thee, / Shall outlive garlands stolen from the chaste tree." In recent times Jonson has had his sprig of bays, perhaps, but hardly his garlands.

In an influential early study of the poetry, Wesley Trimpi described Ben Jonson's achievement as the triumph of a "plain" style that was markedly different from the more obscure and conceited manner of Donne and his followers. Yet the success of many of Jonson's poems is not wholly explicable in terms of their conformity to a supposedly ideal "plain style," nor is the contrast between the "schools of Donne and Jonson" quite as stark as is often represented. Jonson and Donne were close friends and mutual admirers, and their poetic styles are sometimes hard to distinguish. Some scholars have suspected Donne of having written up to four poems of disputed authorship that were published in Jonson's posthumous 1640 collection, *The Underwood,* one of which ("To make the doubt clear that no woman's true," *Und.* 39) had previously been published in the 1633 edition of Donne's *Poems*. Passages elsewhere in Jonson's late verse – in "Eupheme," for example, the sequence of poems written in memory of Venetia Digby (*Und.* 84) – adopt a "metaphysical" style strongly reminiscent of Donne. Indeed when William Drummond, in one of the first known uses of that word in relation to poetic writing of the period, complained of those who had abstracted poetry "to Metaphysical Ideas and Scholastic Quiddities," he may well have been thinking as much of Jonson's practice as of Donne's.[1] And when Samuel Johnson many years later revived the term in his "Life of Cowley" in order to describe "a race of writers that may be termed the metaphysical poets" he chose to include Ben Jonson amongst their number.

Metaphysical or no, Jonson knew (as Donne did) that the greatest poetry was bound to be difficult, and that poetic understanding in any generation was a scarce commodity. The first poem in Jonson's *Epigrams* is addressed challengingly "To the Reader": "Pray thee take care, that tak'st my book in hand, / To read it well; that is, to understand." The second and third poems, "To My Book" and "To My Bookseller," list some of the several ways in which the *Epigrams* will be misconstrued by ignorant readers who glance carelessly at its pages; while the fourth salutes a more distinguished and discerning reader, none other than King James himself, "best of kings" and "best of poets." In this opening salvo of epigrams Jonson is recalling a satire by Horace (*Sat.* I. iv) in which the Roman poet expresses his disdain for the seductions of the plain style (*non satis est puris versum perscribere verbis*, "it is not enough to write out a line of simple words," 54) and of vulgar praise. True poetry is difficult, Horace declares, and will always appeal merely to a few discriminating readers.

> nulla taberna meos habeat neque pila libellos,
> quis manus insudet volgi Hermogenisque Tigelli;
> nec recito cuiquam nisi amicis, idque coactus,
> non ubivis coramve quibuslibet. (71–4)

[I want no stall or pillar to have my little works, so that the hands of the crowd – and Hermogenes Tigellis (a popular poet) – may sweat over them. Nor do I recite them to any save my friends, and then only when pressed – not anywhere or before any hearers.]

Jonson echoes these sentiments closely in the second of his *Epigrams*, "To My Bookseller," but his attitude to the reading public and the question of public fame is in some ways more complex than Horace's.

> Thou that mak'st gain thy end, and wisely well
>   Call'st a book good or bad, as it doth sell,
> Use mine so, too; I give thee leave; but crave
>   For the luck's sake it thus much favour have:

To lie upon thy stall till it be sought;
Not offered, as it made suit to be bought;
Nor have my title-leaf on posts or walls
Or in cleft-sticks, advanced to make calls
For termers or some clerk-like serving-man
Who scarce can spell the hard names; whose knight less can.
If, without these vile arts, it will not sell,
Send it to Bucklersbury: there 'twill, well.

Jonson's booksellers were crucial agents in furthering his career as a professional writer. Jonson's strong distaste for the new print medium and for the bookseller's trade is nevertheless clearly evident in this divided poem. Bucklersbury was a street near Cheapside inhabited by grocers and apothecaries, who would be glad to dismember his book and use it as wrapping paper; a fate that his bookseller (so Jonson implies) would cheerfully tolerate as another form of sale.

Many of Jonson's contemporaries, such as Donne himself, had avoided this marketplace altogether, preferring to circulate their poems in manuscript amongst their friends. Donne's poems were not to be published until 1633, two years after his death, his disliking for print having been strengthened by his decision to take holy orders in 1615. In 1619 Jonson told William Drummond that since Donne was "made doctor" he "repententh highly, and seeketh to destroy all his poems" (*Conv. Dr.* 102–3). In a quite literal sense, Donne's poems might indeed have perished, but the very large number of his extant manuscripts testifies to his contemporary standing as an author amongst the *cognoscenti*, who did (presumably) understand and admire his poetic work. Though Jonson generally chose to present his writings through the medium of print, he was also attracted by the thought of his verse circulating amongst a few judicious readers. *Epig.* 96, for example, is a poem that Jonson evidently sent in manuscript, along with a bundle of other poems, to Donne himself, seeking his friend's judgment and approval. Donne's "best authority" will determine whether Jonson has truly earned the name of poet.

Who shall doubt, Donne, whe'er I a poet be,
When I dare send my epigrams to thee?
That so alone canst judge, so alone dost make;
And in thy censures, evenly dost take
As free simplicity to disavow
As thou hast best authority to allow.
Read all I send: and if I find but one
Marked by thy hand, and with the better stone,
My title's sealed.   (1–9)

It is possible that Jonson here is asking Donne to decide which, if any, of these poems is worth publishing in the Folio edition of his works which Jonson was then preparing, but the poem fastidiously avoids any reference to the culture of print, transporting us instead through its classical allusions to pre-Gutenberg times. The Romans had a habit of marking fortunate days with a white stone. Jonson invites Donne to mark the passable poems in a similar archaic fashion, with "the better stone." The final lines of the poem firmly reject the concept of popular fame that publication might seem to promise: "A man should seek great glory, and not broad." Yet this epigram commending the superiority of private literary transactions, the judgment of a single discerning friend, is then paradoxically published by Jonson in his 1616 Folio, alongside other epigrams which insist that it is the "sole censure" of one judicious critic that Jonson seeks, not the admiration of a wider reading public (*Epig.* 17. 4).

In *Epig.* 94 Jonson writes to the brilliant Lucy Harington, Countess of Bedford – Donne's patroness, and also his own – sending a manuscript "book" of Donne's verse satires.

> Lucy, you brightness of our sphere, who are
> Life of the muses' day, their morning star!
> If works, not the authors, their own grace should look,
> Whose poems would not wish to be your book?
> But these, desired by you, the maker's ends
> Crown with their own. Rare poems ask rare friends. $(1 - 6)$

The poem reveals and celebrates a system of authorship, patronage, circulation, and esteem quite different from that promoted by the book trade. Evidently in response to a hint from his patroness, Donne has passed a manuscript copy of his verse satires to Jonson, who submits them to the Countess on Donne's behalf with a graceful poem of his own suggesting that it is the wish of the poems themselves that draws them to her, the inclination of this exceptional book matching the inclination of this exceptional patron: "Rare poems ask rare friends." Donne as author is courteously, modestly, invisible, *asking* nothing in his own person, though his "ends" are here fulfilled. The light shines on, and from, the patroness, the etymology of whose name (*lux, lucis* = light) Jonson playfully explores: "Lucy, you brightness of our sphere, who are / The muses' evening- as their morning-star." The planet Venus is called Lucifer ("light-bearing") when it appears in the morning before the sun, and Hesperus when it appears in the evening when the sun has set. Jonson praises the rarity of true friendship and true judgment: the *sphere* in which these authors and their patroness move is exclusive, removed, and private. Yet this seemingly intimate poem is subsequently published in Jonson's 1616 Folio for the sake of a wider public, along with those other epigrams written in praise of private friendship, readership, and adjudication. Donne's *Satires,* by way of contrast, are not published until after their author's death. The tensions and contradictions of Jonson's position as an author, and the ambiguous status of the *Epigrams* – as a half-private, half-public collection, offered to discriminating "understanders" yet openly traded on the bookstalls – are fully evident here. Though strongly drawn by the notion of coterie poetry and manuscript circulation, Jonson is even more powerfully attracted by the lure of print. The final destination of the *Epigrams* is a printed book, an object that – unlike Donne's more vulnerable poetic manuscripts – would seemingly never perish.

Stanley Fish has suggestively described the manner in which Jonson's poems create an implied audience of like-minded readers and recipients, an elite but egalitarian discipleship, a "community of the same" who intuitively recognize and understand the central values (of friendship, loyalty, steadfastness, and so on) which the poems celebrate.[2] Such values and such people are hailed but seldom described in detail; their deeper qualities, it is implied, will be known instantly to those worthy of reading the poems. Amongst true friends, friendship requires no explanation; to the virtuous, the nature of true virtue will be at once apparent.

> I do but name thee, Pembroke, and I find
> It is an epigram on all mankind,
> Against the bad, but of and to the good;
> Both which are asked, to have thee understood. (*Epig.* 102. 1–4)

There is often thus a curious absence at the heart of Jonson's poems, Fish argues, as the very qualities which the poems appear most profoundly to commend are summarily noted, or merely gestured at; the richer and more detailed description being reserved for satirical denunciation of their opposites, what such virtues and such people emphatically are *not*. (For this reason, Fish finds the notion of the "plain style," with its implied mode of transparent representation of clearly discernible phenomena, peculiarly inappropriate to an understanding of Jonson's verse.) Fish's concept of "the community of the same" greatly illuminates one aspect of Jonson's poetry and of the *Epigrams* in particular: their sense of exclusivity and private exchange. What it does not quite explain is why Jonson also wished to place his poems in the public domain; why, despite his deep distaste for the activities of the marketplace, he should have entrusted these works to his bookseller. To repeat a central question that Pope was later to ask of himself while tracing and testing his own progress as a poet: "*But why then publish?*" (*An Epistle to Doctor Arbuthnot*, 135).

In Jonson's case at least the answer may lie not merely in the ambitions of authorship but in a deeper consciousness of the need for poems such as the *Epigrams* to perform a civic role by publicly commemorating the virtuous, and publicly berating their opposing vices; a role that could not be entirely fulfilled through the circulation of poems in manuscript. Epigrammatic verse was particularly well suited to these functions. "In short and sweet poems, framed to praise and dispraise, or some other sharp conceit, which are called *Epigrams*, as our country men now surpasse other nations, so in former times they were not inferior," wrote Jonson's old schoolmaster, William Camden, in his *Remains of a Greater Work Concerning Britain* in 1605. Praise and dispraise form the central poetic activities in Jonson's *Epigrams*, in which poems of tribute to named individuals are carefully mixed with poems that satirize generic figures – Court Worm, Old Colt, Groom Idiot, Hazard the Cheater, Sir Cod the Perfumed, Lieutenant Shift, Sir Voluptuous Beast, etc. – whose precise identity is never disclosed. The names of those whom Jonson salutes are formally recited, as in a roll-call of honor, often at the outset of each poem: "Donne, the delight of Phoebus and each muse"; "Uvedale, thou piece of the first times"; "Rudyerd, as lesser dames to great ones use"; "Who now calls on thee, Neville"; "Who, Edmondes, reads thy book"; "Who would not be thy subject, James"; "Jephson, thou man of men, to whose loved name / All gentry yet owe part of their best flame!"; "Roe (and my joy to name)," and so on (*Epig.* 23, 125, 121, 109, 111, 35, 116, 128). Sometimes, in a variation of this pattern, a set of ideal characteristics is first described and a name belatedly and delightedly produced which perfectly encapsulates them, as in *Epig.* 76, "On Lucy, Countess of Bedford": "Such when I meant to feign and wished to see, / My muse bade, *Bedford* write, and that was she." The name may prompt historical, literary, or lexical associations which become in turn the subject matter of the poem, as in *Epig.* 91, "To Sir Horace Vere":

> Which of thy names I take, not only bears
> A Roman sound, but Roman virtue wears:
> Illustrous Vere, or Horace, fit to be
> Sung by a Horace, or a muse as free . . . (1–4)

What power does Jonson find in names, and why does he invoke them so insistently throughout the *Epigrams*? Pope's rather similar practice may provide a clue.

> But why then publish? *Granville* the polite,
> And knowing *Walsh*, would tell me I could write;
> Well-natur'd *Garth* inflam'd with early praise,
> And *Congreve* lov'd, and *Swift* endur'd my Lays;
> The Courtly *Talbot, Somers, Sheffield* read,
> Ev'n mitred *Rochester* would nod the head
> And *St. John*'s self (great Dryden's friends before)
> With open arms receiv'd one Poet more.
> (*An Epistle to Dr Arbuthnot*, 135–42)

Through this ritual call of names Pope evokes a small but powerful company of approving patrons and well-wishers: friends to his work, who have been, significantly, "great Dryden's friends before." All are lovers or practitioners of poetry, and some have influence in other spheres, as "courtly" "mitred" and "polite" may suggest. Listening, reading, nodding, and approving, these influential friends urge the young poet towards publication. In their harmonious endorsement of the poet's genius, they constitute indeed "a community of the same," yet their power rests also in their social diversity. Some are from a stratum of society entirely unlike that of Pope himself. It is a skilful stroke for the Catholic poet, subject to numerous social penalties and disentitlements, to have included an Anglican bishop in his circle of admirers. The names serve to legitimize and authenticate the poet's social function; for these are no mere "friends," but exemplary representatives of society itself.

The names which Jonson invokes throughout the *Epigrams* serve in a similar way through their very diversity to endorse his role as poet, and also to illustrate his notion of an ideal society. To praise such individuals is to praise the larger ideals of the community which they exemplify and sustain:

> These, noblest Cecil, laboured in my thought,
>> Wherein what wonder, see, thy name hath wrought:
> That whilst I meant but thine to gratulate
>> I've sung the greater fortunes of our state. (*Epig.* 64. 15–18)

Jonson creates in the *Epigrams* a kind of pantheon of national worthies, men and women whose virtues are deserving commemoration.[3] The poet, wrote Jonson in *Discoveries* (1045–8), is one who "can feign a commonwealth . . . can govern it with counsels, strengthen it with laws, correct it with judgments, inform it with religion and morals." In the *Epigrams* Jonson "feigns" a commonwealth of exemplary individuals in much this way – statesmen, scholars, soldiers, writers, artists – "leading forth so many good and great names as my verses mention on the better part, to their remembrance with posterity" (*Epig.* Ded. 13–14). The 1616 folio, sometimes viewed as the product of Jonson's personal ambitions, was an apt vehicle for this grand celebratory project, and the men and women it sets out publicly to honor.

The rituals of shaming, like those of celebration, are performed most tellingly in public, and Jonson's poems of dispraise, like his poems of praise, also demand a published form. These might be described as poems of partial exposure. Laconically sketching the nature of a vicious person, they threaten to disclose something more: the person's identity and name. Here is *Epig.* 30, to "Person Guilty":

> Guilty, be wise; and though thou know'st the crimes
>> Be thine I tax, yet do not own my rhymes;
> 'Twere madness in thee to betray thy fame
>> And person to the world, ere I thy name.

What is hidden and private may easily be shown to "the world": this is the *danger* of the *Epigrams* about which Jonson speaks in his dedication to the Earl of Pembroke (line 4). *Epig.* 68 moves in the same liminal territory:

> Playwright, convict of public wrongs to men,
> Takes private beatings, and begins again.
> Two kinds of valour he doth show at once:
> Active in's brain, and passive in his bones.

"Playwright" is a contemptuous coinage whose suffix suggests mechanical labor (cf. "wheelwright"), and chimes ironically with "wrongs." The poem is built upon a series of such simple binary contrasts – "active"/"passive," "brain"/"bones," "public"/"private" – which define and delimit the personality of the victim: like a mechanical toy, this person has a tiny repertoire of tricks: writing plays, taking punishment, starting again. Public wrongs, private beatings: if a quiet cudgeling will not restrain Playwright, then a public exposure in poetry may at least humiliate. But the exposure here remains only partial: for Jonson scrupulously withholds Playwright's name, and any description of the nature of those "public wrongs." Playwright hovers dubiously at the very threshold of Jonson's *Epigrams*, half-admitted and half-excluded: "Playwright, I loathe to have thy manners known / In my chaste book: profess them in thine own" (*Epig.* 49. 5–6).

T. S. Eliot once famously described Jonson's poetry as being "of the surface." The characterization is (for once) not entirely accurate, for Jonson's poetry works in another mode, constantly suggesting, through hints and glances, what lies *beneath* the surface, behind a public face. What is concealed or half-concealed in these satirical epigrams are (moreover) not just the shameful facts and identifications which the poet has chosen to withhold, but that fuller, freer life which the individual himself has chosen to suppress. Thus the nameless lord of *Epig.* 11 has voluntarily contrived – so it is implied – to reduce himself to the status of a neutered "Something that Walks Somewhere":

> At court I met it, in clothes brave enough
> To be a courtier, and looks grave enough
> To seem a statesman. As I near it came,
> It made me a great face; I asked the name;
> A lord, it cried, buried in flesh and blood,
> And such from whom let no man hope least good,
> For I will do none; and as little ill,
> For I will dare none. Good lord, walk dead still.

"Buried in flesh and blood" as in his grand clothes and grave looks, the lord has surrendered all real title to humanity: clinging instead to the title of his rank ("A lord, it cried") he has become a mere "it," bearing no name, walking "dead."

This self-engrossed, self-neglecting automaton resembles "The New Motion" of *Epig.* 97 whose "clothes have over-leavened him" (20), and "Fine Lady Would-be" of *Epig.* 62, who has suppressed her own fertility by use of contraceptives, and with it, in Jonson's view, another and more productive life she might have led:

> What should the cause be? Oh, you live at court:
>   And there's both loss of time and loss of sport
> In a great belly. Write, then, on thy womb:
>   Of the not born, yet buried, here's the tomb. (9–12)

This notion of the buried life is in stark contrast to the various modes of freedom which Jonson celebrates elsewhere in the collection in his poems of praise (*Epig.* 43. 12; 66. 13–14; 95. 17–18; 101. 35, etc.). It is a freedom that his patron Esmé Stuart, Lord Aubigny, has afforded the poet himself through his protection, enabling him to write such verses as these:

> How full of want, how swallowed up, how dead
>   I and this muse had been if thou hadst not
> Lent timely succours, and new life begot . . .   (*Epig.* 127. 6–8)

Praising Robert Cecil, Earl of Salisbury, he similarly rejoices: "But I am glad to see that time survive / Where merit is not sepulchred alive" (*Epig.* 64. 9–10). These lines were written in May 1608, on Cecil's appointment as Lord Treasurer. But as time passed, Jonson grew disenchanted with Cecil, for reasons that remain obscure; and in publishing this epigram and another to Cecil in the 1616 collection he followed them immediately with another epigram, "To My Muse," which begins irately: "Away, and leave me, thou thing most abhorred, / That hast betrayed me to a worthless lord" (*Epig.* 65. 1–2). While the juxtaposition of poems within the collection strongly hints at the identity of this "worthless lord," it is an essential part of Jonson's strategy to withhold the name, allowing the victim to remain, in an ironic fate, "sepulchred alive."

The characters selected for both praise and dispraise throughout the *Epigrams* are described repeatedly in terms of the models they offer for emulation or avoidance. The actor Edward Alleyn and the learned diplomat Sir Thomas Roe are both praised for their "great example," and Sir Thomas Overbury as setting a "fair precedent" for those who follow him (*Epig.* 89. 7; 99. 5; 113. 9). Donne's early verse "Came forth example, and remains so yet," while the honors loved by Sir Henry Cary are "of best example" (*Epig.* 23. 4; 66. 13). Mary, Lady Wroth, "had all antiquity been lost" might serve as a template from which ancient virtue might be recovered: "So are you nature's index, and restore / In yourself all treasure lost of the age before"; and Sir William Uvedale is praised in a similar trope (*Epig.* 105. 1, 19–20; 125). Examples may also however be corrupting: it is the "example" of court practice, for instance, that first encourages "Mill, My Lady's

Woman" to entertain a lover (*Epig.* 90. 4). Such exemplary portraits, good and bad, are carefully distributed and juxtaposed throughout the *Epigrams*. Writing in *Discoveries* about the qualities which a true poet should possess, Jonson (like Milton after him, in *Areopagitica*) stresses the need for the poet to distinguish clearly between good and ill: "We do not require in him mere elocution, or an excellent faculty in verse, but the exact knowledge of all virtues and their contraries; with ability to render the one loved, the other hated, by his proper embattling them" (1048–52; cf. *Epig.* 102. 1–4). While offering personal tribute and (no doubt) settling private scores, the poems of praise and dispraise in the *Epigrams* cumulatively fulfill a more ambitious public aim, displaying such "virtues and their contraries" in their properly embattled state. It is this grand aim that prompts Jonson to describe the poems proudly in the 1616 Folio as "the ripest of my studies" (*Epig.* Ded. 3).

2 Living trees: *The Forest*

The fifteen poems of *The Forest* were first published as a group in the 1616 Folio. Many of them had been written considerably earlier, and some had been previously published in a slightly different form – *For.* 10 and 11, for example, in 1601 in an anthology of poems by Shakespeare, Marston, Chapman and others – or in a radically different context. The Catullan translations, "Come my Celia" and "Kiss me, sweet" (*For.* 5 and 6) had last been heard in the altogether more sinister setting of *Volpone*, 3. 7, where they form part of Volpone's amorous repertoire as he tries unsuccessfully to seduce the unfortunate Celia, wife of the merchant Corvino. Brought together now as a collection and arranged in sequence, they acquire a somewhat different signification, as individual trees (to follow Jonson's figure) acquire a different shape and mass when growing as a forest.

Jonson was evidently much taken by the metaphorical suggestiveness of his title, which he was to exploit again in relation to his later poetic collection, *The Underwood*, and his commonplace book, *Timber, or, Discoveries*. The Latin term *silva* and the Greek term ῾γλη which lie behind these titles were used by the ancients to describe a literary miscellany; or as Jonson puts it in his note "To the Reader" prefixed to *The Underwood*, "works of diverse nature and matter congested, as the multitude call timber-trees, promiscuously growing, a wood or forest." The terms could also be used to denote rough drafts or improvised work: raw materials waiting to be worked up (a sense more evident in relation to *Timber* than either of the two poetry collections). Jonson extends and enlarges these traditional meanings through a subtle play of image and metaphor throughout *The Forest*, which, as we venture in, proves soon to be a forest indeed, and something more than a forest.

"Thou joy'st in better marks, of soil, of air, / Of wood, of water; therein thou art fair," writes Jonson of Penshurst (Lord Lisle's estate near Tonbridge, in Kent) in the second poem of the sequence, surveying the richly wooded landscape.

> Thou hast thy walks for health as well as sport:
> Thy Mount, to which the dryads do resort,
> Where Pan and Bacchus their high feasts have made,
> Beneath the broad beech and the chestnut shade;
> That taller tree, which of a nut was set
> At his great birth, where all the muses met.
> There in the writhed bark, are cut the names
> Of many a sylvan taken with his flames;
> And thence the ruddy satyrs oft provoke
> The lighter fauns to reach thy lady's oak.
> Thy copse, too, named of Gamage, thou hast there,
> That never fails to serve thee seasoned deer
> When thou wouldst feast or exercise thy friends.
> The lower land, that to the river bends,
> Thy sheep, thy bullocks, kine and calves do feed;
> The middle grounds thy mares and horses breed.
> Each bank doth yield thee conies, and the tops,
> Fertile of wood, Ashour and Sidney's copse,
> To crown thy open table, doth provide
> The purpled pheasant with the speckled side . . .   (7–28)

"That taller tree" is the oak (still standing today at Penshurst) grown from an acorn planted on the day of Sir Philip Sidney's birth, November 30, 1554, which appears to symbolize the dynasty itself, deeply rooted on the estate. Jonson would have known that in planting this tree the family was following a classical tradition; Suetonius reports that a poplar had been planted in similar fashion on the day of Virgil's birth (*Vita Vergili*, 5). The scene is topographically precise, but imaginatively elaborated, as classical memories and mythological creatures invade and enliven the native landscape: the forest is Roman as well as English, symbolic as well as literal. The oak tree bears not only the names of lovers carved into its bark, but twinned identity with Sir Philip Sidney himself. Another tree ("thy lady's oak") and copse ("named of Gamage") are identified with Lady Lisle, who according to tradition "was taken in travail under an oak in Penshurst Park, which was afterwards called *My Lady's Oak*," and also fed deer in the copse which bore her name (Gifford's note). The trees of this forest figure, and almost seem to *be,* the people whose names they carry. The "tops" of the wood are "fertile" not just in their production of deer and pheasant, but in their apparent fostering of, and identity with, the Sidney family itself. "Grow, grow fair tree, and as thy branches shoot, / Hear what the muses sing about thy root," Jonson writes to Katherine, Lady Aubigny in *For.* 13, urging her, in a simpler application of the same metaphor, to "raise a family stem" (99–100, 97). In "To Penshurst" the play between tenor and vehicle, between the observed scene and its figurative meaning, between the operation of a seemingly "plain" style realistically charting a known place and a style that works by indirection, association, and negative suggestion is altogether more complex, creating the sense of a landscape that is magically animated, and a family so profoundly at one with that landscape that they are implicit in and represented by the forest itself.

The forest and surrounding countryside of Sir Robert Wroth's estate at Durrants in Essex are depicted in *For.* 3 as lying at a significant remove from the city and the court, with their inevitable corruption. Wroth himself is one who

> . . . canst at home in thy securer rest
> Live with unbought provision blest;
> Free from the proud porches or their gilded roofs
> 'Mongst lowing herds and solid hoofs;
> Alongst the curled woods and painted meads
> Through which a serpent river leads
> To some cool, courteous shade, which he calls his,
> And makes sleep softer than it is! (13–20)

"Courteous" (line 19) means literally "in a manner appropriate to the court"; applied to a rural shade, it may seem mildly surprising. This is a Virgilian *umbra*, a delicious sylvan resting place, but it is also a shadow or simulacrum of James' seat of power – but not in the teasingly derogatory sense of shadowing developed in *For.* 7, "Song: That Women are but Men's Shadows," for Durrants, like Penshurst, is a place from which the king himself draws strength and refreshment, a court in itself whenever he chooses to visit (line 24). The forest here serves a multiple function, providing grateful relief from the strains of courtly and urban life as from extremities of weather: "The trees cut out in log, and those boughs made/ A fire now, that lent a shade!" (45–6). Here is the perfect social and environmental balance – a balance whose absence, in another country estate, is wryly noted by Alexander Pope in a similar trope: "The thriving plants ignoble broomsticks made, / Now sweep those Alleys they were born to shade" ("Epistle iv, To Richard Boyle," 97–8). Jonson's forest provides, in a quite literal sense, the focus of life at Durrants as it does at Penshurst – the Latin *focus* being a hearth or fireplace, traditionally tended by the *Penates*, or household gods.

> That found King James, when, hunting late this way
> With his brave son, the Prince, they saw thy fires
> Shine bright on every hearth as the desires
> Of thy Penates had been set on flame
> To entertain them; or the country came
> With all their zeal to warm their welcome here.   (*For.* 2. 76–81)

The fires of Penshurst are glimpsed again in the "Ode To Sir William Sidney, on His Birthday".

> Now that the hearth is crowned with smiling fire,
> And some do drink, and some do dance,
> Some ring,
> Some sing,
> And all do strive to advance
> The gladness higher;
> Wherefore should I
> Stand silent by,
> Who not the least
> Both love the cause and authors of the feast? (*For.* 14. 1–10)

William Sidney was the eldest son of Robert Sidney, Lord Lisle, the owner of Penshurst, where William's twenty-first birthday was celebrated. Jonson may have acted as tutor to this young man, whose career thus far had been troublesome: at the age of fifteen he had stabbed a schoolmaster, with near-fatal consequences. The moment of his gaining maturity is one for reflection as well as rejoicing. Jonson's ode, opening genially with that "smiling fire," maintains through its dancing rhyme and meter – mirrored in its typographical presentation – a lightness of touch that is wholly appropriate to the festive occasion. In its central stanzas the poem modulates, however, to offer more somber, tutorly, advice ("Your vow / Must now / Strive all right ways it can / To outstrip your peers," etc., 23–6) before returning to elaborate the smiling focal conceit from which it began:

> So may you live in honour as in name,
> If with this truth you be inspired;
> So may
> This day
> Be more, and long desired;
> And with the flame
> Of love be bright,
> As with the light
> Of bonfires. Then
> The birthday shines, when logs not burn, but men. (51–60)

In "To Penshurst" the bark of Sir Philip Sidney's oak is carved with names "Of many a sylvan taken with his flames" (15–16). These are "flames" of love, like those to which Sidney himself had alluded in his poetic sequence, *Astrophel and Stella* (8, 28, 59, 68, 76, 89, etc.). The bonfires honoring the birthday of Sir Philip Sidney's nephew in *For.* 14 are kindled by logs from those same forests at Penshurst, yet "the flame / Of love" which Jonson mentions here is not merely amorous: it is that deeper love for the dynasty, and the traditions of virtue it represents, which must now be maintained by its youngest adult member. While tacitly acknowledging his own poetic as well as moral debts to the Sidneian tradition, Jonson shows mastery here of a technique distinctively his own, generating a wider symbolic suggestiveness through such frequent small exchanges of literal and figurative meaning.

The opening poem of *The Forest* professes to explain "Why I Write Not of Love." Readers have sometimes taken Jonson at his word. "Twas an ingeniose remarque of my Lady Hoskins," noted Aubrey gravely, setting the tone for much later criticism, "that B.J. never writes of Love, or if he does, does it not naturally." Jonson is not however confessing his "failure" and "disqualifications as a poet" in this opening poem, as one critic has suggested, but heralding the more serious themes that will engage him in this collection. The announcement that he writes "not of love" soon proves indeed to be far from true, for love is a constant theme throughout *The Forest*. While the various songs to Celia (*For.* 5, 6, and 9) may be seen as traditional amorous exercises, the "love" about which Jonson chiefly writes in *The Forest* is of a different kind from that encountered in a Petrarchan sequence or (for that matter) the enchanted woods of Shakespearian comedy. Rejecting the bewilderments of "lust's wild forest" (*For.* 10, "Proludium," 9), he develops in the "Epode" an alternative concept of "true love":

> That is an essence far more gentle, fine,
>   Pure, perfect, nay divine;
> It is a golden chain let down from heaven,
>   Whose links are bright and even,
> That falls like sleep on lovers, and combines
>   The soft and sweetest minds
> In equal knots. This bears no brands nor darts
>   To murther different hearts,
> But in a calm and god-like unity
>   Preserves community.   (*For.* 11. 43–54)

The "chaste love" (68) described in this poem is exemplified elsewhere in *The Forest* in the marriages of the various couples whom Jonson praises.[4] As in Shakespeare's *The Phoenix and the Turtle,* chastity and married love are not at odds, but viewed instead as proper bedfellows: Lady Lisle is "noble, fruitful, chaste withal" (*For.* 2. 90), while Katherine, Lady Aubigny will

> pay your lord the pledges of chaste love,
> And raise a noble stem, to give the fame
>   To Clifton's blood that is denied their name. (*For.* 13. 98–100)

Such love "preserves community" in the most literal sense. The graduated progression of *The Forest* leads finally, however, to a poem from which communal concerns are carefully excluded, whose final lines speak of another, higher loyalty:

> Yet dare I not complain, or wish for death
>   With holy Paul, lest it be thought the breath
> Of discontent; or that these prayers be
>   For weariness of life, not love of thee. ("To Heaven," *For.* 15. 23–6)

One of the several disadvantages of Petrarchan sonneteering was that it depicted the poet in various postures of abjection and servility, which had small appeal to Jonson. Throughout *The Forest* Jonson presents himself in quite different terms, as a surprisingly elevated and at times, indeed, ecstatic figure. In the "Epistle to Elizabeth, Countess of Rutland" he is possessed with

> . . . high and noble matter, such as flies
>   From brains entranced and filled with ecstasies,
> Moods which the god-like Sidney oft did prove. . . (*For.* 12. 89–91)

Yet as the brilliantly articulated nineteen-line opening sentence of this poem concedes, after moving with the complexity of a Brandenburg concerto through many registers and variations, Jonson himself did not altogether resemble the god-like Sidney, lacking not merely high birth but the central commodity by which society seemingly functions: "whilst gold bears all this sway, / I, that have none to send you, send you verse" (19–20). This poet may be possessed, but is alas! without possessions. All that he owns is his art, which must accordingly serve as the commodity by which he lives. This unhappy contradiction, of central significance within Jonson's life, was to become a major preoccupation of his later verse.

3 Gifts and debts: *The Underwood*

Jonson must have foreseen the possibility of publishing another collection of his poems at some future date, for in the 1616 folio he describes his *Epigrams* in confidently anticipatory style as "Book 1" of some presumably larger work. Book 2 of the *Epigrams* was never in fact to appear, nor was any other volume of Jonson's poems to be published within his lifetime, though he continued to write verse constantly until the end. In the final decade of his life, however, Jonson began to prepare a second major collection of writings to complement the great folio of 1616. By the time of his death in 1637 these writings had still not appeared. Eventually they were to be published in 1640–1 in two folio volumes, the first of which contains a collection of ninety poems entitled *The Underwood*.

The collection carries a motto from Martial's epigrams, presumably chosen by Jonson's friend and literary executor, Sir Kenelm Digby: *cinera gloria sera venit*. Martial is urging his friend Faustinus to publish:

> ante fores stantem dubitas admittere Famam
> teque piget curae praemia ferre tuae?
> post te victurae per te quoque vivere chartae
> incipiant: *cinera gloria sera venit*. (I. xxv. 5–8)

[Do you hesitate to admit Fame that stands before your doors, and shrink from winning the reward of your care? Let writings that will live after you by your aid also begin to live now; *to the ashes of the dead glory comes too late.*]

Jonson seldom allowed fame to stand before his doors for too long, and it is not altogether clear why, in the last years of his life, he shrank from the rewards of publishing these poems, along with his other writings. It is equally unclear why Jonson chose to describe *The Underwood* in a note "To the Reader" as "lesser poems of later growth" than those in *The Forest*; for this altogether larger and more varied collection contains some of Jonson's finest pieces, including "An Execration upon Vulcan" (*Und.* 43), "A Speech According to Horace" (*Und.* 44), "An Epistle Answering to One that Asked to be Sealed of the Tribe of Ben" (*Und.* 47), and the Cary/Morison Ode (*Und.* 70). The answer may lie partly in the unreadiness of the collection for immediate publication, and partly in the nature of the poems themselves.

A few months after Jonson's death in August 1638 Sir Kenelm Digby wrote to Dr. Bryan Duppa to congratulate him on the volume of poems to Jonson's memory, *Jonsonus Virbius*, which Duppa had recently produced. His letter goes on: "I will as soon as I can do the like to the world, by making it share with me in those excellent pieces (alas, that many of them are but pieces!) which he hath left behind him, and that I keep religiously by me to that end" (HS 9. 102). Digby sounds like an editor with plenty of work ahead of him. "Pieces" is a word that significantly recurs in the titles of two poetic sequences placed symmetrically near the beginning and the conclusion of *The Underwood*: "A Celebration of Charis in Ten Lyric Pieces" (*Und.* 2) and "Eupheme. . . Consisting of these Ten Pieces" (*Und.* 84). Whether the apparently fragmentary nature of these "pieces" is accidental or the product of a considered aesthetic is open to question. Whatever the case, it is reasonable to assume that Digby had some responsibility for the final selection and arrangement of poems in *The Underwood,* whose preliminary shape Jonson must also have pondered.

The poems which Jonson or Digby chose to omit from *The Underwood* are of some interest. They include a scatter of poems from Jonson's Catholic period (1598–1610) addressed to co-believers, the finest of which is the "Ode Allegorike" (*UV* 6), originally prefixed to his friend Hugh Holland's *Pancharis* in 1603. Digby, a Catholic himself, tactfully kept these from the volume, along with others that may have appeared too skittish (such as *UV* 10 and 11, addressed to Thomas Coryate) or quarrelsome (such as the poems addressed to Inigo Jones, *UV* 34, 35, and 36, John Eliot, *UV* 37, and Alexander Gill, *UV* 39) or politically insensitive (such as *UV* 18, congratulating Robert Carr on his marriage with Frances Howard before it was widely known that the couple had contrived to murder Sir Thomas Overbury, who had opposed the match). A more puzzling exclusion is Jonson's great poem to the memory of Shakespeare, which may have been felt to have belonged rightfully in the 1623 first folio where it had first been published. In his 1816 edition of Jonson's works William Gifford chose to insert this poem near the beginning of *The Underwood*, along with eighteen other poems (including some now thought not to be by Jonson), thus further obscuring whatever arrangement Jonson himself may originally have intended.

Some sense of order, however partial, is apparent in the 1640 folio. *The Underwood* begins with a sequence of "Poems of Devotion" which continue the mood of the final poem in *The Forest*, "To Heaven." It moves next to the Charis poems, and thence to a series of pastoral and amorous verses, proceeding through a succession of verse epistles (*Und.* 13, 14, 15, 17), odes (*Und.* 23, 25, 26, 27), and epigrams (*Und.* 30, 31, 32, 33, 34) to the longer poems which stand at the center of the collection: "An Execration upon Vulcan" (*Und.* 43); "A Speech According to Horace" (*Und.* 44); and "An Epistle Answering to One that Asked to be Sealed of the Tribe of Ben" (*Und.* 47). The second half of the collection is largely occupied by poems written during the reign of Charles I; some eloquently reflect Jonson's growing insecurity and rising troubles through the land. The sequence of ten "Eupheme" poems placed near the end of the collection gravely complements the ten Charis pieces as well as the "Poems of Devotion" with which *The Underwood* began. A final series of classical translations, some on the subject of old age and the continuing agitations of love, brings the collection to its conclusion. The last poem in *The Underwood* is Jonson's rendering of Martial's famous epigram on the happy life (I. xlvii), which concludes with appropriate simplicity:

> Will to be what thou art, and nothing more;
> Nor fear thy latest day, nor wish therefore.   (*Und.* 90. 12–13)

Despite these signs of arrangement, *The Underwood* is undeniably a miscellany, less orderly in sequence than *The Forest*, and less homogeneous in formal terms than the *Epigrams*. In comparison with the earlier collections it contains moreover a greater number of poems about friendship and about the difficulties of his personal circumstances. It is possible that Jonson felt that some, at least, of these poems did not urgently demand publication. The numerous poems in the collection about money – about borrowing, lending, giving, receiving, thanking, and needing more – are nevertheless of particular interest, though they seldom receive critical attention.

"He dissuaded me from poetry," noted William Drummond soberly after talking with Jonson in 1619, "for that she hath beggared him, when he might have been a rich lawyer, physician, or merchant" (*Conv. Dr.* 540–1). Unlike his other work for the court and playhouses, Jonson's verse-writing brought him little, if anything, by way of direct income, and was seldom undertaken for gain. *Epig.* 73, "To Fine Grand," seems to suggest, however, that Jonson had written commissioned verses for a patron who failed to reward him: "For which or pay me quickly, or I'll pay you" (22). The form of *payment* which Jonson threatens here is a further and more explicit satirical epigram, verse being the sole currency which the poet has at his disposal. It is a currency which Jonson was to deploy and revalue with great resourcefulness throughout his career and most particularly in *The Underwood*. Many poems in the collection were originally presented as gifts to their recipients, in much the same manner that *For.* 12 had been presented to the Countess of Rutland on New Year's Day 1600 ("I, that have none to send you, send you verse," 19). "My Picture Left in Scotland," for example (*Und.* 9), was sent by Jonson to William Drummond as a thank-you gift after his stay at Hawthornden in January 1619, while *Und.* 79 was presented as "A New Year's Gift Sung to King Charles, 1635." *Und.* 26 was sent to an unknown "High-spirited friend" – Sir Edward Sackville, perhaps, who in 1613 was recovering from the duel in which he had killed Lord Bruce. The "paper" of this gift mentioned in line 10 is not the wrapping around drugs, nor is it money, but (Jonson suggests) something much better, the poem itself, furnishing "wholesome physic for the mind."

Though of small value in cash terms, the poems of *The Underwood* are thus ingeniously commodified and used (so to speak) as items of exchange. In a light-hearted epistle to Arthur Squib, a teller in the Exchequer (*Und.* 54), Jonson announces that he has entered into a wager: if it is proved that he weighs twenty stone (280 pounds), he will win the wager, and if not, he must pay. He is in fact two pounds short of that weight, but with six pounds of money in his pocket, the scales will tip to twenty stone. He has one pound in his pocket already; will Squib now send him, please, five more? and these verses will stand as security against repayment. All that Jonson actually possesses at this moment, it seems, is one pound in cash; inventively employed, however, both his body and the poem itself will serve to earn him more: the wager, five pounds in cash, and a free dinner. Borrowing money and giving thanks are not easy tasks to perform; in *The Underwood* poems, Jonson borrows with wit and humor, and acknowledges his debts with dignity. In "An Epistle to Sir Edward Sackville, now Earl of Dorset" he meditates at length on the ethics of giving and receiving, drawing deeply on

Seneca's work, *De beneficiis*, and gently reminding Dorset that recipients, like benefactors, may exercise free choice:

> And though my fortune humble me to take
> The smallest courtesies with thanks, I make
> Yet choice from whom I take them, and would shame
> To have such do me good I durst not name.   (*Und.* 13. 15–18)

In *Und.* 17 and 37 Jonson deftly argues that states of obligation – owing money, receiving gifts – are in fact indicative of the truest friendship. In another epistle to Arthur Squib (*Und.* 45) he likens friendship to money itself, both of which must be tried and tested, "For there are many slips and counterfeits" (17).

Disabled by illness from the mid-1620s, Jonson found himself increasingly marginalized at Charles' court, and increasingly short of money. In 1616 he had been granted a royal pension of 100 marks a year, a sum that was increased in 1630 to 100 pounds, plus an annual tierce of royal sack. The Exchequer's actual payment of the pension, however, was tantalizingly irregular, and Jonson resorted repeatedly to verse in order to remind the royal officials, and at extreme moments the king himself, of his pressing need for cash. While the petitionary poems scattered through the later stages of *The Underwood* are not to be numbered amongst Jonson's greatest achievements, they testify touchingly to his continuing poetic versatility during this last and difficult period of his life. In *Und.* 57 Jonson writes ruefully to Master John Burgess, a clerk in the Exchequer, and, through him, to Sir Robert Pye, Remembrancer (or paymaster) of the Exchequer – ironically an ancestor of a later poet laureate, Henry James Pye, who was himself destined to run into severe financial problems:

> Father John Burgess
> Necessity urges
> My woeful cry,
> To Sir Robert Pye:
> And that he will venture
> To send my debenture.
> Tell him his Ben
> Knew the time, when
> He loved the muses;
> Though now he refuses
> To take apprehension
> Of a year's pension,
> And more is behind:
> Put him in mind
> Christmas is near;
> And neither good cheer,

> Mirth, fooling, nor wit,
> Nor any least fit
> Of gambol or sport
> Will come at the court,
> If there be no money;
> No plover or coney
> Will come to the table,
> Or wine to enable
> The muse or the poet
> The parish will know it;
> Nor any quick warming-pan help him to bed,
> If the 'chequer be empty, so will be his head.

Jonson uses Skeltonics here not merely to amuse, but as a reminder of the traditions – of verse and of payment – associated with earlier royal poets: a learned Remembrancer might recall that Skelton as *orator regius* had also written sardonically about the "bouge of court" – the rations or reward that supposedly accompany royal appointment.

In the "Epistle Mendicant" directed to the Lord High Treasurer, Lord Weston (*Und.* 71) and a series of poems to King Charles, Jonson skillfully connects the obligations for payment of his pension not merely with other royal duties, but with the duties owed, in the troublesome 1630s, by the people themselves to the crown. The king may easily relieve the "poet's evil" of poverty, just as his touch was thought to relieve the "king's evil" of scrofula; a harder task (Jonson implies) would be to relieve the political disease now threatening the land: "What can the poet wish his king may do, / But that he cure the people's evil too?" ("An Epigram to King Charles for a Hundred Pounds He Sent Me in My Sickness 1629," *Und.* 62. 6, 4, 13–14). In another epigram to Charles on his Anniversary Day, March 27, 1629, Jonson describes – not himself, but the nation, as afflicted by a massive debt:

> 'Tis not alone the merchant, but the clown
> Is bankrupt turned; the cassock, cloak, and gown
> Are lost upon account! and none will know
> How much to heaven for thee, great Charles, they owe!
>
> (*Und.* 64. 19–22)

The nation's debts at this moment were indeed immense.[5] With characteristic loyalty, Jonson ingeniously turns this fact against the people themselves, who have failed to recognize their larger debts to heaven, which has furnished them with such a monarch. The nation (declares the impoverished poet sternly) needs to settle its accounts.

In any critical accounting, Jonson himself must be reckoned a poet who has never received his proper due. For his own neglect, Jonson himself is partly to blame. The verse (in ways already described) is often more difficult than generally supposed, and often seemingly directed to an exclusive readership. Yet the range and achievement of this poetry are truly impressive. The "posterity" to which he commended his poems owes him a belated tribute.

NOTES

1 French Rowe Fogle, *A Critical Study of William Drummond of Hawthornden* (New York: King's Crown Press, Columbia University, 1952), 19; R. H. MacDonald, *The Library of Drummond of Hawthornden* (Edinburgh: Edinburgh University Press, 1971), 27, n. 1.

2 Stanley Fish, "Author-Readers: Jonson's Community of the Same," *Representations*, 7 (1984), 26–58.

3 Jonson told Drummond "That he had an intention to perfect an epic poem, entitled *Heroologia*, of the worthies of his country roused by fame, and was to dedicate it to his country" (*Conv. Dr.* 1–3). A similar intention to celebrate English worthies is evident in *P.H. Barr.* and *Queens.*

4 The facts did not quite live up to the praise. Lord Lisle appears to have had a mistress (see *The Poems of Robert Sidney*, ed. Katherine Duncan-Jones, *English* 30: 136 [1981]: 4), while his daughter, Lady Mary Wroth, bore two illegitimate children to William Herbert, Earl of Pembroke, whom Jonson elsewhere praises as a model of virtue: *The Poems of Lady Mary Wroth,* ed. Josephine A. Roberts (Louisiana State University Press: Baton Rouge and London, 1983), Introduction, 24–5.

5 See Kevin Sharpe, *The Personal Rule of Charles I* (New Haven and London: Yale University Press, 1992), 9–23.

IO

STEPHEN ORGEL

Jonson and the arts

"The pen," Jonson wrote in his commonplace book *Timber, or, Discoveries*, "is more noble than the pencil; for that can speak to the understanding, the other, but to the sense" (1528–30). The invidious comparison here is between the written word and pictorial art; but the synecdoche itself shades the two into each other: Inigo Jones did his drawings in pen and ink, while the books that survive from Jonson's library include many with marginalia in pencil – the instrument of Jones' invention was the pen, that of Jonson's understanding the pencil. In fact, the passage, *Poesis et pictura*, goes on to praise picture more highly than poetry. It is "the invention of heaven: the most ancient, and most akin to nature." The two arts, moreover, are indissolubly linked, just as sense and understanding are; and "whosoever loves not picture is injurious to truth, and all the wisdom of poetry" (1536–8).

But what pictures does Jonson have in mind? Many of them are certainly, if not fictitious, at least exclusively textual, such as those lost masterpieces of Apelles and Xeuxis described by Pliny, or Philostratus' gallery of *Icones*. Jonson's sense of modern masterworks similarly derives from descriptions and catalogues – it is unlikely that he read Vasari, though he certainly knew people who did; but his account of ancient and modern painting comes quite directly from Antonio Possevino's *Bibliotheca Selecta*, published in 1593, a guide to the history of the arts and sciences. *Timber* is, after all, a collection of authoritative opinions; but the authority behind them is rarely Jonson's. In this sense, his praise of picture is a praise of ekphrasis, and the pen and the pencil are one.

In a peculiarly indicative passage Jonson cites a list of the best artists of his own time, "six famous painters who were excellent, and emulous of the Ancients." The six are in fact seven: Raphael, Michelangelo, Titian, Correggio, Sebastiano del Piombo, Giulio Romano and Andrea del Sarto.[1] The list – including the erroneous number – is copied from Possevino, who in turn is copying G. B. Armenini's *De' Veri Precetti della Pittura* (Ravenna, 1586), and the slip in the numbering suggests that Possevino's sense of painting is no less textual than Jonson's: Armenini in fact names eight excellent artists, and implies that there are many more; his list starts with Leonardo, who is his benchmark, includes the seven cited by Jonson, and concludes with "molti altri." Possevino, however, translating the passage into Latin (and perhaps working from an edited transcription), streamlines Titian's name as it appears in Armenini, "Titian da Cadoro," (i.e., from his birthplace, Cadore) to simply "Titiano," and omits the comma between him and "Antonio Corrigiensi," making Titian and Correggio appear to be a single artist, Titiano Antonio Corrigiensi – though they would appear so, obviously, only to someone who had never heard of Correggio and knew too little about Titian to know his full name. This, therefore, must be the case with Possevino, unlikely as it would seem in a late sixteenth-century Italian Jesuit writing a handbook of the arts.[2] Jonson, on the other hand, clearly knows that Titian is not Correggio, because he reinserts the comma; but he still follows Possevino in numbering the seven great painters six. Authority is not to be lightly rejected.

What visual experience is there behind this textual praise of painting? What pictures would Jonson have seen? Not, certainly, many originals by the artists on his list – though also not necessarily none. The collecting instinct was starting to burgeon in England. Leicester was said to have owned some Venetian paintings, though there is no record of what they were, and Sidney knew enough to sit for Veronese when he was in Venice, though he was not happy with the result, and the portrait has since disappeared. Robert Cecil, Earl of Salisbury, Jonson's patron on more than one occasion, was a notable connoisseur (he was furnishing Hatfield House), and owned works by both Italian and Netherlandish artists, as did two other patrons of Jonson's, the Earl of Somerset and the Duke of Buckingham. Prince Henry, under Salisbury's guidance, became a passionate collector of paintings and bronzes. The Earl and Countess of Arundel formed the greatest art collection in Jacobean England, and acquired works by Leonardo, Michelangelo, Raphael, Giulio Romano and Annibale Carracci to display beside their inherited Holbeins – Jonson praises Arundel in *The Gypsies Metamorphosed* by calling him "father" and "nurse of the arts."

There was, in fact, a good deal of information circulating in Jonson's England about who were the right artists to admire and invest in – Possevino would have been, for Jonson, at most a convenience. Richard Haydocke, translator of an artistic handbook by Paolo Lomazzo, published in English in 1598, noted "many noblemen then furnishing their houses with the excellent monuments of sundry famous and ancient masters, both Italian and German"[3] – it is perhaps indicative of how essentially literary Jonson's sense of the artistic canon is that it includes only Italian names. But Jonson's best source of information, along with whatever entrée he may have had to the works themselves, would certainly have been Inigo Jones, at least as long as they remained on friendly terms. Jones was a genuine expert; he had traveled in Italy observing and sketching, and was advising first the Earl of Rutland on artistic matters, and later the Prince of Wales, the Arundels and Prince Charles.

Still, whatever pictures Jonson saw, he mentions painters but no paintings. The only actual works he refers to by any of the artists he singles out for praise are Giulio Romano's notorious set of sexual positions, *I Modi*, which circulated as prints, accompanied by the salacious sonnets of Pietro Aretino. Lady Politic Would-Be uses them in *Volpone* to show off her familiarity with Italian culture: "But for a desperate wit, there's Aretine / Only his pictures are a little obscene" (3.4.96–7). If Jonson had left it there, this would be simply a joke at the expense of the expatriate nouveau-riche Englishwoman. But three scenes later the uxorious Corvino, who certainly knows his Italian pornographers, worries about "some young Frenchman, or hot Tuscan blood, / That had read Aretine, conned all his prints" (3.7.59–60). And five years later in *The Alchemist*, the world's expert on pornographic painting Sir Epicure Mammon imagines his "oval room / Filled with such pictures as Tiberius took / From Elephantis, and dull Aretine / But coldly imitated" (2.2.43–4). Jonson, in short, seems to be under the impression that the pictures are by Aretino. Possibly Jonson had read the sonnets, which were easily available, but had not seen the prints, which were suppressed; nevertheless, turning Aretino into a visual artist and eliding Giulio Romano is surely the most complete triumph of ekphrasis the Renaissance offers.

Ignorance is, of course, no impediment to the deployment of artistic allusion. Giulio Romano is, notoriously, the only modern artist named by Shakespeare, who knew so little about him that he made him a sculptor, the creator of Hermione's lifelike statue in *The Winter's Tale*. Giulio did no sculptures; but the name of the great artist alone is sufficient to establish Paulina's (or Shakespeare's) credentials as a connoisseur. Jonson's list of names from Possevino would doubtless have been similarly sufficient to certify Jonson's expertise – even, perhaps (since *Timber* is his own commonplace book), to certify it to himself.

I pause over this only because Jonson's praise of "picture" is so genuinely magnanimous, but at the same time so relentlessly unspecific. For comparison, Donne, in "The Storm," reveals an equally unspecific but nevertheless much more direct knowledge of contemporary painting: ". . . a hand or eye / By Hilliard drawn, is worth an history / By a worse painter made . . ." (3–5). The engraved frontispiece portrait of Donne in the 1635 *Poems* is apparently based on a lost Hilliard miniature, and a superb Isaac Oliver portrait of Donne survives. Donne and Jonson were close friends, and moved in the same circle; Oliver was Jonson's neighbor when both lived in Blackfriars, he painted at least two ladies in the costumes they probably wore in Jonson's masques, and he and Jonson must have known each other. But Jonson, Hilliard and Oliver seem not to have inhabited the same cultural world. The only surviving portraits of

Jonson, whether painted or engraved, all apparently derive from a single original by Abraham Blyenberch, done shortly before Jonson's stroke in 1628, and recorded in the 1635 inventory of the Duke of Buckingham's pictures at York House – the original is lost, but the painting of Jonson in the National Portrait Gallery is an early copy. Visually, this is Jonson's immortality, but no allusion to Blyenberch or the portrait survives in Jonson's work – apparently it simply did not mean much to him. The only portraits memorialized in his work are two lost ones, one by his friend Sir William Borlase, Sherriff of Buckinghamshire and not otherwise known as a painter, of which Jonson says in *Underwood* 52, "You made it a brave piece, but not like me" (14), and the one left by his beloved Charis in Scotland in *Underwood* 9, presumably a miniature, and entirely too much like him, recording his "hundred of grey hairs" and "rocky face" at the age of 47. It is surely not irrelevant that in his prefatory poem to the Shakespeare Folio – with its author's portrait, quite anomalously, displayed on the title page rather than facing it as a frontispiece – Jonson admonished the reader to "look / Not on his picture, but his book" (9–10).

And yet, Jonson does occasionally deploy the technical language of Renaissance pictorial art quite conspicuously, if not always quite precisely. The painted front curtain of *The Masque of Blackness* (1605) is described as a work of art, though not as a painting: "First, for the *Scene*, was drawn a *Landtschape*, consisting of small woods" – thus the Quarto; the technical term is subsequently corrected in the Folio to the proper Dutch Landtschap, and printed, appropriately, in black letter. The word meant specifically a painted landscape; it had in fact already appeared in English in the form "landskip," but Jonson clearly wants his expertise to be etymologically and typographically apparent. His description of the whole setting, moreover, reveals a sophisticated understanding of the optical principle governing Inigo Jones' stage: "the scene behind seemed a vast sea . . . from the termination or horizon of which (being the level of the State, which was placed in the upper end of the hall) was drawn by the lines of prospective, the whole work shooting downwards from the eye . . ." (24–5, 82–7). The technical term for Jonson here is "prospective" – he uses the word elsewhere in *Poetaster* (1601) and *The Fortunate Isles and their Union* (1625).[4] "Perspective" is the more common form in the period, and is used by Jonson in *Oberon* (1611) and *The Vision of Delight* (1617),[5] which indicates that he was not at all consistent in his usage; but it is probably to the point that "prospective" is the term Jones used: that is where Jonson started, and where he ended.[6] In short, the only Renaissance painting Jonson describes in any detail and with any real understanding and enthusiasm is Jones' scene painting. The scene painters of *The Masque of Beauty*, with which Jones was not involved, get short shrift: "The painters, I must needs say . . . lent small color to any, to attribute much of the spirit of these things to their pencils." Jonson goes on to acknowledge that only the execution, not "the invention or design," was at fault, but he has so little interest in the designer that he does not even identify him (lines 272–6).

In fact, Jonson's most obvious expertise in the pictorial arts is not in painting but in the bookish world of iconologies, hieroglyphs, emblems, impresas – the rich and complex visual language of Renaissance symbolism. This imagery figures ubiquitously throughout Jonson's career as poet, playwright and masque writer, and in this respect, picture was unquestionably one of his natural languages. *The Masque of Blackness* and *The Masque of Beauty* locate beauty not in the imitation of nature, and even less in the hand of some Italian (or Italianate) master, but rather in the abstraction of beauty into the most abstruse symbolic forms – Euphoris, Aglaia, Diaphane; the geometrical figure icosohedron, "an urn sphered with wine"; Venustas, Serenitas, Perfectio; "the Throne of Beauty divided into eight squares and distinguished by so many Ionic pilasters." The artistic authorities here are not Raphael, Titian, Giulio Romano – or Inigo Jones – but the codifiers of Renaissance iconography: Cesare Ripa, Vincenzo Cartari and Giovanni Pierio Valeriano.

And yet, the extraordinary title page to the 1616 Folio of Jonson's *Workes* (see p. iv above) reveals a mind intensely involved with the visual arts, and specifically with the translation of text into an imagery that is certainly imbued with tradition but not at all dependent on standard iconologies – a mind that we might call counter-ekphrastic. William Hole's engraved symbols are obviously designed to Jonson's order. This is what Jonson chose as the entry to and embodiment of his work, not his own portrait (which did not appear as the frontispiece until the posthumous 1640 Folio), but a triumphal arch framing his name and the title of his book. The arch is adorned with figures representing the history of theatre and his place within that history. On either side stand the figures of Tragedy and Comedy; above, the third of the classic genres, the satiric or pastoral is anatomized into the figures of satyr and shepherd. Between them is a Roman theatre; above this, at the pinnacle of the arch, stands the composite figure of Tragicomedy, flanked by the tiny images of Bacchus and Apollo, patrons of ecstatic and rational theatre respectively. On the base of the arch are two scenes illustrating the ancient sources of drama, the *plaustrum*, or cart of Thespis, legendary inventor of tragedy, with the sacrificial goat, the tragedian's prize, tethered to it, and an amphitheatre with a choric dance in progress. The figures participating in both these originary scenes, however, in contrast to the classical figures above, are in modern dress – they are Jonson himself and his contemporaries.

This title page is specifically designed for this book, a visual summary of Jonson's sense of his art, defining drama in relation to its history and its kinds, and postulating a set of generic possibilities. The crucial art displayed here, however, is not drama: the arts of Jonson's title page are symbolism, engraving, and perhaps most significant of all, architecture. There is more than irony in the fact that Jonson's detractors were fond of reminding him that he had, in his youth, been apprenticed to a bricklayer. David Riggs has shown that Jonson renewed his lapsed membership in the bricklayers' guild in 1599, after his imprisonment for the murder of Gabriel Spencer.[7] Doubtless his emergent condition as a convicted felon dictated the move, which was an expensive one; but despite his disdain for the craft, he remained a guild member long after his success as an actor and playwright was assured. There were practical reasons for this, as I have suggested in *Impersonations*, having to do with the structure of the theatrical companies and their relation to the guild system,[8] but there were symbolic reasons too: poetry was a craft, and the craft that most resembled it, Jonson wrote in *Timber*, was building. "As a house consisting of diverse materials becomes one structure and one dwelling, so an action composed of diverse parts may become one fable epic or dramatic" (2791–4). The critical move here, however, as the bitter quarrel with Inigo Jones ultimately revealed, was not the move from bricklaying to poetry, but the move from bricklaying to architecture: from the artisan's craft to the artist's Design. Design had been, in *The Masque of Beauty*, synonymous with invention, both a structural and originary principle, something that united poet and architect and that both could take credit for. By 1630, however, when Jonson wrote his "Expostulation with Inigo Jones," design, he claimed, had been pirated, and was nothing but "a specious, fine / Term of the architects" (55–6).

Jonson's earliest architectural associate was not Inigo Jones but Stephen Harrison, creator of the triumphal arches erected for James I's coronation procession through London in 1604. Arches of triumph are symbolic and ephemeral structures. Unlike houses, they have no practical function, and Jonson's praise of Harrison's architecture, which, as Per Palme has amply shown, is full of a knowledge of Vitruvian and Palladian notions of organic wholeness,[9] nevertheless construes architecture as a basically celebratory art:

> The nature and property of these devices being to present always some one entire body or figure consisting of distinct members, and each of those expressing itself in the own active sphere, yet all, with that general harmony so connexed and disposed as no one little part can be missing to the illustration of the whole: where also is to be noted that the symbols used are not, neither ought to be, simply hieroglyphics, emblems or impresas, but a mixed character partaking somewhat of all, and peculiarly apted to these more magnificent inventions . . .   (HS 7: 90–1)

Harmony and decorum govern both form and symbolism here, but they do so in the service of a purely visual meaning beyond words:

> Neither was it becoming, nor could it stand with the dignity of these shows . . . to require a truch-man [narrator], or (with the ignorant painter) one to write "This is a dog" or "This is a hare," but so to be presented as upon the view they might, without cloud or obscurity, declare themselves to the sharp and learned.
>
> (HS 7:91)

The architect-poet addresses his ideal audience here through structures and images, not language. The poet's words are relegated to a secondary and retrospective function, memorializing the event and reporting it to those who were not present – or who were not "sharp and learned." Is the symbolic arch really Jonson's ideal of poetry, a silent, visual world of pure meaning? It may well be, at least from time to time: he told Drummond "that verses stood by sense without either colours or accent" – that the essence of poetry was meaning, not the figures of rhetoric and the rhythm of metrics – "which yet," Drummond adds, "other times he denied."[10] A. W. Johnson argues cogently for the relevance of Vitruvian principles and Pythagorean proportion to Jonson's thinking, but locates it primarily in the early masques.[11] There is unquestionably something in this: Jonson's copy of Vitruvius is heavily annotated, and his interest in neoplatonic philosophy has long been recognized. But the debt can be overemphasized – Johnson's claims are, in fact, relatively modest, and though he finds a great deal of abstruse number theory informing the masques before 1610, he also shows Jonson abandoning the system by the time of *Oberon*, and finds such matters hardly relevant at all to Jonson's plays of the period. Indeed, it is difficult to see how the rich mess of *Every Man out of his Humour* (to say nothing of *Bartholomew Fair*) could have much to do with Pythagoras and Vitruvius. Nevertheless, architecture remained a controlling metaphor for Jonson's sense of his career, as the title page of his *Works* attests. In the last of his masques for the Stuart court, *Chloridia* (1631), Architecture appears along with Poetry, History and Sculpture as handmaids of Fame. These are the arts that survive. Jonson, parodying Jones under the names of Iniquo Vitruvius and Vitruvius Hoop, reveals more than anything else how much he feels he has lost in the loss of Vitruvius. The contempt expressed in the "Expostulation," "O to make boards to speak! There is a task!/ Painting and carpentry are the soul of masque" (49–50), is the dark side of Jonson's intense admiration for the genius of Jones' stage.

The masque was a quintessentially collaborative artistic enterprise, and the collaboration extended well beyond Jonson and Jones. It was, to begin with, a collaboration with the royal or noble patron, who had to approve the conceit, and on occasion (as with the masques of *Blackness*, *Queens* and *The Gypsies Metamorphosed*) even provided it. It is to the point that in the Jonson masque that deals most directly with the use and misuse of art, *Mercury Vindicated from the Alchemists at Court* (1616), the misuse of art is the search for gold and the parthenogenetic creation of life, and its proper function is the praise of the king at the center of the spectacle – the true source of both gold and life is royal patronage. For the aristocratic performers and spectators, however, Jonson's text was a relatively insignificant element in a large and complex whole, the principal components of which were spectacle, music, and above all a great deal of dancing. A masque in performance might occupy four hours or more, while Jonson's text rarely extended to fifteen pages. Jonson analogizes his text to the soul of the work, which survives after the bodily part disappears, but the elevation of the text to the masque's divine essence would have made little sense to the participants. The poetic soul's survival, in any case, was entirely a function of its re-embodiment in print – to a contemporary, Jonson's text might have seemed more like the masque organism's skeleton than its soul.

Just as Inigo Jones' settings, machines and costumes comprised the visual context for Jonson's words, the harmonic and choreographic context was no less essential; and for all Jonson's insistence on the primacy of his invention, his concern with the music and dance was neither casual nor uninformed. In a number of places he specifies the voices and orchestration: for the first song in *Blackness* a tenor and two trebles sing "loud music"; the Cyclope's song in *Mercury Vindicated* is accompanied by cornets; in *The Irish Masque*, a Bard sings to two harps and the antimasquers dance to "the bagpipe and other rude music"; the antimasque of *The Golden Age Restored* is danced to "two drums, trumpets, and a confusion of martial music"; in *Pleasure Reconciled to Virtue*, Mercury speaks the final speech, "which is after repeated in song by two trebles, two tenors, a bass and the whole chorus"; in *Neptune's Triumph*, "the fleet is discovered while three cornets play." The musicians are frequently incorporated into the stage action: in *Pleasure Reconciled* "the whole music is discovered sitting at the foot of the mountain"; *Hymenæi* begins with a procession of "musicians diversly attired, all crowned with roses" who perform the opening song; in *Neptune's Triumph* "Apollo, with Mercury, some muses and the goddess Harmony make the music"; in *The Haddington Masque*, "the musicians attired in yellow, with wreaths of marjoram and veils, like Hymen's priests, sung . . . the epithalamion"; in *The Masque of Augurs*, the priestly augurs are an onstage chorus leading in the dancers. Jonson is in general less explicit about the dances, but on occasion specifies their form, and is unstinting in his enthusiasm for both the choreography and the performance:

> Here they danced forth a most neat and curious measure full of subtlety and device, which was so excellently performed as it seemed to take away that spirit from the invention which the invention gave to it, and left it doubtful whether the forms flowed more perfectly from the author's brain or their feet. The strains were all notably different, some of them formed into letters, very signifying to the name of the bridegroom, and ended in manner of a chain, linking hands.
>
> (*Hymenæi*, 310–17)

Dance in *Pleasure Reconciled to Virtue* embodies the highest ethical wisdom,

> For dancing is an exercise
> Not only shows the mover's wit,
> But maketh the beholder wise,
> As he hath power to rise to it. (269–73)

Two epigrams to Alphonso Ferrabosco, who provided the music for both masques and plays, declare Jonson's unqualified admiration for him, though in terms that are, characteristically, both hyperbolic and unspecific. Peter Walls has written well about the high degree of collaboration poet and composer achieved in the masque, with Ferrabosco's settings, which are often declamatory, underlining and providing dramatic emphasis for Jonson's verse. But Ferrabosco's music also took its own way: "Some songs," Walls observes, "could even be described as anti-declamatory. In 'If all the ages of the earth' [from *Queens*] the vocal line is so strongly syncopated that it virtually dislocates the sense of the verse: relatively unimportant words (notably 'of') are thrown into prominence . . ."[12] It is perhaps to the point that Jonson, or his patrons, turned to other composers for the masques after 1611. Ian Spink suggests that Jonson may have quarreled with Ferrabosco as he did with Jones,[13] but it is equally possible that the kind of music required for the masque changed as Jonson's concept of the form evolved.

In particular, the opening lines of *The Vision of Delight* (1617) are "spake in song, *stylo recitativo*," and in *Lovers Made Men*, in the same year, "the whole masque was sung (after the Italian manner) *stylo recitativo* by Master Nicholas Lanier, who ordered and made both the scene and the music" (26–8). A great deal of musicological heavy weather has been made over this: was it *really* recitative, or merely some form of extended declamation? Could true recitative have been known in England at this time? Would Jonson have known recitative if he heard it? But all this is surely beside the point: the music was something Jonson called recitative, and as Walls observes, the real question is, "*why* did Jonson state that recitative had been used? For anyone interested in Jonson's literary aims, this is an important question and would be even if it could be established that Lanier definitely did not set those texts in *stylo recitativo*" (p. 88). In fact, both Lanier and Dowland had traveled in Italy by this time, and Italian monody had been heard and published in England by 1610. Music theorists of the period associated *recitativo* with the music of classical Greece; Walls remarks that this would obviously have appealed to Jonson, who claimed that his masques too "were grounded upon antiquity and solid learnings."[14] "Above all," Walls concludes, "he would have been enthusiastic about recitative style as a heightened form of speech" (p. 101). In short, Jonson was interested in the new musical style because it served his poetic ends. There are all sorts of reasons to love music.

Jonson's use of music in his plays has been discussed in detail by Mary Chan.[15]

There is in fact not much. Only *Cynthia's Revels*, written for the Children of the Chapel, a professional choir school, includes a significant amount of music – though oddly, since Echo is a character, it includes no echo song (there are two echo songs in *The Masque of Blackness*). Here Jonson is quite expert at parodying currently fashionable musical styles, and is apparently also familiar with the theoretical literature. In 4.3, Hedon and Amorphus perform songs they have written. When Amorphus sings his, he finds Hedon insufficiently enthusiastic:

> Why, do you not observe how excellently the ditty is affected in every place? that I do not marry a word of short quantity to a long note? nor an ascending syllable to a descending tone? Besides, upon the word "best" there, you see how I do enter with an odd minim, and drive it through the breve, which no intelligent musician, I know, but will affirm to be very rare, extraordinary and pleasing. (327–34)

As Chan shows, this is based on a quite thorough knowledge of how contemporary music theorists advised the composer *not* to set words.[16] The correct use of music, as not simply expressive but as an ordering and moralizing element, is exemplified in Echo's song in 1.2, "Slow, slow, fresh fount, keep time with my salt tears," in which she mourns the ennui and decay of Cynthia's court. The song is accompanied, and validated, by "music from the spheres" – the musicians above the stage. The play, Chan argues, involves "ambitious and rather complex experiments with different modes" of music – experiments that were clearly not entirely successful, and were not to be repeated.

Jonson uses more practical theatre music in *Volpone*, when Volpone, attempting to seduce Celia, sings "Come my Celia, let us prove," presumably accompanying himself on a lute (3.7.165ff.). The poem is a translation of the most famous seduction piece in classical literature, Catullus' "Vivamus mea Lesbia," and would have been instantly recognized as such; but Volpone obviously believes that its affective power will lie in the music, not in the allusion, hence he sings it rather than reciting it. As an aid to seduction, it should be added, music is regularly ineffective in Jonson: Wittipol wooing Mistress Fitzdottrel in *The Devil is an Ass* with the song "Do but look on her eyes" (the second stanza is the famous "Have you seen but a white lily grow"), has no more success than Volpone (2.6.94–113). One would expect *Epicœne* (1609), written, like *Cynthia's Revels*, for the Children of the Chapel (now called the Children of the Revels), to make significant use of music, the more so since it concerns a protagonist, Morose, who hates speech and noise. But the only song in the play is Clerimont's song "Still to be neat," sung by a page not to Morose but to Clerimont's friend Truewit (1.1.91–102), who merely responds by disagreeing with the sentiments expressed in Clerimont's verse, and completely ignores the musical setting. Obviously audiences heard a great deal more music during the performance of any Renaissance play than these examples suggest – introductory pieces, fanfares, interludes, closing jigs – but it is music that Jonson takes no account of. The indispensable music was the music of the masque.

Jonson's admiration for the visual and musical arts is clearly deep and genuine, even when, as with the case of painting, it is relatively uninformed. It also resonates with the sounds of early modern capitalism. The beauty and ingenuity of Inigo Jones' stage machines, the music that moves the spirit and replicates the music of the spheres, epitomize the Renaissance dream of ordering and controlling the natural world. Along with this dream went the impulse to acquire and display the rarest things in the world, not the least of which were those products of human wit and craftsmanship that reproduced and refined the natural. Jonson the connoisseur, in a note in *Oberon*, praises "that famous piece of sculpture in a little gem or piece of jasper observed by Monsieur Casaubon in his tract *De Satyrica Poesi* . . . wherein is described the whole manner of the scene and *chori* of Bacchus, with Silenus and the satyrs. An elegant and curious antiquity, both for the subtlety and labor, where in so small a compass (to use his words), there is 'rerum, personarum, actionum plane stupenda varietas' [a quite astonishing variety of things, persons and actions]."[18] Casaubon's text includes an exquisite engraving of the gem, and Jonson's praise is really praise of the engraving, which delivers the tiny masterpiece to him in a book. Volpone enumerating the lavish jewels he offers Celia, Sir Epicure Mammon imagining what wonders he will possess when the Philosopher's Stone is his, speak some of Jonson's most passionate verse. The collecting instinct goes hand in hand with the development of artistic taste.

In 1609 the Earl of Salisbury commissioned an entertainment from Jonson to celebrate the opening of Britain's Burse, the new market he had erected in the Strand as an outlet for the riches the East India Company was importing to London. The performance was attended by King James, Queen Anne, Prince Henry and a large group of court ladies and gentlemen. The show was called *Britain's Burse*, and has only recently been rediscovered.[19] Jonson gave the longest and most striking speech in it to a character called The China Man, a dealer in porcelain and other exotic wares, who produces a loving, extended hyperbole in praise of his merchandise. The speech is a marvel of linguistic invention and profligacy. Its primary technique is Jonson's favorite, enumeration and accretion – it is a verbal display of a multitude of treasures recalling Sir Epicure's endlessly material desires. The inspiration that animates Jonson's catalogue of rarities is profoundly, unabashedly materialistic, as he celebrates china "translucent as amber and subtler than crystal," "a conceited saltcellar: an elephant with a castle on his back," carpets "wrought of paraquitos' feathers, umbrellas made of the wing of the Indian butterfly," fans made of flying fishes' fins, as well as optical instruments that analyze and revise the appearance of things – refracting prisms, concave and convex mirrors, a "perspective" or telescope. We are rhetorically in the world of *Volpone,* but the harangue of the mountebank here shades again into the discourse of the connoisseur. The point is not to gull the public or even to sell the Burse's wares, but to establish for the royal audience the immense value of the treasures available to them and of the gifts they are about to receive. These are prototypical collectors – in fact, Prince Henry had already begun acquiring paintings, and was actively negotiating for pictures, bronzes, ingenious devices, anything rich and rare. Jonson speaks with the voice that animated the first great art collections in England.

NOTES

Citations from Jonson's plays and masques are from C. H. Herford and P. and E. Simpson, *Ben Jonson,* 11 vols., Oxford, 1925–52, cited in the notes as HS; texts have been modernized. Citations from the poems and the *Conversations with Drummond* are from Ian Donaldson, *Ben Jonson* (The Oxford Authors, 1985).

1 HS 8:612.
2 See HS 11:260.
3 From the Preface to his translation of Paolo Lomazzo's *Trattato, A Tracte containinge the Artes of curious Painting, Caruinge & Buildinge* (Oxford, 1598), 6.
4 "I studie architecture too . . . I'd haue a house iust of that prospectiue." (*Poetaster* 3.1.35); "the first Prospective, a Maritime Palace," "the second Prospective, a Sea" (*Fortunate Isles,* lines 568, 577).
5 "within a farre off in perspectiue, the knights masquers sitting in their seuerall sieges" (*Oberon,* lines 293–4); "A Street in perspective of faire building discovered" (*Vision,* line 2).
6 E.g. on Stonehenge, "The whole Work in Prospective, as when entire"; "The Ruin yet remaining drawn in Prospective" (*Stonehenge Restor'd,* 1725, p. 42).
7 David Riggs, *Ben Jonson, A Life* (Cambridge, MA: Harvard University Press, 1989), 53.
8 Stephen Orgel, *Impersonations* (Cambridge: Cambridge University Press, 1996), 65.
9 Per Palme, "Ut Pictura Poesis," *Sandblad* (1959), 96.
10 *Conversations with Drummond,* ll. 323–4.
11 A. W. Johnson, *Ben Jonson: Poetry and Architecture* (Oxford: Oxford University Press, 1994), 9–51
12 Peter Walls, *Music in the English Courtly Masque* (Oxford: Oxford University Press, 1996), 59.
13 Ian Spink, *English Song: Dowland to Purcell* (London, 1974), 45–6.
14 *Hymenæi,* line 16.
15 *Music in the Theatre of Ben Jonson* (Oxford: Oxford University Press, 1980).
16 Ibid., 58–61.
17 Ibid., 69.
18 *Oberon,* line 17, note d.
19 The manuscript was found in the Public Record Office by James Knowles, and described in the *Times Literary Supplement* of February 7, 1997. I quote from the transcription kindly supplied by James Knowles. See James Knowles, "Jonson's Entertainment at Britain's Burse," in *Re-presenting Ben Jonson: Text, Performance, History,* ed. M. Butler (London: Macmillan, 1999).

II

JAMES A. RIDDELL

Ben Jonson's Folio of 1616

It may fairly be said that Ben Jonson was one of the most self-conscious of poets and also a man not noticeably plagued by self-doubt. For publication in 1616, he gathered together a collection of his plays, poems, and other pieces and changed forever the world's (or at least the English-speaking part's) perception of what constituted a man's works. "Works," the word that Jonson selected as the title for his collection, was itself an act of audaciousness. No one before had thought, perhaps dared to think, that such a grand word, even translated (from the Latin "Opera") into English, could be used to describe a collection that included mere plays. Seven years later, the collection of Shakespeare's plays bore the more modest title *Comedies, Histories, and Tragedies*, and in 1647 Beaumont's and Fletcher's, similarly, were *Comedies and Tragedies*. Jonson's use of the word "Works" was enough to provoke some contemporary derision, of which the following may be taken as a representative sample:

> *To Mr. Ben Johnson demanding the reason*
> *why he called his plays works.*
> Pray tell me Ben, where does the mystery lurk,
> What others call a play you call a work.
> *Thus answered by a friend in Mr.*
> *Johnson's defense.*
> The authors friend thus for the author says,
> Ben's plays are works, when others works are plays.[1]

As the example demonstrates, Jonson's audacity had defenders as well as attackers, a consequence of the very high reputation that he enjoyed among many of his contemporaries.

But at the heart of his undertaking there was almost certainly much more involved than Jonsonian audacity. By calling attention to the material he gathered together as "Works," Jonson seems to have invited his readers to assess the unity of the whole.[2] This piece is meant to be a study of the 1616 Folio itself, and is therefore perhaps not the proper place to speculate about what, strictly speaking, are Jonson's unknowable intentions. Given, however, the extraordinary care that he must have devoted to the arranging of the parts of the Folio, best exemplified by the placing of *Every Man in his Humour* first in the volume, the placing of *The Golden Age Restored* last may be taken as an example of Jonson's seeking to give a particular shape to the volume.[3] It would be remiss of me not to suggest, at least, that the word "Works" was intended to bear its full share of meaning. Jonson often invested ordinary-seeming words with particular meaning. Richard Peterson has demonstrated convincingly and fully the particular ways that Jonson employed such words as "stand," "circle," or "understanding";[4] more recently, Judith Anderson[5] has called attention to two passages from *Discoveries* that bear directly on the point:

> For a man to write well, . . . he must first think, and excogitate his matter; then choose his words, and examine the weight of either. Then take care in placing, and ranking both matter, and words. . . . The congruent, and harmonious fitting of parts in a sentence, has almost the fastening, and force of knitting, and connection: as in stones well squared, which will rise strong in a great way without mortar.[6]

To be sure, the building of sentences is not the present issue; the choosing of words is, and "weight" and "stones well squared" call attention precisely to the choosing of words, of which "Works," I suggest, would provide a good example, both for its "weight" and for its architectural function. It is not too much to say that "WORKES" dominates the engraved title-page of the Folio (see p. iv above). Not surprisingly the word is set entirely in capital letters; however, the word is in letters much larger than any other on the page, and is further distinguished by the rather dramatic amount of white space that surrounds it. If one compares the title page with those of comparable volumes published in roughly the same period, one is bound to be struck by just how prominent on the Jonsonian title page "WORKES" is. In *The Comely Frontispiece*, Margery Corbett and Ronald Lightbown provide a convenient range of relevant examples.[7] It seems unlikely that Jonson merely went along with a decision made by his publisher, William Stansby, in the choice of type for the word, as unlikely as the notion that he did not consult with the engraver, William Hole, on the elaborate design that Hole produced, or as unlikely as the notion that he did not choose the quotation from Horace: *neque, me ut miretur turba, laboro: Contentus paucus lectoribus.* The quotation is not verbatim, but is adapted from *Satires*, I.x.73–4: "I do not work so that the crowd may admire me: I am content with a few readers."

Jonson and the printing of the Folio

The portion of the Folio to which Jonson seems to have paid the closest attention is the poems, *Epigrams* and *The Forest*. There are a couple of reasons for holding this view, one based on physical evidence, the other on conjecture. First, there are few examples in the poems of corrections, and those are rare. My argument requires that the two elements of this sentence be taken in conjunction. Because it would be reasonable to expect that about ten percent or so of sheets would be printed before stop-press corrections were made, uncorrected sheets (about ten percent) would appear in various copies of the Folio.[8] It seems that in the case of the poems, Jonson insisted – or at least tried to – that the proof reading be carried out before the press run started. That he was not altogether successful (see below) should not be surprising. Indeed, that lack of success accounts for the rarity of sheets in the uncorrected state. The only correction cited by Herford and Simpson in their section on the "Survey of the Text" (9. 71) is that on sig. 3T4, *Epigram* 23, line 5, "with" is corrected to "wits"; they are wrong, however, to assume that the correction (or corrections) is to be found only "in a fragment of the Folio used as a press-copy," for this and the following two corrections are to be found in complete copies of the Folio. David Gants has pointed out to me four more corrections in *Epigrams*, all of them in bound copies of the Folio, but all rare. On sig. 3T1v, *Epigram* 6, "ON ALCHYMISTS," corrected to "TO ALCHYMISTS"; on sig. 3T6, *Epigram* 40, "Marble," corrected to "Marble" (line 1); on sig. 3V6, *Epigram* 76, the title "ON LUCY COUNTESSE OF BEDFORD." corrected to "TO LUCY COUNTESSE OF BEDFORD."; on sig. 3X2v, *Epigram* 94, "Then, they," corrected to "They, then," (line 11). Dr. Gants has seen but one example each of the first three original readings; he has seen four examples of the fourth. In his dissertation, he has been able to add about 1,000 to the roughly 1,500 variants (including resettings) that were identified by Herford and Simpson. His view, in contrast to mine, is that Jonson paid little attention to the printing of the poems.[9]

The second, or conjectural, reason that I believe Jonson paid especially close attention to the printing of his poems in the Folio is his well-known characterization of them, the *Epigrams* in particular, as "the ripest of my studies"; if there were a section of the volume that he would prefer to have made as nearly perfect as possible it would be this one. While discussion of small changes in printed texts, such as I have given above, may seem particularly abstruse, they are necessary to illustrate how the modern idea of an "author" – one who takes particular care with the exact physical appearance of his words – began with Jonson.

The *Entertaynments and Masques*, on the other hand, although they follow immediately after the poems, constitute the portion of the Folio that received the least attention by Jonson and by the printer's men as well. Everywhere one looks in these sheets one finds instances of neglect. Herford and Simpson are surely correct, at least for the most part, when they state: "Jonson cannot have read the proofs." They may also be correct in the reason that they assign for the neglect: "It is probable that the printer, registering the work in 1615 [a number of

Jonson's masques were first registered with the Stationers' Company in 1615] and producing it in 1616, hurried the printing" (9:72). It is altogether reasonable to suppose that Stansby's shop was operating at a frenetic pace in the last couple of months of 1616, when he finished the printing of the Folio. Not only was it finishing the Jonson folio, but, as Kevin J. Donovan demonstrates, some of the sheets of Aaron Rathborne's *The Surveyor* were being printed simultaneously,[10] and there is evidence that various other volumes were also in one form of production or another at the same time.[11] As a slight exception to their view that "Jonson cannot have read the proofs," the Oxford editors posit that the one place in this part of the volume where Jonson may have taken a hand was in the last two pages, "where he transposed effectively the final speeches, making Astræa decide that she would return to earth in order to bask in the sunshine of King James's court." In this observation they are half right and half wrong. Jonson must have been the one who reordered the sequence of the two speeches because no one in the printing house would be in a position to imagine that once the order of the speeches was established it could be wrong. But the reordering was in the direction opposite to that set out by the Oxford editors. They were mistakenly convinced that the text found in large-paper copies always represented the version that Jonson intended to be the final one.[12] The reordering of the two speeches does imply something about Stansby's practice as he was printing the last part of the Folio. Strictly speaking, the evidence applies only to the last quire, constituting but two sheets; given the haste that the entire section reflects, however, the inference I draw here seems reasonable. Because the speeches of Astræa and Pallas are in two separate formes (that is, the individual plates set up by the printer for each page to be printed) and because the speeches were rearranged one for the other without being altered, one must assume that the two formes were being machined simultaneously – thus, another reason to suspect speeded-up printing in Stansby's shop.

The typography of the Folio

When Jonson saw the plays of the Folio into the press, he took pains to present them in a regularized format. Some years ago W. David Kay, asking why Jonson placed *Every Man in His Humour* at the beginning of his *Workes*, offered the following answer, which also has implications for the printing of the full volume. "I would suggest," says Kay,

> that [the answer] is to be found in his continuing attempt to interpret himself to his age as a writer whose individual works formed a unified corpus animated by his conception of the poet's function. . . . The action would seem to have been a retrospective attempt to give his work a striking unity, an application of his architectonic skill to the form of his career itself.[13]

If Kay is right, and he certainly seems to be, we can see why Jonson took pains to present the plays in a consistent manner, and the entertainments and masques as well, though the latter to a lesser extent than the plays. He altered a number of details in the format of earlier printings of both. In their general introduction to the plays, Herford and Simpson point out one significant change: "in the Folio . . . [he] pruned severely the lavish stage directions given in the Quartos" (folio and quarto are, very conveniently, terms used to distinguish between the formats of a printed book: folio is roughly twice the size of quarto); they offer speculation about why: "He liked the look of a clean page in which the text stood out clear" (3. xiv). The quartos of Jonson's plays represent their first printing; the Folio, the "Workes," presented Jonson with an opportunity for revision. In the absence of Jonson's own manuscript copies of his texts, the changes made from quarto to folio give us the best opportunity to see his creative mind at work.

The same speculation may also apply to the cleaned-up version of *Sejanus* that appears in the Folio, from which all of Jonson's elaborate historical notes that appeared in the quarto version have been banished. (I have not thought it worthwhile to try to present more than a few examples of Jonson's changes from quarto to folio in this rather general description of the Folio; those changes can be found in the textual notes to the plays in Herford and Simpson). On the other hand, a number of typographical changes must have been introduced for the sake of uniformity itself. For instance, in the Epilogue to *Volpone* there are a couple of changes from italic type to roman. Percy Simpson points out that in the quartos "place-names are in lower-case italic . . . so are technical terms . . . quotations, songs, foreign words and phrases, Greek derivatives, and words which, in their context, have a special point." This is much altered in the Folio. These changes would do little to affect the general impression of the printed page upon the eye. And one does find throughout the Folio numerous examples of italic. We may ask, then, why would Jonson make the changes at all? The question is, of course, rhetorical, as I have just suggested the answer: Jonson seems to have gone to some lengths to impose upon the works in the Folio a uniformity that would bear up under some fairly close scrutiny. I realize that about this issue there has been considerable discussion by eminent bibliographers, largely, however, having to do with the choice of copy-text for a printing of Jonson's works. I take some comfort from one of Fredson Bowers' characteristically forceful observations: "For the Folio Greg mentions three stages of supervision of the revised edition [of any given play]: Jonson's markings of alterations in the copy sent to the printer; Jonson's revision of the Folio proofs; and finally his correction of the sheets while they were in process of printing. The first and third of these are incontrovertible."[14] I recognize that there is a certain circularity in my argument, but not, I hope, a ruinous one. We can see that there are a number of alterations of text from quarto to folio; the alterations seem to reflect an attempt to impose regularity; why would Jonson make them?

In the plays of the Folio, names of characters, abbreviations of names, and even alternative names (such as "Foxe" for "Volpone"), whether they be to identify speakers' parts or to refer to a given character in the dialogue, are all set in caps and small caps, a practice that Jonson partially introduced in the quarto *Sejanus*; "partially" because nowhere in any of the quartos are characters' names always rendered in caps and small caps in the dialogue. (In a play as late as *The Alchemist* [1612] one finds this introduction of characters: "FACE. SUBTLE. DOL Common." [sig. B1].) If in the entertainments and masques, on the other hand, Jonson attempted to attain a regularity similar to that of the plays, he was only partly successful. In *The Masque of Queens*, for instance, the inconsistent practice in the quarto is somewhat regularized in the Folio. The speech headings "6. CHARME."; "DAME."; "7. CHARME." of the quarto [sigs. C4v-D1] become "6. CHARME."; "DAME."; 7. "CHARME." [Fol. sig. 4L4], but elsewhere the "HAGGES." of quarto [sig. B4] is simply retained as "HAGGES." [Fol. sig. 4L1v]. The entertainments and masques, as I have already mentioned, were not so carefully attended going through the press as were other parts of the Folio. A certain amount of regularization was achieved, however, in that throughout the masques, songs, usually set in italics in the quartos, were consistently set in roman in the Folio. Whether this was the result of Jonson's wishes or simply the practice of Stansby's men one cannot now say; at the risk of undercutting my argument I must say that the latter seems likely. The dropping of some parts of the text from quartos must have been Jonson's doing, though not for the purpose of imposing uniformity of appearance. In *Hymenæi*, for instance, all references to the original performance were stricken because of the scandalous divorce of the Earl of Essex and his wife. There are three other excisions: the dedication to Prince Henry of *The Masque of Queens* and notes to both parts of the *Kings Entertainment in Passing to His Coronation* and *The Entertainment at Althorpe*. (All are cited in the textual notes of HS.)

In addition, there are changes in the typography of the Folio that were introduced with the purpose of making it less rather than more uniform in appearance. Mark Bland talks of

> [examples] of typographic thoughtfulness [that] are to be found throughout the Workes: the setting of Ed Knowell's letter [in *Every Man in his Humour*] in great primer italic, the lacuna in the text as the boys draw the short straw in *Cynthia's Revels*, and the setting of [the names] Ulen and Ulen Spiegel in black-letter in *The Alchemist*, are three examples of carefully mediated moments where the printer's art and the poet's intentions cohere.[15]

As in virtually all matters having to do with Jonson, one must come to grips with a temperament that defies categories; Jonson complicates and simplifies at the same time. F. H. Mares puts the matter succinctly when he says: "there are differences in typography between F and Q, and, as with the punctuation, the folio is both more elaborate and more systematic than the quarto."[16]

One fairly striking change from quartos to Folio is that Jonson dropped most of the commendatory poems that had appeared with some of the plays in their earlier printings. He retained only a few that had originally appeared with the quarto versions: poems by George Chapman and Hugh Holland on *Sejanus*; poems in Latin by John Donne and Edmund Bolton on *Volpone*; and three poems by Francis Beaumont, one each on *Volpone*, *Epicœne*, and *Catiline*. *Sejanus* (1605) was the first of Jonson's plays to be accompanied by commendatory poems; it had nine. *Volpone* (1607) had eleven, *The Alchemist* (1612), one, and *Catiline* (1611), three. The commendatory poem for *Epicœne* may have come from a now lost quarto.[17] In addition, Jonson procured two poems for the Folio itself, one in Latin by John Selden and one in English by Selden's "chamber-fellow," Edward Heyward. The first quire (that is the first gathering, or section) of the Folio, containing all of the preliminary matter, was, as one would expect, the last to be printed. There was not room enough in it for all of the commendatory poems from the quartos; we cannot tell exactly why Jonson chose just the poems that he did, but the space available almost certainly meant that he could not choose them all.

The order of materials printed in the Folio

There are three distinguishable general title pages (that is, title pages for the entire Folio), and a varying number of title pages for each of the first three plays to be printed: *Every Man out of his Humour* has no fewer than seven, *Cynthia's Revels* two, and *Poetaster* three (one of which is seemingly to be found only in large-paper copies). The extraordinary number of titles for *Every Man Out* may imply that Stansby was uncertain about the direction in which he was headed as he began the printing of Jonson's Folio, and Jonson himself may have been party to the uncertainty. It is clear that at the outset of the printing Stansby did not intend to employ the bookseller John Smithwicke's name, nor did he when he rounded off the printing of *Every Man Out*. The first two title pages that Stansby printed for that play – all, admittedly, rare – do not bear Smithwicke's name. The next four (one of them rare) does. And the final title page for the play (not at all rare) does not bear it. Herford and Simpson partially explain what may have been going on in Stansby's shop: "For the right to print [much] of the volume he had to negotiate with various booksellers" (9. 14). But no one now seems able to explain completely the nature of those negotiations, and a number of plays for which Stansby may not have owned the rights are to be found in the Jonson Folio. Both of the title pages of *Cynthia's Revels* have only Stansby's name, so for this play the issue of a part owner whose name must be included on the title page does not exist. By the time that *Poetaster* was printed, Stansby (or, perhaps, Stansby and Jonson) settled upon the format that was to prevail in the title pages for the rest of the volume.

So far as the three general titles are concerned, an examination of the various states of the imprint reveals that it was redone twice. That is, the cartouche (the device on the title page that contains the printer's name) in which the imprint appears was twice burnished clear – or nearly clear, but in one case not entirely – and subsequently re-engraved. Therein lie the clues to the sequence of the three imprints. This somewhat oversimplifies the case, but because certain fragments of an earlier imprint can be accounted for only in one way, we can determine the correct order of the three resultant states, which is:

(1) Imprinted at / London by / Will Stansby
(2) London / printed by W: / Stansby, and are / to be sould by / Rich: Meighen.
(3) LONDON / Printed by / William Stansby.[18]

It would seem that all large-paper copies of the Folio have the first general title, as do many small-paper copies. The other two general titles appear only in small-paper copies. I know of one exception to this statement; there may be more. Huntington 62100 is printed on large-paper stock, but bears the second of the three imprints instead of the first, the imprint found in all of the large-paper copies that I have seen. I don't know how to account for this anomaly.

I mentioned above that the matter contained in the first quire would have been the last to be brought together and that this is what one would expect of a book printed in the early seventeenth century – or for many years to come. I also mentioned that the numerous title pages that appear with *Every Man Out* suggest that with this text Stansby seemed to be finding his way. What is left out of the equation is that *Every Man In* appears first in the volume. This, however, can be accounted for. A portion of Every *Man In*, the first quire (to Folio, I.iii.104 in HS), was printed after Stansby had finished his work with *Volpone*; subsequently, it was not until he had completed all of the plays and turned his hand to the next section, *Epigrams*, that he returned to *Every Man In*. That is to say, William Stansby set aside six full quires, A through F, to accommodate *Every Man In* and started his work at the beginning of quire G with *Every Man out of his Humour*.[19]

As *Every Man In* was extensively rewritten between its quarto and Folio printings, the two are substantially different plays. Most influential modern critics follow Herford and Simpson in agreeing that the Folio version is the better. And most also agree that Jonson's parings near the end of the play are a part of his general strategy to improve it.[20] But there may be another reason for Jonson's having cut substantial portions of the text when he revised it for the Folio.[21] First, there is the question implied in Stansby's having set aside six quires to accommodate the revised *Every Man In*: would these six provide sufficient but not too much space for the play? How did he arrive at the number six – and this before type for any part of any of the plays had been set? Printers were no doubt skillful at estimating how many folio pages would be the equivalent of a certain number of quarto pages, but to suppose that even the most skillful estimator could judge that seventy-six pages of quarto would work out to be exactly sixty-seven pages of folio is to suppose too much. There are additional complications, the most important being that Jonson was certainly revising, or had revised, the play; Herford and Simpson demonstrate that most likely the Folio was set from a marked-up copy of the quarto (9. 293–4). Not all authorities, however, agree with this view. Lever suggests that, although the quarto may have been the basis, "it is more plausible to suppose that [instead of marking up that text of the play] Jonson had the Quarto before him while preparing his manuscript revision and inadvertently repeated some slightly defective punctuation [which provides the basis for the Herford and Simpson judgment]."[22] Furthermore Jonson's manuscript additions, deletions, and other corrections, even if they were known to the printer well in advance of the six quires being set aside for the play, would be cause for a good deal of guesswork. Jonson could have made the very extensive cuts in the last pages of the Folio version of *Every Man In* – and let them persist – for artistic reasons alone, and I am certainly not arguing that he made cuts without the most serious consideration of their implications. However, it is no doubt the fact that *Every Man In* was, for the most part, the last play printed, first quire A and some time later quires B through F. The play was, more to the point, confined to a space that was to some degree arbitrarily set, exactly six quires – and those six quires for a play that was to differ markedly from its earlier printed version. The extensive cuts made in the last few pages of *Every Man In* might have been, no doubt to Jonson's dismay, an example of the print shop exerting control over the author.

NOTES

1 From *Wits Recreations* (1640), cited by C. H. Herford and Percy and Evelyn Simpson, *Ben Jonson* (Oxford: Clarendon Press, 1925–52), 9. 13; all quotations of Jonson, unless otherwise noted, are from this edition; quotations have been modernized.

2 See Richard Dutton, *Ben Jonson: To the First Folio* (Cambridge: Cambridge University Press, 1983) and David Kay, "The Shaping of Ben Jonson's Career: A Reexamination of Facts and Problems," *Modern Philology*, 67 (Feb. 1970).

3 See W. W. Greg, "The Riddle of Jonson's Chronology," *The Library*, 6th Ser. (1926), 343–4; HS 10: 545–6.

4 Richard Peterson, *Imitation and Praise in the Poems of Ben Jonson* (New Haven and London: Yale University Press, 1981), passim.

5 Judith Anderson, *Words That Matter: Linguistic Perception in Renaissance English* (Stanford: Stanford University Press, 1996), 103, 104; and Chapter 4, 101–23.

6 HS, lines 1697–1704; 1976–80.

7 Margery Corbett and Ronald Lightbown, *The Comely Frontispiece: The Emblematic Title-Page in England, 1550–1660* (London: Henley, 1979).

8 See Charlton Hinman, *The Printing and Proof-reading of the First Folio of Shakespeare* (Oxford: The Clarendon Press, 1963), 1, 229, n.1; Philip Gaskell, *A New Introduction to Bibliography* (Oxford: The Clarendon Press, 1972), 353; and my "The Concluding Pages of the Jonson Folio of 1616," *Studies in Bibliography*, 47 (1994), 150.

9 David Gants, "A Descriptive Bibliography of The Workes of Benjamin Jonson" (London: William Stansby, 1616), Ph.D. Dissertation, University of Virginia, 1997, 325.

10 See Kevin J. Donovan, "The Final Quires of the Jonson Workes: Headline Evidence," *Studies in Bibliography*, 40 [1987], 119–20. He considers that "late November or early December, 1616 seems a likely date for the completion of the Jonson 1616 Folio."

11 See Gants, "Descriptive Bibliography," 349–56.

12 See HS 5: 148–9; 9. 40 and, also, William A. Jackson, *The Carl H. Pforzheimer Library, English Literature, 1475–1700* (New York: The Merrill Press, 1940), II, 573. For the contrary view, that is that the large-paper sheets were not always the last through the press, see Johan Gerritsen, "Stansby and Jonson Produce a Folio: A Preliminary Account," *English Studies*, 40 (1959), 54; Donovan, "Final Quires," 109, n.6, 118; my "Concluding Pages," 147–54; Gants, "Descriptive Bibliography," 321–4.

13 W. David Kay, "The Shaping of Ben Jonson's Career: A Reexamination of Facts and Problems," *Modern Philology*, 67 (February 1970), 236.

14 Fredson Bowers, "Greg's 'Rationale of Copy-Text' Revisited," *Studies in Bibliography*, 31 (1978), 110–11. See, also, W. W. Greg, "The Rationale of Copy-Text," in *Collected Papers*, ed. J. C. Maxwell (Oxford: The Clarendon Press, 1966), 374–91.

15 See Mark Bland, "William Stansby and the Production of the Workes of Beniamin Jonson, 1615–16," *The Library*, 6th ser., 20 (March 1998), 26.

16 See F. H. Mares, ed., *The Alchemist*, The Revels Plays (Cambridge, MA: Harvard University Press, 1967), lxxiv.

17 See: HS 9: 142–3; W. W. Greg in *A Bibliography of the English Printed Drama to the Restoration* (London: The Bibliographical Society, 1939–1959; rpt. 1970), I, 442–3; and, for a much fuller discussion, Greg, "Was There a 1612 Quarto of Epicene?" *The Library*, 4th Ser., 15 (1934), 306–15.

18 See my note: "Variant Title-Pages of the 1616 Jonson Folio," *The Library*, 6th Ser., 8 (June 1986), 152–6.

19 Gerritsen, "Stansby and Jonson Produce a Folio," 52–5.

20 For instance, Jonas Barish, *Ben Jonson and the Language of Prose Comedy* (Cambridge, MA: Harvard University Press, 1960), 130; J. A. Bryant, Jr., "Jonson's Revisions of *Every Man in his Humour*," *Studies in Philology*, 59, (1962), 646–7; Richard Dutton, *Ben Jonson: To the First Folio* (Cambridge: Cambridge University

Press, 1983), 31; Alexander Leggatt, *Ben Jonson: His Vision and His Art* (London and New York: Methuen, 1981), 90–91; Anne Barton, *Ben Jonson, Dramatist* (Cambridge: Cambridge University Press, 1984), 54.

21 I discuss this more fully in "Jonson and Stansby and the Revisions of *Every Man in his Humour,*" *Medieval and Renaissance Drama in England*, 9 (1997), 81–91.

22 J. W. Lever, ed., *Every Man in his Humour: A Parallel-Text Edition of the 1601 Quarto and the 1616 Folio*, Regents Renaissance Drama Series (Lincoln: University of Nebraska Press, 1971).

12

JOHN MULRYAN

Jonson's classicism[1]

I

The term *classicism* is used here in two senses – as a literary and philosophical system that asserts and celebrates the existence of a series of timeless, unvarying principles of conduct and thought: attention to form, decorum, knowledge, the past, imitation, consistency, fidelity, personal worth; and as an acknowledgment that those principles are embodied in the writings of ancient Greece and Rome, which should be taken as models by all later writers aspiring to repeat the process.

It is clear that Jonson embraced classicism in the second sense. He consciously imitated ancient Greek and Roman authors (although mainly Roman), and called attention to his debt in learned notes to his plays and masques. But he was also a classicist in the first sense, for he yearned to associate himself with the stability of the classical tradition, and the prestige of its authors. One could argue about the wisdom of attempting to translate certain classical concepts into seventeenth-century artifacts, but to consider Jonson outside of the classical tradition would be as anomalous as to ignore Herman Melville's interest in the sea.

Historically, seventeenth-century poets in general and Jonson in particular aspired to classicism because they were influenced by the movement known as Renaissance humanism, the rebirth of learning in literature and the arts that began in Italy and spread its way across Europe, and which was characterized by a devotion to Greek and Roman literature, and, more specifically, to the restructuring of all literature on the model of the classical genres: epic, satire, lyric, drama, elegy, and so forth. Humanist principles also traveled from the north with Desiderius Erasmus (1466?-1536), the great Dutch scholar and educator, whose *Colloquies* and *Adages* earned a place in the curriculum along with the more philosophical pronouncements of the great Italian educational theorist, Juan Luis Vives (1492–1540). William Grocyn (ca. 1446–1519) and Thomas Linacre (1460–1524) imported the movement to England and it was popularized by Roger Ascham (1515–68), Queen Elizabeth's tutor. Under the aegis of the Oxford reformers (Grocyn, Linacre, John Colet [1466–1519], and Wiliam Lyly [ca. 1468–1523]) a system of classical education was set up in England, from grammar school through university, which was expanded and perfected in the seventeenth century. Jonson himself was trained at Westminster School by the great antiquarian and humanist William Camden (1551–1623). He benefited directly from the educational system set up by the Oxford reformers, acquiring a sound grounding in the classics and a love of learning that never deserted him.

It is also true that there was some resistance among the English toward the classics and classicism, primarily due to their association with Italy and Roman Catholicism. Ascham's own enthusiasm for the classics was subdued by this bias, but Jonson's interest in Roman Catholicism may have helped him to avoid this provincial trap. Jonson obviously wanted his own work to be regarded as "classical" in the sense of an œuvre that can stand the test of time. Classicism has come to be regarded as pedantic because it is associated with the schools and emphasizes imitation of select models rather than striking out on one's own. It also carries the connotation of conservative and here the label fits as well, since Jonson was conservative if not reactionary in his thought. It also carries the idea of restraint, a conscious effort by the bellicose Jonson to control both his life and his art. It is, in addition, exclusive or elitist; one becomes a classicist because others are not. Perhaps, too, the ex-bricklayer and convicted felon liked the status conferred by his association with the best that had been known and thought in Greece and Rome. Roman moralists also set up a dichotomy between the depraved multitude and the wise and virtuous elite, providing Jonson with a pat explanation for the failure of his more learned, recondite plays to entertain or enlighten the groundlings among Jacobean theatregoers. In fact, Jonson identified himself so closely with the classical tradition that he was willing to sacrifice his popularity with his audience, rather than compromise his exacting standards. According to William Blissett, Jonson failed to integrate his knowledge of the classics with other aspects of his learning, especially in the Roman plays, in which the parallels between Rome and England were too intricate for the ordinary playgoer to follow. In *Catiline*, for example, the lengthy speech by Cicero denouncing Catiline is out of all proportion to its dramatic effect.[2]

William Kupersmith speaks of a reverse type of influence in Jonson, whereby instead of adjusting his vision of ancient Rome to contemporary London, he turns seventeenth-century Londoners into ancient Romans. Jonson's satire, Kupersmith writes, is conditioned by Christian morals and a kind of elitism that is missing in Juvenal. In other words, his satire is always responsive to contemporary models and needs, reshaped and reworked into something that is quite originally his own. Stubborn antiquary though he may be, Jonson still uses the classics rather than being used by them.[3]

Ironically, Jonson's creative adaptations of the classics have had a positive effect on the classics themselves. As Thomas M. Greene observes, Jonson's adaptations of Martial increased awareness of the great Roman epigrammatist, and "Englished" him so finely that he will never be forgotten.[4] Moreover, Jonson's translation of Horace's *Art of Poetry* and many adaptations of Catullus and other Roman lyricists enhanced the stature of these poets in English eyes, particularly among Jonson's own imitators.

Apart from his own contributions to classicism, Jonson inspired the "Tribe of Ben" – Andrew Marvell, Robert Herrick, Sir John Suckling and others – to continue experiments in adapting Catullus, Horace, Tibullus, Ovid and Propertius to the English language. Thus the whole tradition of carpe diem poems in the seventeenth century (a favorite subject of his "tribe" or "sons") stems from Jonson. In fact Jonson seldom used a classical genre or imitated a classical poem without improving on it and setting a new standard of generic excellence in his own language. In his great poem, "To Penshurst," for example, he adapts the epideictic conventions of Statius' *Silvae* (1.3, 2.2) from the praise of the Roman villa to the manor house of the Sidneys, introducing the "great house" genre into English poetry. Jonson's identification of house and man is, in fact, a better "fit" than Statius'. He follows Statius in fusing description of the house and praise of its owners, but, unlike Statius, he avoids turning the design of the "great house" into a symbol of ostentation and greed.[5]

Most of the elegies collected after Jonson's death under the title *Jonsonus Virbius* stress his mastery of Greek and Latin authors, but particularly his elevation of the English language to a new status as equal if not superior to the classical languages. Indeed, according to one anonymous elegist, Jonson's imitations of the classics are so well wrought "That Ages hence, Critics shall question make / Whether the Greeks and Romans English spake" (HS, vol. 11, Elegy 23, "*Upon the Death of* Mr. Ben. Jonson," 43–4). In comparison to Jonson, Shakespeare, according to H. Ramsay, could barely understand Latin: "That *Latin He* reduced, and could command / That which your *Shakespeare* scarce could understand?" (Elegy 26, 13–14). The elegies also stress his careful, slow, painstaking writing, his immense learning, his plain style, and the inadequacy of the elegists to match it. Jonson transformed the classics, made them his own, and then surpassed them. Six of the elegies are in Latin, and one in Greek, a conscious attempt to associate Jonson with the classical tradition.

Sometimes Jonson appropriated the classicism of others. For example, some politicians who were disenchanted with the politics of the Jacobean court and the rule of James I himself took refuge in a form of neostoicism drawn from the precepts of Seneca and the cynical musings of Tacitus. The great Flemish scholar Justus Lipsius (1547–1606), pioneering editor of Tacitus (1574) and Seneca (1605), had attempted to develop a stoic code of ethics that would permit a free man to participate in an absolutist government like James', but his English followers (including Jonson's mentor William Camden and the great antiquarian and book collector Sir Robert Cotton [1571–1631]) were not so adept at translating the writings of Seneca and Tacitus into a prudent political philosophy. As for Jonson, it was widely suspected that the disgraced Robert Devereux, second Earl of Essex (1567–1601), was the model for the protagonist of *Sejanus*, the favorite of the emperor Tiberius. It also seemed obvious to many that Jonson was drawing ironic parallels between Rome in its last century as a republic and the first of James' imperial rule.[6]

Aristotle's definition of poetry as the art of imitation (*Poetics* 1447a) is at the heart of Jonson's classicism, and in our own time it is difficult to reconcile ideas of originality and creativity with such a view of poetry. In addition to the assumption that an imitative poet is unoriginal, there is the added stigma of plagiarism. Jonson himself distinguished between slavish and true imitation of the classics. In fact Martial, one of Jonson's favorite authors, wrote a number of epigrams on poets who had stolen his work or the work of others. John Dryden, in his "An Essay of Dramatic Poesie," speaking through Crites, defender of the ancients, seems to damn the poet with faint praise, when he refers to Jonson as a "learned Plagiary" of Horace and "all the other" ancient authors. On the one hand Crites praises Jonson by saying that "He invades Authors like a Monarch, and what would be theft in other Poets, is only victory in him," and on the other he notes, condescendingly, that "there are few serious thoughts which are new in him." Dryden also recognized Jonson's grasp of the plain style, which eschewed rhetorical ornament and embraced brevity, concision, and correctness. Thus "In his works you find little to retrench or alter," but his language was "too closely and laboriously" concise. In a final hit, Neander, another participant in the dialogue, attacks Jonson's originality directly: "As he did not want imagination, so none ever said he had much to spare."[7]

Although he was mocked for his presumption by the playwright Thomas Dekker (1572?-1632?) and others, Jonson, in a piece of extreme self-fashioning, modeled himself on Horace, both in personality (as he understood it) and poetic method. Jonson announces this without subtlety in his play the *Poetaster*, where, in imitation of the *Sermones* of Horace, he presents Horace (obviously a substitution for himself) as a virtuous poet who responds with dignity to the schemes directed against him by the enemies of poetry who are themselves subjected to ridicule and punishment in the play.

II

Jonson wrote an astonishing amount of material during a busy and hectic life, but he excelled in three forms: criticism, poetry, and drama (including comedy, tragedy, and the masque). Rather than presenting a detailed list of multiple borrowings from classical authors in the totality of Jonson's works, I shall limit myself to a detailed discussion of one work of criticism (*Timber, or, Discoveries*); three poems from two collections (from the *Epigrams*, 45 "On My First Son" and 19 "On Sir Cod the Perfumed," and from *The Forest*, 9 "To Celia"); one tragedy (*Catiline*); one comedy (*Volpone, or The Fox*); and one masque (*Pleasure Reconciled to Virtue*).

Jonson's *Timber, or, Discoveries* reveals him to be an aggressive reader as well as writer, for these revelations are presented "*As They have flowed out of his daily Readings* . . ." (HS 8: 561).[8] His many prefaces and annotations to his own works suggest an almost pathological attempt to control the interpretation of his own text, not only by making his meaning as plain as possible, but also by creating barriers between the naked text and the reader, and also controlling the interpretation of Jonson's own sources (e.g. Horace, Seneca, Aristotle). Even the annotations Jonson made in the books in his personal library point to a pattern of attempted control over both the reading and the writing of texts, particularly the classics. Jonson's remarks on critical theory are scattered through his plays and the conversations with Drummond as well as in the *Discoveries*, but this is the only one of his works devoted to literary criticism. Even so, there are as many remarks on character and morals as there are on writing.

With fine Jonsonian irony, he informs the reader that the ancients are "Guides, not Commanders" (HS 8: 567), a remark lifted from Juan Luis Vives among others. According to Katherine Eisaman Maus, "This declaration of critical and artistic independence is in fact translated from Vives, who adapts it from Quintilian and Seneca, who in turn derive it from Cicero."[9] Almost all of the other remarks on poetry are drawn from the ancients, and for the most part from the Latin authors, with the noted exception of Aristotle. Most of his remarks relate to the *res et verba* controversy, the duel between words and matter, itself a product of close study of classical authors like Cicero and Quintilian. Roger Ascham spoke sharply to his teacher audience on this subject: "Ye know not what hurt ye do to learning that care not for words [*verba*] but for matter [*res*] and so make a divorce betwixt the tongue and the heart."[10] On the opposite side of the debate, Francis Bacon wryly observes that this fascination with style "grew speedily to an excess; for men began to hunt more after words than matter. . . ."[11] Jonson is clearly in Bacon's camp: for him, the author "must first think, and excogitate his matter; then choose his words, and examine the weight of either. Then take care in placing, and ranking both matter, and words, that the composition be comely; and to do this with diligence, and often" (HS 8: 615). Thus one begins with the matter and proceeds to clothe it in words, a decorum of language as well as thought. Language should be plain, unadorned, in a kind of universal style that can be understood by all ages. Jonson criticizes those who read without a principle of selection; those who, like Montaigne, are most convinced by the last work that they read; those who attack reading itself; those who pretend to read what they have not; those who place a premium on their own ignorance; and those who write down everything they know in order to seem more learned than those who have made a judicious selection from their readings before they put pen to paper. His absolute conviction that poetry, as envisioned by Aristotle, is the art of imitation is epitomized in the sentence, "Nay, sometimes it is the reward of a man's study, the praise of quoting another man fitly" (HS 8: 616–17). Take the wisdom of the ages, and hammer it into a new form appropriate to one's own age.

Jonson's epigrams, which he referred to as *"the ripest of my studies"* (Dedication to William Earl of Pembroke, HS 8: 25), are his most successful attempt to organize, schematize, and control experience through the discipline of form. All the principles of the plain style – brevity, concision, lucidity, clarity, and thematic point – come together in the epigram. Jonson, for the most part, substitutes the serene voice of Horace for the mocking jeers of Martial, a voice characterized by restraint, human sympathy, and understated eloquence. His epigram "On My First Son" (45) is a model of the form. Unlike the two epigrams of Martial on which it is based (12.34, 6.29), the poem nicely balances personal grief and public responsibility. For Martial, a friend is simply a hostage to Fortune, one's partner in a series of experiences in which the pleasant ones out-number, barely, the unpleasant. And the loss of a young male occasions the stoic advice, "Whatever you love, pray that it not please too much."[12] While Jonson echoes this sentiment in the last two lines of the epigram ("For whose sake, henceforth, all his vows be such, / As what he loves may never like too much"), he does not allow his classical model to suppress the intense, intimate nature of his grief. In a tone of Christian submission, Jonson accepts the fact that all earthly goods and attachments are intrinsically ephemeral and must be returned "on the just day" (4). But this calm spirit of resignation is overturned with the powerful "O, could I loose all father now" (5). With masterful concision, Jonson memorializes what should be obvious: nothing is so particularly painful as the loss of one's offspring; better to be a stranger than a father at a son's funeral. Although the poem is a fine integration of conventional Latin phrases ("Vale," "Requiescat in pace," "Hic jacet" (1, 9) and contains its own epitaph (". . . here doth lie / *Ben. Jonson* his best piece of *poetry*" [9–10]), it is still a personal address to his departed son – wishing him well, wishing him peace, and remind-ing him that the answer to who or what lies in his grave is Jonson's finest piece of art. The poem's epitaph has carried the memory of the son and the grief of the father over three hundred troubled years of history. Jonson has both univer-salized and personalized the experience of grief, with an authenticity and emotive power that are derived from the measured language of his poem.

Jonson, however, could not fully imitate his model Martial without including some scurrilous or quasi-obscene epigrams, since about a fourth of Martial's poems are of this type. Although he fiercely denied that there was any obscenity in his epigrams, there is some evidence, especially in his *Conversations with William Drummond of Hawthornden,* and in the annotations he made in his personal copies of Martial, that he was himself of a bawdy turn of mind. The epigram, which had displaced the sonnet in popularity, had been moving also in a bawdy vein from 1590 to 1630, but Jonson wanted to disassociate himself from other English epigrammatists who focused only on the scatological side of Martial. In Epigram 19, "On Sir Cod The Perfumed," Jonson makes the best of this dilemma by expressing moral indignation at the generically named Sir Cod (testicles or a receptacle for perfume), whose corrupt stench envelops both body and soul: "That *Cod* can get no widow, yet a knight, / I scent the cause: He woos with an ill sprite [spirit or breath]." Here, indeed, is "much in little": the mockery of being a *Sir* Cod, the physical corruption betokening the corruption within, the double entendre of a stinking *breath* and a corrupt *spirit*, the swift and pleasantly rhetorical turn from fetid breath to fetid soul – and all in two lines of poetry!

Jonson's uncanny ability to imitate an author so closely that it almost seems like plagiarism (a charge often laid against him – see Dryden's remarks above), and yet to create something totally new, is epitomized in his great Song "To Celia" (HS, vol. 8, *The Forest* 9). Based on three poems (2, 32, and 33) from the "Love Letters" of Philostratus, two lines from poem 33 are direct translations: the Loeb edition translates ἐμοὶ δὲ μόνοις πρόπινε τοῖς ὄμμασιν as "drink to me only with your eyes," or as Jonson has it, "Drink to me only with thine eyes" and πλήρου φιλημάτων τὸ ἔκπωμα καὶ δίδου τοῖς δεομένοις as "fill the cup with kisses and so pass it to the thirsty" which becomes in Jonson "Or leave a kiss but in the cup, / And I'll not look for wine." Lines 9–12, on the "rosy wreath," are, with the exception of four words deleted by Jonson, a direct translation of Letter 2.[13] The context, however, is radically different. Philostratus alternates these poems in praise of sexual attributes between boys and women, while Jonson has chosen to imitate only the poems in praise of women, and to transform three poems concerned with physical lust into a single poem of delicate courtly compliment, praising Celia's ability to defeat decay and satisfy the deep thirst of the soul. Jonson has also transformed Philostratus' reference to Zeus and his catamite Ganymede (Letter 33), the one who bears the cup, into a comparison between Celia's inviting eyes and nectar, the drink of the gods: "But might I of *Jove's Nectar* sup, / I would not change for thine" (7–8).

Both the faults and the genius of Jonson in developing his art from classical materials are obvious in *Catiline.* While the titular source of the play is Sallust, with significant background from the speeches of Cicero on the Catilinarian conspiracy, the tone is Tacitean and the assemblage of embarrassing and vulgar details in the garrulous manner of the gossipy Suetonius. The ghost of Sylla, whose declamation begins the play, informs us of Catiline's "incests, murders, rapes . . .," his "forcing first a *Vestal* nun" (a capital crime in Rome, resulting in, despite the blamelessness of the victim, the live burial of the vestal), and his intent to seize control of Rome by torching the landscape and drenching it in human blood (1.30–1, 65–6). Tacitus, in his account of the Emperor Claudius, harpooned the good Emperor with savage irony, juxtaposing Claudius' function as custodian of public morals with his wife's promiscuity and unfaithfulness: "Claudius, meanwhile, ignorant of his own matrimonial fortune [his wife Valeria Messalina is having an affair with the boy Gaius Silius] and engrossed by his censorial functions, reprimanded in austere edicts the license shown in theatres by the populace" (*Annals* 11.13).[14] Similarly, Sylla's ghost mocks Catiline's incest as a kind of parental economy ". . . that act of thy incestuous life, / Which got thee, at once, a daughter and a wife" (1.35–36). The bloodthirsty Catiline piles up bodies like Clint Eastwood's (*A Fistful of Dollars, For a Few Dollars More*) Man with No Name, who dumps the bodies of his victims in a buckboard before collecting his bounty. As Jonson's Cathegus remarks in the play, Charon had to call on a whole navy to transport the bodies Catiline left in his bloody wake, a comic parallel worthy of Suetonius:

> The rugged CHARON fainted,
> And asked a navy, rather than a boat,
> To ferry over the sad world that came:
> The maws, and dens of beasts could not receive
> The bodies that those souls were frighted from;
> And even the graves were filled with men, yet living,
> Whose flight, and fear had mixed them, with the dead.　　(247–53)

As noted earlier, Jonson's version of Cicero's speech to the Senate taxed the patience of his audiences and contributed to the play's failure. Yet the issue is more complex than it first seems to be. Jonson meant his plays to be read as well as seen (hence the elaborate Folio edition of 1616), and the reader in possession of the facts about Cicero's life and times might take a certain relish in it. Cicero spent much of his career congratulating himself on quashing the Catilinarian conspiracy, and generations of unwilling students of Latin would concur that Cicero can be a bore. Thus his loquaciousness in the play is quite in character with the historical figure, and Catiline's riposte is both stinging and just: "He has strove to emulate this morning's thunder, / With his prodigious rhetoric" (4.464–5). These two lines also recall Aristophanes' mockery of the rhetorical contest between Aeschylus and Euripides, how they tossed rivers and mountains about in an effort to be judged the most bombastic of the dramatists (*The Frogs*

1379 ff.). A later speech by Jonson's Cicero is so piously self-serving that it is difficult to believe that Jonson did not intend it as a parody of Ciceronian rhetoric: "My fortune may forsake me, not my virtue: / That shall go with me, and before me, still, / And glad me, doing well, though I hear ill" (4.821–3).

The references to Mercury, the slightly disreputable god of speech and occult wisdom, remind us of the superficiality of Cicero's particular talent. Jonson's Catiline, perhaps recalling Vincenzo Cartari's remark (in his *Images of the Gods of the Ancients*) that the tongue was the appropriate sacrifice for Mercury, taunts Cicero by referring to him as "a boasting, insolent tongue-man" (4.161). Or as Cartari puts it: ". . . the ancients dedicated the tongue to Mercury; in addition to all of the other sacrifices in his honor, the ritual of drinking a little wine while sacrificing the tongues of victims to Mercury was his own particular and fitting form of worship" (translation mine).[15] The desecration of the historical Cicero's body, with his severed hands and head nailed to the apex of a speaking platform, the same hands that had written the *Phillipics* against Marc Antony and the loose-tongued head that had spoken against the tribune (Plutarch, *Lives*, "Cicero," sec. 49), form another part of the fine web of historical detail that Jonson has woven into this play. And Cicero, as an up-and-coming "new fellow" (501) or "upstart" is an unfortunate parallel to the gifted Jonson, forced to flatter those who were his betters in birth and station, but not in talent or genius. Thus the play is certainly based on classical sources, but the integration of contemporary themes with the incidents of the ancient past is almost seamless, and the subtlety of its allusions to related scraps of history as well as its evocation of the troubled, conspiracy-ridden Jacobean court reward the pains of the attentive playgoer or "the Reader extraordinary" that Jonson evokes in the preface to the play (HS 5: 432).

While *Catiline* has obvious classical roots, *Volpone, or The Fox*, a much more successful play, is less obviously indebted to the classics. Reminiscent of the quarrels between ancients and moderns in the seventeenth century, some critics, citing this work among others, would deny that Jonson was classical at all, and attempt to prove that all or most of his so-called classical effects emanate from the English tradition, ignoring Jonson's own declared esteem for the classics. The immense complexity and range of the sources for this play are noted by W. David Kay, who focuses on "the imaginative transformation Jonson worked on his sources":

> He elaborates Petronius' metaphor of legacy hunters as carrion-eaters into an extended beast fable in which the greedy Voltore, Corbaccio, and Corvino (vulture, raven, and crow) are outwitted by his Fox, whose willingness is inspired in part by Caxton's *The History of Reynard the Fox* and by Aesop's fables. Additional details of the cheats played by and on his unscrupulous suitors are derived from Horace and from Lucian's *Dialogues of the Dead*, which also supplies hints for Volpone's parasite Mosca. . . . The Venetian setting is linked to the world of his audience by

his sub-plot of the English travelers, Sir Politic and Lady Would-Be – the latter a version of the domineering, talkative women ridiculed by Juvenal and the Greek rhetorician Libanius, the former a satire on pretenders to intelligence about political intrigues. The pair are integrated into the beast fable by their parrot-like chatter and by Sir Pol's absurd device of disguising himself as a tortoise, while the whole play is further unified around the Erasmian theme of folly.[16]

Others see a balance in Jonson's work, in which he invokes the classics only when they are appropriate to the contexts of his writings. In *Volpone, or the Fox*, in fact, David C. Macpherson indicates how Jonson develops the myth of Venice to deal with both ancient Rome, which Protestant Englishmen felt had migrated to Venice, and contemporary Venice, known for its theatricality. While much of the plot is a careful imitation of the character Eumolpus in Petronius' *Satyricon*, and Volpone's behavior is modeled on the extravagances and depravities of the emperors Nero and Caligula, as communicated by Suetonius, the play also focuses on the theatricality of modern Venice, as well as the crimes, intrigues and power struggles of the Venetian court. Sir Pol, the Italianate Englishman, displays his ignorance of Venetian power politics, while Lady Politic Would-Be lacks both the beauty and the eloquence of the Venetian courtesan. In effect, Jonson has juxtaposed ancient Rome and contemporary Venice, but has rendered both meaningful to his English audience by showing basically English types displaying their greed, vanity, and incompetence in an exotic setting.[17] Jonson also makes extensive use of Lucian's *Dream, Or the Cock*, a satire on legacy hunting; many other Greek sources are mentioned or cited in *Volpone*, but most of them had already been cited by Lucian.

Jonson turns his art of imitation from authors to images in his masques, from classical history and literature to classical mythology. The loose form of the masque and its trivial purpose (court entertainment) allowed Jonson to be more overt in his classicism than in his other works. In *Pleasure Reconciled to Virtue*, for example, Jonson chooses a subject that might be termed the ultimate challenge of his career: to entertain as an artist, while promoting virtue as a moralist, or, to put it in Horace's terms from the *Art of Poetry*, to mix the useful with the sweet. Or, as Jonson puts it in his translation of *Horace His Art of Poetry*, The writer ". . . can apply / Sweet mixed with sour, to his Reader, so / As doctrine, and delight together go" (514–16).

Hercules confronts Comus, the god of revelry and celebration, whose attendants are bearing away Hercules' drinking cup. Mercury intervenes, and assures Hercules that Pleasure will be reconciled to Virtue, after they climb Atlas, the "hill of knowledge." This should remind the learned reader that Hercules was not permitted to reconcile the two: in fact, in the famous episode of Hercules at the Crossroads (retold from Prodicus in Cicero's *De Officiis* 1.32.118), the demigod Hercules had to choose between following the inviting *Voluptas* down the smooth path of Pleasure or the matronly *Virtus* down Virtue's rocky road. At the same time, the alternative tradition of Hercules as a womanizing glutton whose drinking cup was the size of a large boat, renders suspect his complaints about Comus' irreverence. Indeed, Mount Atlas was once Atlas himself, a devoted seeker after knowledge, who misspoke to Perseus and ending up becoming the mountain he used to climb to gaze at the stars. To pile irony upon irony, the truth seekers will be led across the mountain by Dædalus, the man who invented the labyrinth, the path that leads to nowhere, and that is sometimes identified with the complications of a work of art. And Mercury, who reassures Hercules about the reconciliation of Pleasure and Virtue, is, in a way, talking to himself, for the Gallic Hercules, the patron of learning and wisdom, was often confounded with the messenger god.

Here as elsewhere, Jonson draws on Renaissance sources of classical mythology as well as the classical authors themselves, including Natale Conti (*Mythologiae*, Venice, first edn. 1567), Vincenzo Cartari (*Imagini*, Venice, first edn. 1556 – see above), and some of the emblem writers, a genre that was initiated by Andrea Alciato's *Emblemata* (first edn. Venice, 1531). Jonson mentions these and other authors in the annotations to his poems and plays, introducing yet another complication in defining the nature of his classicism: do the sources he identifies constitute an actual record of his reading, or are they inflated testimonies to his self-proclaimed erudition? Both so and thus: Jonson was a proud man with much to be proud of. The breadth of his knowledge of classical literature impregnates every page of his writing, and leaves the critic in awe of his learning and the unfeigned joy he took in displaying it.

NOTES

1 I would like to thank Professor W. David Kay for assisting me in defining this concept.
2 William Blissett, "Roman Ben Jonson," in *Ben Jonson's 1616 Folio*, ed. Jennifer Brady and W. H. Herendeen (Newark: University of Delaware Press, 1991), 90–110.
3 William Kupersmith, "Ben Jonson, Juvenal, and Horace," in *Roman Satirists in Seventeenth-Century England* (Lincoln: University of Nebraska Press, 1975), 1–17.
4 Thomas M. Greene, *The Light in Troy* (New Haven: Yale University Press, 1982), 127, 132.
5 Carol C. Newlands, "Statius' Villa Poems and 'To Penshurst,'" *Classical and Modern Literature*, 8 (1988), 291–300.
6 J. H. M. Salmon, "Stoicism and Roman Example: Seneca and Tacitus in Jacobean England," *Journal of the History of Ideas*, 50 (1989), 199–225.
7 Samuel Holt Monk, ed., *The Works of John Dryden*, vol. 17 (Berkeley: University of California Press, 1971), 21, 57, 80.
8 All quotations from Jonson's works are from the edition of Herford and Simpson; they have been lightly modernized.
9 Katharine Eisaman Maus, *Ben Jonson and the Roman Frame of Mind* (Princeton: Princeton University Press, 1984), 18.

10 Lawrence V. Ryan, ed., *The Schoolmaster* (1570). *By Roger Ascham* (Ithaca, New York: Cornell University Press, 1967), 115.

11 Francis Bacon, *Advancement of Learning*, in *The Works of Francis Bacon*, ed. James Spedding, R. L. Ellis, and D. D. Heath (London, 1879), 3: 283–4.

12 Martial, *Martial Epigrams* (Cambridge, MA: Loeb Classical Library, 1952), 6.29.8.

13 Philostratus, *The Letters of Alciphron, Aelian And Philostratus* (Cambridge, MA: Loeb Classical Library, 1949).

14 Tacitus, *Annals* (Cambridge, MA: Loeb Classical Library, 1963).

15 Vincenzo Cartari, *Le imagini de i dei de gli antichi* (Venice, 1571), 329.

16 W. David Kay, *Ben Jonson: A Literary Life* (London: Macmillan, 1995), 89.

17 David C. McPherson, "Theatricality and the Myth of Venus in *Volpone*" in *Shakespeare, Jonson, and the Myth of Venice* (Newark, Delaware: University of Delaware Press, 1990), 91–116.

13

STANLEY STEWART

Jonson's criticism

I

Browsing among the shelves of Jonsoniana leaves no doubt that Jonson is known primarily as a playwright. It would not be surprising if, of the thousands who remember *Volpone* or *The Alchemist* with amusement, most have never heard of "Penshurst," and as many may have forgotten or never learned that the lyrics they sang in childhood ("Drink to me, only, with thine eyes, / And I will pledge with mine") are Jonson's. Even so, literary tradition has been more generous to Jonson the poet than to Jonson the critic; he is firmly established as the premier courtly poet of Jacobean and Caroline England, and, as such, progenitor of self-proclaimed "Sons of Ben," who sought, even during the Civil War and Interregnum, when courtly values were not in vogue, to emulate Jonson's poetic style. While loyal to the principles of his poetic practice, the Cavaliers were not so enamored of Jonson's interest in literary theory and philosophy. Critical theory was not for fearless prisoners and exiles like Lovelace and Suckling. And yet Jonson looked to his Roman predecessors for more than models of poetic and dramatic forms.

The greatest English literary critic of his time, Jonson, like many critics practicing today, made no keen distinction between literary theory and philosophy. He considered poetry the product of an acquired skill ("Who casts to write a living line must sweat"),[1] but he did not believe that discipline alone would produce real poetry. Only "a good poet" could do that, and "a good poet's made, as well as born" (455). Literary creation involved, not just facility with language, but the totality of the poet's being. "[I]f men," he wrote, "will impartially, and not asquint, look toward the offices and function of a poet, they will easily conclude to themselves the impossibility of any man's being the good poet, without first being a good man" (1). At first glance, this aphorism from the dedicatory epistle to *Volpone* might look like an obligatory bow to the two great universities for granting Jonson Honorary Master of Arts degrees. But Jonson took the occasion "to justify the bounty of [their] act," suggesting that, since society afforded "too much licence [to] poetasters," decent subjects might ask whether, in matters more important than the granting of honorary degrees, university authorities exercised their power responsibly. Like Sidney, Jonson thought poetry in need of defense; but, unlike him, he aligned his apology *with*, rather than *against*, attitudes registered in Gosson's *School of Abuse*. Both nay-sayers thought the art corrupt; but, for Jonson, the corruption of "poetasters" had deprived "the poet" of his rightful status. And here, he echoed Sidney rather than Gosson:

> He [i.e., the poet] that is said to be able to inform young men to all good disciplines, inflame grown men to all great virtues, keep old men in their best and supreme state, or as they decline to childhood, recover them to their first strength; that comes forth the interpreter and arbiter of nature, a teacher of things divine no less than human, a master in manners; and can alone (or with a few) effect the business of mankind . . . (1–2)

Current practitioners, with their "inverted" natures, were not "poets" in the "supreme" sense just described, but scribblers jotting trivial marks on pages, putting powerless words in the mouths of actors. It is the playwright *manqué* who most traduced the name of poetry with "ribaldry, profanation, blasphemy," and by whom "all licence of offence to God and man is practised" (2).

For reasons integral to his conception of poetry, Jonson takes the calumny heaped on the theatre personally, bristling especially at offenses perceived in productions over which he exercised little control. Not only does Jonson deny that his plays traduce anyone, but he insists that his satire assails only "creatures . . . worthy to be taxed". In this way, Jonson distances himself from the immorality endemic, "especially in dramatic or (as they term it) stage poetry." Indeed, he issues a public disclaimer: "I can (and from a most clear conscience) affirm that I have ever trembled to think toward the least profaneness; have loathed the use of such foul and unwashed bawdry as is now made the food of the scene." Jonson defends himself because his detractors, by "deciphering of everything," look at base characters in his plays, and perceive gossip about real people, "utter[ing] their own virulent malice under other men's simplest meanings"(1–2). Despite the fabricated charge of scandal, *Volpone* is, for Jonson, an ostensive definition of poetry fulfilling its "principal end, to inform men, in the best reason of living"(3), and, as such, a restoration of poetry "to her primitive habit, feature, and majesty" (4). It is true that *Volpone* deals with mimics, cheats, bawds, and buffoons, but only in accord with "the office of a comic poet," which is "to imitate justice, and instruct to life, as well as purity of language, or stir up gentle affections" (3).

In the hurly-burly of the real world, true poetry is often misunderstood. "The ends" may be "to profit, and delight," but sometimes people take "impertinent exception" to "things (like truths) well feigned," believing themselves libeled under the guise of a stage character (HS 5:164). Whether a playwright – knowing and loving the Truth – "well feigns" the actualities of the world outside the poem is an ethical no less than an artistic question. The Sir John Daw of *Epicœne* is not only a bad poet, but also a plagiarist and a liar. Likewise, in *Poetaster*, Jonson makes poetry, quite literally, the stuff of dramatic character. Ovid, Horace, and Virgil recite lines from *Amores*, the *Odes* and *Epodes,* and the *Æneid*, which Jonson translates or adapts, in effect, dramatizing character traits by making the authors' poetry available to the audience in English. Jonson puts fatuous and pompous language in the mouths of his stand-ins for Dekker and Marston; but Ovid's "fancies and furies" are not the subject of ridicule. Instead, Jonson uses Ovid to advance a critical principle: Without ethical restraint, even a talented poet fails to merit the highest praise. Jonson does not "tax" Crispinus (Marston) and Demetrius (Dekker) because they are bad poets. They can't help that. But they demean themselves *and* the art by thinking of poetry only as a means to advancement at court.

With Ovid, we have a different story. Not a poetaster, but wallowing in an excess of youthful passion, he flouts the will of Julia's father, Cæsar Augustus, hence, Roman law. This makes him an unfortunate lover, but not a bad poet. At the same time, not all decent men are good poets or literary critics. Ovid Senior wants his son to give up poetry for law studies, in order to make his way in the world. To his son, this practical wisdom seems like a craven and coercive assault on love *and* art. The audience knows that it is neither. The older man thinks Homer a fool, and so shows little promise as a literary critic. But he does urge his son toward an honorable pathway to worldly success, which is no trivial artistic concern. For by ignoring the real world, the poet puts everything, including art, at risk. The audience knows, too, that Ovid's reputation as a poet would be very different were it to rest solely on the *Amores*. Cæsar's first impulse, in reaction to Ovid's defiance, is to kill him. This makes the dramatic contrast all the more pointed as literary criticism: Horace and Virgil align themselves with Cæsar's law, becoming justly, by their mastery of poetic technique *and* of themselves, the arbiters of *ars poetica*.

II

Jonson's characterization of Ovid, Virgil, and Horace by English translations or adaptation of their verse is consistent with his belief that authors reveal themselves in their work. Just as Dekker and Marston recognized themselves in Crispinus and Demetrius, they also saw Jonson's attempt to represent himself as Horace in *Poetaster*,[2] perhaps in signature lines like these:

> Swell me a bowl with lusty wine,
> Till I may see the plump Lyaeus swim
> Above the brim:
> I drink, as I would write,
> In flowing measure, filled with flame, and sprite.   (HS 3.1.8–12)

Apparently, translation says as much about the poet-translator as about the poet translated. Not only did Jonson imitate Horace by shaping the poet-critic for the stage, but he also translated the *Ars Poetica*, and in fact, with the possible exception of Aristotle's *Poetics*, made that work more a part of his critical personality than any other. In prefatory remarks to *Sejanus*, he claims that he was working on "Observations upon Horace his *Art of Poetry*" (HS 4:350), and in "An Execration upon Vulcan," we read that the fire destroyed "All the old Venusine in poetry, / And lighted by the Stagirite, could spy / Was there mad[e] English" (367). After the fire, Jonson translated the *Ars Poetica* again, but his Aristotelian remarks on the work were, as far as we know, not revived. We must conclude that, for Jonson, then, translation of the *Ars Poetica*, more than a labor of love, amounts to a statement of his critical manifesto.

Although Jonson's translation of *Ars Poetica* has had its detractors, in 1666, Alexander Brome "borrowed [it] to crown the rest" in *Poems of Horace . . . Rendered into English Verse By Several Persons* (A5ᵛ), which takes as the "standard-bearers of wit and judgment, Denham and Waller" (A6ᵛ). In opening remarks to the collection, which includes Fanshaw and Cowley, Brome answers the Earl of Roscommon's reproof of Jonson for translating Horace into heroic couplets, a choice that links Jonson's *Ars Poetica* to the Augustan taste which, by mid-century, was gaining ascendance. While our ear may favor Roscommon's lively blank verse, or the prose of Christopher Smart's translation, the age of Dryden and Pope was dawning. And just as Denham's *Coopers Hill* and Waller's *On St. James's Park* are the forerunners of *Windsor Forest* and Thomson's *The Seasons*, Jonson's verse translation of *Ars Poetica* (HS 8:305–37) is the Caroline precursor of Pope's *Essay on Criticism*:

> Take, therefore, you that write, still, matter fit
> Unto your strength, and long examine it,
> Upon your shoulders. Prove what they will bear,
> And what they will not. Him, whose choice doth rear
> His matter to his power, in all he makes,
> Nor language, nor clear order ere forsakes. (54–9)

Brome correctly sensed "the style and ear of these times" (A2), and, likewise, with its emphasis firmly on circumspection and decorum, Jonson's translation of Horace anticipates the critical trend. The strong, monosyllabic, imperative mode suggests the confidence and experience of the elder mentor: "Take," "fit," "write," "still," "strength," "long," "it." The virtue admired here is clarity – "clear order" – and Jonson anticipates the perspective of *Coopers Hill*, to whose speaker the Thames appears to flow "so transparent, pure, and clear, / That had the self-enamored youth gazed here, / So fatally deceived he had not been, / While he the bottom, not his face had seen."[3] In this distinctly Royalist context, clarity goes hand in hand with truth and restraint. As in Denham and Pope, so in Jonson's translation of the *Ars Poetica*, end-stopped couplets convey a sense of the poet's confidence in settled principle.

Given its importance to Jonson, *Ars Poetica* deserves a close look. For "clear order" notwithstanding, whether translated into couplets, blank verse, or prose, the work is not a rigorously organized "theory of literature." Rather, as its verse epistle form suggests, a family friend offers advice on the pleasures and perils of poetic composition "To the Pisos, Father and Sons." There are, though, dominant themes around which Horace organizes the poem. The first of these is structural unity. What, he asks, would the Pisos think of a painter who drew a woman's head attached to a fish's tail by a bird's torso, stuck with feathers? Credulity depends on a serious acquaintance with reality and the proper means of representation. The poet represents life truly, not as in a sick man's distorted dreams, but putting things together appropriately, with the parts fitting the whole. If he takes care to match the subject to his talent, the right words come in the right way at the right time. For diction is important, and Homer is the model. Since some words lose their meaning, as others that have died return to life, it is risky to depart from tradition.

Style matters, too, so the poet keeps the second important standard – of decorum – in mind. Comedy and tragedy sound different because diction fits character, lest the audience laugh *at*, rather than *with*, the poet. Imitation is the key to consistency and decorum. In keeping characters true to life, the poet follows either nature or tradition. Since originality is hard to achieve, it is better to take a familiar tale – say, the fall of Troy – than to dream up something entirely new. By imitating the ancients correctly, while avoiding rote repetition, the poet can salvage a measure of individuality in a poem. Again, much depends on study and decorum. The poet must know how the subject behaves and speaks before sending actors on stage. Just as old men don't talk like young ones, every epoch has its own norms of speech and behavior. Horrors should never be witnessed on stage; and propriety insists that endings should not occur gratuitously, with God descending in a basket to set things right. Instead, events should develop through interaction of believable characters, who are, depending on their actions and motives, either supported or criticized by a properly integrated chorus.

Originally, the chorus was backed by the delicate strains of the flute, but as cities grew with military conquests, music became a more clamorous part of the drama, and overblown religious matter and speeches found their way to the stage. Drinking and carousing led to a confusion of tragedy with inappropriate comic speech and apparel. While some comic relief might work in tragedy, the form never lowers itself to tavern speech. At the same time, tragedy should never be so high-blown that the audience can't tell whether a king or a slave is talking. Again, success comes from the proper treatment in the proper order of believable events and common usage, with the study of Greek models guiding the poet to proper metrical expression.

Poets aim to teach or delight, or both at once. So the poet, brief and to the point, never taxes the audience with impossible situations, and never dwells to distraction on minor errors. Even Homer wasn't perfect. Poems, like pictures, differ: some please at once, while others require time and repetition. The youngest, even with a father to guide him, should pay special attention. Mediocre expression ruins the entire work. Unmindful of this principle, perversely, people who know nothing about poetry insist upon writing, often using their social position to justify what they say. It would be wiser to submit one's writing to a loving father or to an honest critic (Horace), but only after it has sat for nine years. For once published, harmful words can't be withdrawn.

People ask whether the poet creates by nature or nurture. The answer is: both. Besides study, the poet needs to revise his work, for it is better to correct minor errors than face public derision. Successful poetry is more than the rantings of a madman, although remembering that Empedocles jumped into Etna's volcano should give men pause. If a poet wants to destroy himself, it is best not to interfere, for the savior easily becomes the poet's victim.

Clearly, Jonson enjoyed this ending of *Ars Poetica*, which comes close to the guarded threat in his own *Ruines of Time*. Powers that be must beware of the poet, for he is, finally, a power unto himself, whom it is risky to oppress or ignore. As in *Poetaster*, so in *Ars Poetica*, ethical and creative integrity are values in the real world, which seems, at times, oblivious to the fact that "Orpheus, a priest, [was] speaker for the Gods," that "Amphion . . . built the Theban towers" (479, 483), that, as Shelley would put the Horatian dictum centuries later, "poets are the unacknowledged legislators of the world."

III

If we can justly consider Jonson's verse translation of *Ars Poetica* a precursor of Pope's *Essay on Criticism*, then *Timber* is, *a fortiori*, the prose analogue to Pope's *Essay on Man*. O. B. Hardison fairly describes *Discoveries* as "fragmentary" in structure, but still "Jonson's most complete critical statement," and "one of the most significant literary documents of its time."[4] Printed with the 1640 Folio of *The Works of Benjamin Jonson: The Second Volume, Timber, or Discoveries* is paginated with *Ars Poetica* and *The English Grammar*. Critics have been wary of the fact that Jonson's literary executor, Sir Kenelm Digby, probably "gathered up Jonson's loose papers and handed them over to the publisher just as he found them" (HS 8:558). Not only has the 1640 Folio never enjoyed the authorial prestige of 1616, but there are undeniable signs of incompleteness in this work in particular, the entry from Martial on which the work abruptly ends, for instance. Nor is Maurice Castelain alone in arguing that *Discoveries* be "left out of the Jonsonian canon" on the grounds that "practically, the book is not his."[5] By Castelain's reckoning, only some hundred lines "belong to Jonson." In the same vein, J. E. Spingarn pronounced *Discoveries* "merely a commonplace book."[6] We might recall that Lady Mary Montagu made the same complaint about Pope's *Essay on Criticism* – that it was "all stolen."[7] Pope, of course, made no secret that he wrote the *Essay* in imitation of Horace.[8] Like Pope, Jonson had an idea of imitation in mind very different from the one that came to dominate, with Romanticism, a century and a half later. Still, thanks to the indefatigable efforts of scholars like Castelain and Spingarn, we know that a good part of Jonson's *Discoveries* is translated from mostly Latin authors: Seneca, Horace, Cicero, Plutarch, Quintilian, Martial, Juvenal. Jonson drew also from Renaissance forebears – Erasmus, Vives, Machiavelli, Lipsius, and Bacon – as he did from Aristotle's *Poetics*. Furthermore, he translated numerous passages from Heinsius, whose edition of Horace he probably used in translating *The Art of Poetry*.

We can appreciate knowing the exact sources of *Discoveries* without acceding to the "negative conclusion" that "[t]he deep and noble thoughts" admired by Swinburne, who lavished praise on the work, belong, not to Jonson, but "to their right owners" (Castelain xxiv). Nor should we be surprised that a commonplace book preserves traces of its sources. The problem is that, when Castelain tenders those Latin sources, line by line, he undoes the process – the ebb and flow of reading, translation, reflection, and adjustment – that characterizes the *Explorata*. In effect, Jonson tells us how to read the work: *Timber, or, Discoveries, Made upon men and matter, as they have flowed out of his daily readings, or had their reflux to his peculiar notion of the times* (521). Titles, subtitles, and epigraphs from Persius and Statius converge in such a way as to make *Timber*, *Discoveries*, *Silva*, and *Explorata* situational synonyms. Jonson's motto, which he affixed to most of the books in his library, was *tanquam explorator* – always the explorer. In tandem, they suggest that Jonson's intellectual landscape is perpetually exploding out of or imploding into his reading experience, as the author's reflections either "flowed out of his daily readings," or flowed ("had their reflux") back into them, through his individual ("peculiar") perceptions of surrounding events.

By juxtaposing the title and subtitles of his reflections with references to Persius and Statius, Jonson provides a glimpse into the way in which this process of literary exchange works. Reading relates to conduct, and writing, in such a way as to induce awareness of the area or aspect of appositeness, between reading and quotidian events. Thus, in the epigraph from Persius, the poet, in the guise of Socrates, rails at Alcibiades for his ethical blindness. Alcibiades would govern, but he lives the life of a sybarite. So the wise man ends his railing with an explicit imperative on the title page of *Discoveries*: "Live in / Your own house and learn what a bare lodging it is."[9] The nexus between the Fourth Satire of Persius and Jonson is, again, in the *Ars Poetica*. As Schelling, Herford and Simpson, and Donaldson point out, Jonson is alluding to the Socratic dialogues. In form as well as content, Persius draws from Xenophon, Cicero, Epictetus, and Plato, but especially from a context which Persius shares with "[t]he well known precept in the *Ars Poetica*," which owes much to the wealth of attention given to the First Alcibiades of the pseudo-Plato.[10] Jonson translates:

> The very root of writing well, and spring
> Is to be wise; thy matter first to know;
> Which the Socratic writings best can show:
> And, where the matter is provided still,
> There words will follow, not against their will.
>
> (HS 8:325, 440–4)

In the tradition of "Socratic writings," Socrates was the true savant. Thus, in the Fourth Satire, Socrates reproaches Alcibiades for his appalling failure in self-knowledge. In Jonson's time, *Nosce teipsum* was a pervasive motif in poetry and drama. Scholars trace the sources of Sir John Davies' poem by that name to a host of sources, including Spenser, but the wellspring of the Delphic instruction was in Plato, especially as Christianized by Pico and Ficino. Thus, in the front matter of *Discoveries*, Jonson assumes a connection between the title, subtitle, the Fourth Satire of Persius, the *Silvae* of Statius, and the rich intellectual background surrounding the Socratic dialogues of the pseudo-Plato. The comprehensiveness of the reading involved suggests the intellectual and moral values of a literary temperament marked by self-awareness and self-discipline.

Properly regulated poetic temperaments express themselves in different ways. Many seventeenth-century poets call collections of their poems, including translations in verse, *silva*, modelled on the *Silvae* of Statius. On the verso of the title page of *Discoveries*, we read that *silva* is a Latin synonym for "timber." So Jonson places *Discoveries* in the tradition of Renaissance *silva*, which includes *The Forest*, *The Underwood*, Fletcher's *Silva Poetica*, Herbert's *Lucus*, Cowley's *Silva*, Dryden's *Silvae*, and, of course, the famous collection by the most famous "son of Ben," Robert Herrick's *Hesperides*.[11] These collections aren't "miscellanies" in the same sense as *Tottel's Miscellany* (1557). The subtitle of Cowley's *Silva* (1636) emphasizes the occasional nature of his "Verses," several of which

182

are quite personal. Dryden justifies his *Sylvae* (1685), occasioned by "Lord Roscommon's Essay on translated Verse" (A2^v), with his own theory of translation and decorum (A3^v). The definition provided in Latin for *sylva* in *Discoveries* seems to support O. B. Hardison's view that "Jonson's most complete critical statement" is a "fragmentary" or "indiscriminate" collection of aphorisms, meditations, sketches, proverbs, and essays (269). Critics have tried to impose order on the work by numbering, rearranging, deleting, and altering entries. Such editorial choices are not necessarily incompatible with the view that Jonson's recurrent interests impart to a sequence of discrete readings a cumulative thematic coherence. For in Jonson's time, students learned in part by acquiring the wisdom of the past in the manner of the *Adages* of Erasmus and of Cicero's *Sententiae*, in commonplace books. Related to Renaissance miscellanies and florilegia, the commonplace book, as employed in English schools, was aimed at developing the student's character and writing style as well as at providing a solid ground of authority and wit in argument.[12] If the aim of the commonplace book was to accumulate Latin quotations representing common wisdom, *Discoveries* employs translation into English of those quotations which, for Jonson, best suit the development of a poet.

Jonson's method involves translation into English, but its typicality in other respects explains why remarks in *Discoveries* apply to his translation of *Ars Poetica* as well as to questions about the "originality" of the prose work. Both are products of translation, and both exhibit a Horatian theory of the poet's use of tradition:

> The third requisite of our poet or maker is imitation, to be able to convert the substance, or riches of another poet to his own use. To make choice of one excellent man above the rest, and so to follow him till he grow very he, or so like him as the copy may be mistaken for the principal. (585)

Castelain cites the source of this passage in *Ars Poetica* (131–5), in which Horace cautions against adhering too closely to literary precedent to prove Jonson's slavish dependence. We must expect even a poor translation to betray its source, but in fact what follows the passage quoted is a Jonsonian amalgam of disparate readings. The successful poet will not ingurgitate the chosen author in the way a wild beast "swallows what it takes in crude, raw, or undigested." The idea is "to concoct, divide, and turn all into nourishment" (2495–8). Here, Horatian lines emerge in a figurative context of proper diet. In the *Ars Poetica*, we read that one ought not to "imitate servilely (as Horace saith)," and Jonson agrees. But he adjusts that admonition with a gustatory figure of imitation as a transformative mode. For him, there is no way to avoid the exercise of critical judgment, or discernment. Jonson does more than translate Horace in the manner typical of commonplace books, as if to preserve or prove a point. He makes Horace's *Ars*

Poetica so much his own that he "becomes very he," so imbued by the substance of Horace's thought that he is able to compound and improve upon it by his recognition of the relevance of Macrobius. Even some dreams, regardless of their cause, impart oracular wisdom.[13] To ask whether, figuratively, this means that Horace becomes Jonson, or the other way around, is to miss the point of how important intelligent reading is in Jonson's critical scheme.

The proper poet, no less than the proper critic, chooses one above all other texts – "one excellent man above the rest." That choice is the first step only in a process of conversion of what is important in that right author "to [the poet's or the critic's] own use" (2492–3). This emphasis on "one man" indicates Jonson's insistence on "understanding," no less than on good taste. The poet must make the right choice, and when he does, the "occasion," properly ingested and digested, leads through nourishment to a new creation – not just the "matter" of Horace, but the substance of Horace's thought as it "flowed out of [Jonson's] daily Readings," having their "reflux to his peculiar notion of the times." In Jonson's recognition of the relevance of Horace and related readings to the immediate circumstances, Horace becomes more than just another dead Latin poet. His text finds new life, as Jonson follows Horace following his ancient models following Nature. But, as Castelain's impressive source hunting leaves no doubt, Jonson isn't just recycled Horace, any more than Virgil is a Latin translation of Homer. Jonson's "peculiar notion of the times" creates a new amalgam of thought.

We should note that Jonson doesn't advise or practice reading and rereading *only* one "excellent" author. On the contrary, he favors a "multiplicity of reading, which maketh a full man" (2507–8). In a manner typical of Renaissance syncretism, he thinks exposure to a wide range of predecessors opens the way for a new perspective. Of course, he devours, as it were, one text at a time, but it is Jonson whose inner world and poetic expression is shaped by these readings. In a similar vein, centuries later, T. S. Eliot would agree that the widest possible reading negates the pernicious influence of a single strong author or outlook, opening the way for an informed and independent moral judgment.[14]

Just as Jonson chose to translate Horace rather than Longinus, and *Ars Poetica* rather than *To Augustus,* so every choice of reading and translation into a commonplace book of wisdom expresses Jonson's unique perspective. Yes, many, but not all, entries in *Discoveries* are translations of Jonson's readings. But the marginal headings and the subtitles of the work proclaim his indebtedness in such a way as to characterize the shaping of a unique literary being. Jonson thought that the best writing took its rise from dedicated reading, especially, but not solely, of the classics. He was an avid reader of poets of his own time, and of the recent past. In *The English Grammar*, he rejects the notion that English literature was "diseased" by "rudeness and barbarism" (HS 8:465). His study of the

English language assumes that, by learning English, foreigners would overcome their prejudice against Britons. The examples of English that Jonson uses to appeal to "experience, observation, sense, [and] induction," are, like the readings and "reflux" in *Discoveries*, not randomly recorded from daily life. They come from the best of English authors: Chaucer, Gower, Lydgate, More, Foxe, Norton, Jewell, and, finally, "out of that excellent oration of Sir John Cheeke" (HS 8:553). So, Jonson says, the best English writing represents the English people in the most favorable manner. In the same way, Jonson's examples of orators in *Discoveries* are a telling individual judgment of Jonson's standard of "excellent" men, in whom the state may wisely invest its destiny. That Jonson knows he is following in the footsteps of Plato and Seneca hardly lessens the selection of virtuous orators, who know and govern themselves.

Without insisting on sharp dividing lines, we can see how Jonson's readings and reflections cluster around the gravamen of three perspectives. Most of the entries in the first cluster (say, lines 1–530) are shorter, more general, and more cryptic than those that follow, and they touch on a wide range of topics related to principles, instances, and practices of good order in life and writing. They lead up to a disquisition on "Memory, of all the powers of the mind . . . the most delicate and frail" (535, 487–8), the very capacity that the commonplace book was designed to aid.

Section two of the work (531–1712) deals with "truth," which is "man's proper good" (540–1). The wise man knows the truth and acts upon it. Truth is the central concern of all good writing and speaking. No doubt differences among men in wit and judgment affect statecraft and poetry. For instance, actors show themselves poor critics when they praise Shakespeare, claiming that he "never blotted out line" (660). Proper discrimination in literature eludes them and the multitude, who prefer Heath and Taylor to Spenser. In their vulgarity, they miss the aim of writing, valuing "rude things greater than polished" (652–3). The nexus between discriminate reading and proper conduct lies here – in one's judgment: "This is the danger, when vice becomes a precedent" (720–1). Adulation of the multitude is no guarantee of literary judgment, for this very vice appears in esteemed authors, including "all the essayists, even their master Montaigne" (736):

> These, in all they write, confess still what books they have read last, and therein their own folly, so much, that they bring it to the stake raw and undigested; not that the place did need it neither, but that they thought themselves furnished, and would vent it. (737–41)

So what do critics mean when they speak of Montaigne as a writer whose "naturals" excel? Unfortunately, he is like those critics who "turn over all books . . . without choice," surrendering their judgment to nonsense, "by which means it happens that what they have discredited and impugned in one work, they have before or after extolled the same in another" (731–5).

Having said this, Jonson takes positive examples, including More, Wyatt, Surrey, Sidney, Hooker, and Ralegh, into consideration. Above them all stands "one of the greatest men, and most worthy of admiration, that had been in many ages" – the greatest of Englishmen and the greatest speaker and writer, Sir Francis Bacon. For Jonson, the sign of a true patriot and statesman, and Bacon was one, was his loyalty to "the commonwealth of learning." He understood that "schools [were] the seminaries of state" (935–6). So Jonson praises Bacon for writing *De Augmentus scientiarum*, believing that his magnum opus aimed at the highest literary goal: to "instruct to good life, inform manners, no less [to] persuade and lead men" (1040–1). Bacon, then, is Jonson's contemporary example of the wise man, through whom knowledge of the truth shines out in his speech and writing.

Just as Bacon laid out a plan for a "seminary of state," so the final section (1651–2843) begins with a personal address to a nobleman on the subject of educating the young, and amounts to a version of Jonson's *Poetics*. Following Horace's *ad Pisos*, Jonson writes to a noble father about the education of his sons, "and especially to the advancement of their studies" (1652–3), with a mind to teaching them to write. Throughout this section, Jonson resorts to his recurring themes: To write well, one must both read and imitate the best authors, work hard to perfect one's own style, and exercise proper judgment regarding a novice's age and experience. In diction, the orator exercises restraint and common sense, following the ancients as they follow Nature. Bacon taught that "the study of words is the first distemper of learning; vain matter the second; and a third distemper is deceit, or the likeness of truth" (2110–12). To ignore his advice is to risk appearing "either sluttish or foolish" (2114). For, as Bacon writes, truth comes, not from Aristotle, but from "discrediting falsehood" (2124–5). By the same token, good judgment is never swayed by the whim of fashion. Properly deemed a "maker," the poet creates fictions that imitate life. By offering "a dulcet and gentle philosophy,"[15] the poet delights while he instructs, informed by "natural wit" (2434), which he must exercise in order to perfect.

NOTES

1 *Ben Jonson*, ed. Ian Donaldson (Oxford: Oxford University Press, 1985), 455; unless otherwise indicated, all citations from Jonson in my text are from page numbers in this edition. Throughout, following Donaldson, I modernize the text, ignore obvious printers' errors, meaningless italics, capitals, and small capitals. Unless otherwise indicated, all texts published before 1700 bear a London imprint.

2 For a discussion of this exchange, see David Riggs, *Ben Jonson: A Life* (Cambridge, MA: Harvard University Press, 1989), 72–84.

3 *The Poetical Works of Sir John Denham*, ed. Theodore Howard Banks (New Haven: Yale University Press, 1928), 79.

4 O. B. Hardison, Jr., *English Literary Criticism: The Renaissance* (New York: Meredith Publishing, 1963), 269.

5 Maurice Castelain, *Ben Jonson. Discoveries; A Critical Edition with an Introduction and Notes on the True Purport and Genesis of the Book* (Paris: Librarie Hachette, 1906), vi.

6 J. E. Spingarn, "The Sources of Jonson's 'Discoveries,'" *Modern Philology* 2.4 (1905): 10.

7 John Conington, "The Poetry of Pope," *Oxford Essays* (London, 1858), 15.

8 See E. Audra and Aubrey Williams, *Pastoral Poetry and An Essay on Criticism* (London: Methuen, 1961), Introduction, esp. 223.

9 *The Satires of Persius*, trans. W. S. Merwin (Bloomington: Indiana University Press, 1961), 81.

10 Cynthia S. Dessen, *Iuntura Callidus Acri: A Study of Persius' Satires* (Urbana: University of Illinois Press, 1968), 103, 104.

11 Alastair Fowler, *Kinds of Literature: An Introduction to the Theory of Genres and Modes* (Cambridge: Harvard University Press, 1982), 134–5.

12 Ann Moss, *Printed Commonplace-Books and the Structuring of Renaissance Thought* (Oxford: Clarendon Press, 1996), 215.

13 Macrobius, *Commentary on the Dream of Scipio*, trans. William Harris Stahl (New York: Columbia University Press, 1952), chapter 2.

14 T. S. Eliot, *Essays Ancient and Modern* (London: Faber and Faber, 1936), 102–8.

15 Here, perhaps, Jonson echoes Strabo, who held that "poetry is a kind of elementary philosophy" (*The Geography of Strabo*, trans. Horace Leonard Jones, 8 vols. [London: William Heinemann, 1917–49], 1:23).

14

ROBERT C. EVANS

Jonson's critical heritage

Ben Jonson's reputation stands higher now than at any time since his own era, when it perhaps surpassed Shakespeare's. Today he ranks second in the great age of English drama and is considered one of its very best poets. He continued in high esteem after the 1660 Restoration, but later his fortunes fell as Shakespeare's rose. By the early 1800s his influence languished: his works were sometimes read and respected, occasionally admired, but almost never staged and perhaps as rarely loved. The Romantics seldom valued this professedly classical author, but it was now (ironically) that his fortunes rebounded. He found a devoted editor (William Gifford) whose defenses, though fierce, were usually factual. By now, too, Shakespeare's clear triumph made further battles pointless. Thus began a fairer, more methodical assessment of Jonson. By the mid-twentieth century a renaissance was in full swing, helped by the superb Oxford edition (1925–52). Finally, at century's end, Jonson once again seemed truly central to discussions of his period. Scholarship proliferated; his best plays were regularly (if not widely) performed; and even his "dotages" won some renewed respect. If Jonson were living at this hour, even he might be pleased.

In the past century, Jonson has benefitted from diverse analytical attention. Judd Arnold, for instance, stressed the playwright's regard for his fictional "gallants," while Jonas Barish explicated his jagged prose. Anne Barton surveyed every play, particularly rehabilitating the "dotages" (as had Larry Champion). Helena Baum studied Jonson's satire and didacticism; L. A. Beaurline and J. G. Sweeney (among others) discussed his complex relations with audiences; Daniel Boughner related him to Machiavelli; and J. A. Bryant, Jr. examined his satiric moralism. Like C. R. Baskerville, Alan Dessen placed Jonson in the morality-play tradition; Aliki Dick and Coburn Gum connected him to Aristophanes; while Douglas Duncan related him to Lucian. Richard Dutton studied his development, dealings with censorship, and innovative criticism, while John Enck surveyed the comedies and Willa McClung and Mary Chan studied his use of music. Like David McPherson, James A. Riddell, and Stanley Stewart, Robert C. Evans explored Jonson's reading, even as he also followed the lead of Martin Butler (and many others) in trying to situate Jonson historically. Wesley Trimpi, Judith Gardiner, George Johnston, Earl Miner, and Sara van den Berg thoughtfully surveyed the poems, while Jonathan Haynes studied the social relations of some plays, and Richard Helgerson related Jonson to the literary system. Gabriele Jackson studied his vision and judgment; L. C. Knights pioneered an economic approach; Mina Kerr traced Jonson's influence; and Alvin Kernan contributed seminal ideas on satire. Robert Knoll stressed the playwright's Christian humanism, while Calvin Thayer provided an excellent overview of the dramas. Alexander Leggatt emphasized common ideas used in varied genres; Joseph Loewenstein examined the "echo" myth; Katharine Eisaman Maus and Richard Peterson studied debts to Rome; while Russ McDonald (among others) explored links with Shakespeare. John Meagher and Stephen Orgel broke ground in studying the masques, as did Allan Gilbert, Leah S. Marcus, and Dale Randall, while Edward Partridge spotlighted imagery. George Rowe and Robert Watson scrutinized rivalries; Frances Teague traced performances of *Bartholomew Fair*; and Freda Townsend studied Jonson's comic artistry. Robert Wiltenburg looked at self-love, William Slights at secrecy, Anthony Johnson at architecture, C. F. Wheeler at classical myth, Peter Womack at dialogical impulses, Barbara Johnson at women in the poems, Bruce Boehrer at digestive metaphors, and Richard Allen Cave at Jonson's theatricality. A superb survey was prepared by Claude Summers and Ted-Larry Pebworth, and similar works were offered by Rosalind Miles and others. Miles wrote a basic biography, following a fine lead by Marchette Chute. David Riggs published the best recent (and most strongly psychological) biography, while Ian Donaldson plans to cap his varied, life-long focus on Jonson with a major biographical study.[1]

Most modern attention focuses on *Volpone, Epicœne, The Alchemist*, and *Bartholomew Fair*, although *Sejanus* is also widely respected, as is *Every Man in his Humour. Every Man out of his Humour, Cynthia's Revels,* and *Poetaster* still tend to be seen more as data than as art, although *Poetaster* can be highly entertaining. The same is true of *The Devil Is an Ass*, often considered the first "late" play, while *The New Inn* and especially the uncompleted *Sad Shepherd* are also much admired. *The Case Is Altered* is considered promising early work, while such late dramas as *The Staple of News, The Magnetic Lady*, and *A Tale of a Tub* have generally been more disdained than praised. So has *Catiline*, although that work *was* apparently widely read and esteemed in the seventeenth century.

The following survey of responses to the four greatest plays emphasizes especially both the earliest and the most recent reactions.[2]

Volpone

Volpone, Jonson's first masterpiece, succeeded immediately. When it was first published, Jonson was commended for his skill, genius, toil, wit, craft, grace, subtlety, innovation, and sense of structure, and was hailed for emulating the ancients, attacking vice, and observing the unities of time and place.[3] Later commentators claimed he had been inspired (perhaps by wine). His ghost was imagined boasting about the work, and John Cotgrave quoted *Volpone* nine times in his 1655 *English Treasury of Wit and Language*. In 1662 Margaret Cavendish, wife of one of Jonson's patrons and herself an author, defended her own writing by observing that the play violated the unity of time, and she even considered both *Volpone* and *The Alchemist* too long. Yet she still called *Volpone* a masterpiece of wit and "laboring thought."

In 1665, Samuel Pepys termed *Volpone* "a most excellent play; the best I think I ever saw," and although John Dryden in 1668 questioned its double climaxes, he nonetheless termed it excellent, especially in continuity of scenes. Despite criticizing the farcical tortoise-shell episode in 1683, a year later he defended modern dramatists by observing that even Jonson had written such a superb play only after much practice. Meanwhile, *Volpone* had already inspired close imitation by Thomas Killigrew in 1654 and by Aphra Behn in 1678 and was widely valued for decorum, language, and "well humoring of the parts" (an assessment by Edward Phillips in 1675 repeated by others in 1684 and 1694). Only at century's end was muted dissent heard. In 1695 William Congreve, admiring the play's humor, nevertheless objected to its apparent mockery of deafness, an opinion echoed in 1696 by John Dennis, who also faulted its allegedly inaccurate judgment, unintegrated subplot, unconvincing relations between Mosca and Bonario, and inconsistent protagonist. More typical, however, was the praise in 1698 and 1699 of Jeremy Collier, who (like William Mountfort in 1691) lauded Jonson for attacking vice. Yet Dennis' charges were frequently debated in coming decades, when supposedly extraneous matter was often cut from performances. In the nineteenth century *Volpone* was vigorously defended by Gifford, but even critics who partly admired it (such as William Hazlitt and S. T. Coleridge) objected to its allegedly cold, mechanical construction. Only later, influenced by J. A. Symonds and Charles Swinburne, did the tide begin to turn, although even Symonds questioned the subplot.

Some modern critics have seen *Volpone* as almost darkly tragic, especially in treating Celia and in the final fate of the tricksters. The comedy is often compared to *Sejanus* – an ironic, satiric, sardonic tragedy. Critics sometimes claim that *Volpone* emphasizes evils rather than follies, and while some regret the virtuous characters' thinness, others see Jonson deliberately mocking stiff, stick-figure goodness. Many admire his unflinching, witty portraits of depravity and praise his implicit moral satire. Meanwhile, the supposedly "extraneous" elements are now often defended as parts of a complex design, and the Would-be subplot (in particular) has been championed as comic relief, as connecting Venetian vice to English folly, and as a lighter variant on the main plot.

Commentators often admire the play's allegory, hyperbole, centripetal structure, classical allusions, ironic grandiloquence, lack of sentimentality, clever stage-business, clear and detailed characterization, oscillating scenic rhythms (including indoor and outdoor scenes), and abandonment of obvious authorial spokesmen. They praise its combination of learning and popular art; its ever-quickening pace; and its effective use of imagery linked (for instance) with religion, animals, love, money, sex, abnormality, and especially feeding. Debts have been traced to Aristophanes, Avian, Catullus, Erasmus, Gower, Lewkenor, Lucian, Machiavelli, beast fables, emblem books, morality plays, and city comedies. Volpone himself is seen by some as perverse, cold, narcissistic, vacuous, and morally sick, but by others as witty, energetic, vital, and imaginative – as an artist whom Jonson partly admired. His ambiguous relations with Mosca are often emphasized, as are the ironic portraits of the play's lawyer, judges, and families (including Volpone's freakish "children").

Major themes emphasized by modern critics include acting, avarice, conspiracy, corruption, disguise, excess, folly, homoeroticism, inversion, lust, manipulation, materialism, misanthropy, mimicry, misogyny, monstrosity, over-reaching, paranoia, patronage, pride, sadism, scheming, secrecy, self-control, self-love, sensuality, sexuality, sickness, sin, sloth, spying, theatricality, trickery, voyeurism, worldliness; broken bonds, corrupt authority, false romance, fluctuating fortune, impotent innocence, perverse art, subverted expectations, unnatural conduct, personal and topical satire, conflicts with audience, and unstable generic tones. Many critics also stress our supposedly simultaneous attraction and repulsion toward Volpone and Mosca (sometimes seen as Satanic). When assessing these characters (some critics contend), we inevitably assess ourselves.

Volpone has inspired translations or adaptations into Catalan (1957), French (1929, 1934, 1948, 1950), German (1925, 1928), Hungarian (1961), Italian (1930, 1943), Polish (1962), Portuguese (1958), Russian (1954), and Spanish (1929 [twice], and 1953). It was adapted for Broadway in 1976 and has also been the basis of several films.

Epicœne

Recent responses to *Epicœne, or The Silent Woman* have usually seemed less enthusiastic than those in the seventeenth century, when it was often highly praised. Although one aristocrat thought the play mocked her, Francis Beaumont in 1612 praised it for avoiding personal satire and for instead encouraging honest self-examination. Jonson himself reported that the play was originally mocked, but before long it was widely admired. Already in 1616 Beaumont and Fletcher casually alluded to it in a drama, and throughout the century (for example, in

1639, 1654, 1668, 1671, 1673, and 1690) others followed their lead, often focusing on its fools. Its only song was frequently recopied and reprinted (for instance, in 1663, 1671, 1699), and in its own century the play inspired both a Spanish translation and an English imitation. It was often performed – perhaps because it anticipated (and helped create) the Restoration fashion for comedies of manners. Samuel Pepys, who attended at least four stagings (in 1660, 1664, 1667, and 1668), was highly pleased with nearly all. In 1660 he called the work "excellent"; in 1668 he termed it "the best comedy, I think, that ever was wrote," and he noted that Thomas Shadwell was also "big with admiration." In 1662, Margaret Cavendish likewise called it a masterpiece.

Similarly, Dryden wrote (in 1668) that Jonson's play not only surpassed recent French drama in variety but almost perfectly observed dramatic laws while combining complexity and unity. He commended its wit and fancy; its convincing imitation of gentlemanly conversation; its unities of action, time, and place; its continuity of scenes; its elaborate yet easy plot; its surprising but convincing ending; its excellent contrivance; its varied characters and credible humors; its habit of describing characters before introducing them; its integration of motives; and its constantly rising, increasingly complicated action. Jonson wrote (said Dryden) like a chess-master, especially in creating Truewit, whom Dryden in 1672 called masterly (if perhaps more bookish than contemporary gentlemen). A year earlier, he praised *Epicœne* for strict poetic justice since it depicted the "naughty" Dauphine as a victor and Truewit as his "pimp."

In 1698, however, Jeremy Collier vigorously dissented, defending Dauphine and commending Jonson for decorously depicting the clergy. Meanwhile, the play was also cited in 1675, 1684, and 1691 as among Jonson's finest for decorum, language, and humor, and in 1691 Gerald Langbaine said it was "accounted by all, one of the best comedies." Charles Gildon echoed Langbaine in 1699 and similarly noted Peter Hausted's stage imitations. Admittedly, some writers debated whether Morose was properly comic (John Oldham in 1681 thought he was, but William Congreve in 1695 considered him too farcical), and in 1696 John Dennis, although admiring the ending, found the work less morally edifying than either *Volpone* or *The Alchemist*, agreeing with Congreve that Morose's flaws were too unusual to be instructive. In 1673 Dryden even suggested that the play had begun to slip from fashion. In general, however, *Epicœne* was widely known and admired, as incidental allusions (in 1637, 1651, 1665, 1669, 1690, and 1691) suggest. It was continuously performed (if often altered) between 1660 and the late 1700s, and Coleridge even called it Jonson's most entertaining comedy. In the nineteenth century, however, it mostly went unstaged.

In the twentieth century, *Epicœne* has been frequently studied, especially in relation to such themes as abnormality, conspiracy, cross-dressing, deception, deviance, disguise, elitism, excess, exuberance, factionalism, festivity, friendship, gallantry, gossip, imagination, individuality, marriage, misanthropy, misjudgment, moderation, privacy, reputation, rigidity, secrecy, self-display, self-interest, self-possession, shame, silence, surprise, superficiality, torment, wit, amoral relativism, corrupt speech, ethical ambiguity, failed festivity, fake stoicism, feminine corruption, moral vacuity, individual and group competition, inversions of sex and status, male bonding, male dominance, male fears of women, meaningless speech, misogyny (or its limitations), moral complexity, role-playing, social detachment, stereotypes of gender and sex, upper-class vanity, wasting time, gradations of good and evil, relations between art and morals, sexual equality and freedom, violations of decorum, appearance vs. reality, art vs. nature, public vs. private, and true vs. false art.

Techniques often cited include the play's use of disguise, surprise, suspense, adroit prose, allusive language, apt English settings, clever dialogue, discordant music, pestering visitors, sexual innuendo, good ensemble scenes; and imagery of animals, clothes, coldness, metal, prodigality, stone, and strangeness. Analysts have also noted how it controls its audience, emphasizes prose paradoxes, juxtaposes closed and open worlds, uses child actors to mock adult pretensions, satirizes through ironic praise, transforms conventional plots, and manipulates sources. Analogues studied include Aretino, Juvenal, Machiavelli, other satirists, Ovid, Plautus, Shakespeare, and the Biblical legend of the prodigal son. Critics have particularly debated whether the play is torn between Ovidian polish and Juvenalian fierceness.

Epicœne's tone has been variously termed amusing, comic, cruel, dark, disturbing, entertaining, farcical, frigid, genial, light, playful, pleasing, realistic, satirical, secular, sophisticated, and thoughtful. Its structure has also been variously perceived: as centering around two major changes in Epicœne; as modifying classical four-part designs; as parodying wedding masques; and as masque-like in general. Some critics see it as less unified than *Volpone* and some as more, although most consider it far more unified than the comical satires. Some think it more narrowly aristocratic than Jonson's other plays, while some consider it lighter than *Volpone* because it focuses more on folly than on vice.

Response to the play depends heavily on reactions to its characters, especially Morose, Dauphine, and Truewit. Some critics see all the characters as variously foolish; others see distinct differences between the fools and gallants. Truewit has been perceived both as clever and witty and as amoral, cruel, cynical, superficial, and worldly-wise. Dauphine has been seen either as a witty, ethical master-plotter or as calculating, cynical, foolish, and solipsistic. Meanwhile, Morose, although usually viewed as antisocial, extreme, intolerant, misanthropic, misogynistic, sadistic, trivial, and tyrannical, has also been regarded as complex, sometimes correct, and partially sympathetic. Persons who pity him as a target of excessive torment by selfish, loutish youths also regard the play either as unintentionally cold, immoral, and joyless or as deliberately unsettling (since it raises uncomfortable questions about wit's relation to ethics). In fact, some think the play implicitly interrogates audience morals, with sympathy for the wits indicating shallow values. Others, however, see the gallants as clear-headed heroes inflicting deserved humiliation on the unlikeable Morose, while still others regard almost all the characters as unsympathetic, the play as a failed comedy, and the ending as either a trick or a total surprise.

Topical discussions usually center on possible allusions to Simon Forman, John Harington, Thomas Overbury, and especially Arbella Stuart. The work inspired a French adaptation (ca. 1733); a Russian translation (1921); a German comic opera (1830); and a German adaptation (1935). Modern performances have rarely been as well received as recent stagings of *Volpone* or *The Alchemist*, and today *Epicœne* is, perhaps, the least popular of Jonson's greatest comedies.

The Alchemist

The Alchemist, conversely, is probably Jonson's most popular work. Already in the 1600s it was obviously loved: Thomas Carew (c. 1629) called it the playwright's apex, while James Howell thought it even more inspired than *Volpone*. In 1638 Jasper Mayne recommended repeated viewings, claiming it "laughed [one] into virtue" and provoked hatred of one's own vices even while avoiding personal satire. Sir John Suckling ranked it (with *Volpone* and *Epicœne*) as one of Jonson's best dramas; James Shirley (c. 1637–40) extolled its wit and art and compared it with the best Greek and Roman drama; Edmund Gayton in 1654 praised its satire; and William Davenant in 1660 admired its solid judgment and sublime wit and wondered whether "so rare a Masterpiece" could now be properly acted.

Inevitably dissent was voiced: although John Gee in 1624 valued the play as evidence about actual alchemists, Philip Kynder in 1656 considered its Puritans caricatures. Robert Herrick claimed (before 1648) that audiences had "once hissed" Jonson's "unequalled Play"; Aphra Behn, in 1673, said it often bored audiences delighted by Shakespeare; while Margaret Cavendish (whose husband alluded to the play in 1649 in one of his own) in 1662 called *The Alchemist* perhaps too long for staging and used it (and, as we have seen, *Volpone*) to justify her own violations of the unity of time. Yet she still considered it a masterpiece produced both by "Wit's Invention" and by "laboring thought," an opinion widely shared. Pepys in 1661 termed it "most incomparable" and in 1664 and 1669 praised a lead actor. Dryden in 1668 also called it masterful, commending its varied humors, apt verse, continuity of scenes, and generally complex but unified design. In 1683 he suggested it might even surpass *Volpone* by lacking farce, and in 1685 he mentioned it again more generally. Meanwhile, in 1671 he used its ending to justify his own disinterest in strict poetic justice. Likewise, in that same year, Edward Howard also used *The Alchemist* to guide modern playwrights: it showed (he claimed) that comedy need not be strictly realistic and could deal effectively with plebians.

In fact, Jonson's characters were often mentioned, with references (for instance) to Mammon (in 1662), Dapper (in 1673), Surly (in 1682), Face (in 1640 and 1660), Subtle (before 1635 and in 1637 and 1660), and especially Dol (in 1655, 1664, 1668–9, 1672, 1673, 1684, and 1687). Debts to Chaucer and Erasmus were noted in 1664, while echoes of Aristophanes were mentioned in 1692. In 1675 Edward Phillips called *The Alchemist* one of Jonson's top three or four works for its decorum, language, and "well humoring of the parts," an opinion echoed in 1684 and 1694. In 1691 William Mountfort commended it for exposing crimes, and in 1696 John Dennis similarly praised its ethics and artful plot (although he found its resolutions somewhat forced). Finally, Jeremy Collier in 1698 predictably disagreed with Dryden's view of its lax poetic justice, arguing instead for a moralistic conclusion: both Lovewit and Face (he asserted) finally confess and seek pardon. Thus Jonson's precedent did not (he thought) justify unpunished vice.

The Alchemist impressed early commentators and audiences alike. It was Jonson's most performed drama in the 1600s and 1700s, and, although often cut, it was never altered as drastically as *Volpone*. Abel Drugger was especially popular after 1750 (thanks largely to David Garrick's performances), and his role was emphasized in re-writes such as *The Tobacconist* and *Abel Drugger's Return*. Inevitably, though, the play dated, thanks to its arcane subject and to changed tastes, and after Garrick retired in 1776 few performances occurred. Not until 1899 was *The Alchemist* staged again, despite Coleridge's claim that its plot was one of literature's three best.

Modern criticism has discussed *The Alchemist* in relation to such varied themes as avarice, cleverness, conscience, desire, disguise, fantasy, greed, hypocrisy, imitation, ingenuity, initiation, lust, language, money, monomania, pride, and rivalry. Critics have explored its treatment of arbitrary justice, art and nature, false creation, grand visions, hidden desires, male arrogance, role-playing, self-deception, unstable scheming, and the dangers of capitalism. Jonson here allegedly depicts an inverted universe, shows the ubiquity of acting, exposes deceit in law and religion, links literal and moral sickness, contrasts true artists and false tricksters, reveals how factions betray community, satirizes alchemy as a fake religion and bogus business, parodies conventional happy endings, and generally mocks the popular literature (especially romance) that influenced ignorant fools. The play allegedly highlights the dilemmas of widows; subverts monological discourse; uncovers self-delusion in both magic and theatre; implies both the dangers the plotters face and the threats they pose; demonstrates how concealed knowledge weakens when revealed; discloses society's refusal to benefit even when nature subverts vice; suggests that the true punishment the schemers suffer is stasis; and reveals how the fools seek to become knaves even as the knaves become fools.

Stylistic and stage techniques discussed include disguises, exaggeration, irony, jargons, scatology, tricks, abundant action, apparent improvisation, paired characters, realistic diction, sudden shifts, varied tones, vivid quarrels, chaotically allusive language, perverted but energetic rhetoric, violations of decorum, and inflated (then deflated) imagery of war, royalty, religion, and sex, as well as images of dogs (and other imagery likening humans to animals). Commentators also note how effectively Jonson exploits clashing jargons to prevent real communication while nonetheless building a unified over-all tone. Structurally, the play has been admired for fusing classic form and realistic matter; for avoiding excessive digressions; for employing separate, similar, but accelerating episodes; for clever costume changes that keep plot lines distinct; for increasingly complex subplots; for adroitly exploiting a classical four-part structure; for strictly observing unities of action, time, and place; and for dynamic suspense. *The Alchemist* has been called more coherent than *Volpone* or *Epicœne*, and critics have admired how Jonson makes each fool increasingly corrupt; how he opens and closes by deceiving Dapper (the stupidest gull); how, as each crisis ends, a greater begins; and how he separates the gulls to build tension, allowing everyone finally to appear on stage only near the end.

Much has also been written about the play's characters. Thus Mammon has been called a great imaginative creation, the best non-Shakespearean comic figure in English drama, a reflection of Jonson's own enormous imagination, an embodiment of the deadly sins, an ambitious dreamer needing no encouragement from the knaves, and a parody of Christopher Marlowe's over-reachers. Like the comedy's Puritans, he also has been termed a transgressor of serious social responsibilities. Subtle, meanwhile, has been seen as a blasphemous, perverse exploiter of self-deceiving fools who subverts any possibility of real perfection, and also as a false artist or perverted poet. Face, Dol, and Subtle have been likened (respectively) to the world, flesh, and devil, while Face has been called comedy embodied, a manipulative stage-director, and a symbol of capitalist flux. Interestingly, much comment centers on Surly, whom some critics consider a Jonsonian innovation – an ambiguously amoral (or immoral) satirist who is competitive, skeptical, negative, and unsympathetic; who fails by acting alone and by blindly enacting a prescribed role; and who embodies the audience's suspicions while being (at best) principled but ineffective. Greater debate swirls around Lovewit, alternately viewed as more realistic, admirable, and successful than Surly; as an old, sly symbol of comic order whose superior mind, self-knowledge, and self-contentment allow him easily to dominate Face; as a symbol of the play's shift from linguistic chaos to plain talk; as just another scheming imposter; as a con man backed by the law; as a poor authority figure; as a symbol of the ignorant, foolish audience; as Jonson's ambiguous alter-ego; as a potential cuckold; and as just another dupe. Some critics think Jonson endorses Lovewit's triumph, while others find the ending highly ironic. In general, though, the characters have been praised both for their realism and individuality and for their effectiveness as caricatures or stereotypes. Jonson has been commended for creating characters who are both detailed and hollow and for devising persons whose hunger for transformation makes them either pathetically ironic or oddly hopeful.

General interpretations have predictably varied. *The Alchemist* has been perceived as both comic and antiromantic, as both realistic and unrealistic, as both lighter and darker than *Volpone,* and as both genuinely humorous and corrosively ironic. Some think it exhibits Jonson's worst villains thus far (plus his widest spectrum of gulls). For others, it displays a unique failure of law and rare tolerance of evil. Some find the ending highly disturbing, while others argue that by reaffirming order (and even affection) the play is ultimately positive. Others praise it for lacking any tidy moral, and for some its ironies implicate even Jonson (as trickster and rogue). Many see the epilogue as aggressively indicting an audience tainted by foolishness and vice, while others see this work as Jonson's least antagonistic play. Still other interpreters contend, however, that the drama tests and sharpens judgment, transforming the audience even if not the characters. *The Alchemist* has been called less intense than *Volpone* and more dated than it or *Epicœne,* yet it has also been termed Jonson's liveliest, funniest comedy (although one critic argues that the more we ponder its ethics, the less we can simply enjoy it).

Sources or parallels discussed include Chaucer, Erasmus, Lucian, Machiavelli, Plautus, as well as alchemical tracts, morality plays, contemporary con-games, law cases, ballads, and pamphlets (especially on cony-catching), hieroglyphic and emblem traditions, and the Biblical parable of the talents. Topically, the play has been interpreted as mocking Elizabethan nostalgia, magical Protestantism, the rise of capitalism, or such real figures as Thomas Rogers, John Dee, and Edward Kelley, and as reflecting Jonson's own dabblings in occult trickery. Besides inspiring two eighteenth-century spin-offs, the play has also been adapted or translated into Czech (1956), French (1933, 1957, 1962), Italian (1948), and even modern English (1973) and has been frequently staged.

Bartholomew Fair

Bartholomew Fair, Jonson's fourth "great" comedy, inspires similar modern interest, although initial references (for instance, in 1613, 1614–15, 1631, 1640,

1661, 1662–4, 1663, 1667, 1668–9, 1674, 1688, 1690) were largely incidental (perhaps because the play was not published in the 1616 Folio or acted for decades after 1620). Substantive comments mostly begin with Pepys, who saw the play at least seven times in the first ten years of the Restoration (four times in 1661 alone). Although he disliked its puppets and found its anti-Puritan satire inflammatory, he loved the play, in 1664 calling it "the best comedy in the world" and in 1668 terming it "excellent," its wit more impressive with each new viewing. In that same year, Dryden praised its "variety," noted that it typically described characters before introducing them, and commended its decorum, especially its subtle heightening of a "vile" subject. In 1667 he had already alluded to Cokes debating the puppets, and in 1700 he mentioned Littlewit. Indeed, several characters were cited specifically by various writers. A reference to Ursula and Overdo by Richard Flecknoe was published in 1653; one by Richard Brome to Overdo appeared in 1658; an allusion to Ursula by Francis Kirkman and Richard Head saw print in 1668; an anonymous reference to Cokes appeared in 1675; one to Busy by Thomas Shadwell was published in 1676; another to Busy and other matters (by Thomas D'Urfey) appeared in 1690; and another to Cokes (by Henry Higden) was published in 1693. Other early references include an account (by Robert Boyer in 1670) of injuries resulting when scaffolding collapsed just as the play mocked the clergy; commendation (by Edward Howard in 1671) of its proper handling of lower-class characters; praise that same year by Thomas Shadwell for Jonson's ability to make such characters speak wittily in "one of the wittiest plays in the world"; Edward Phillips' ranking of the play (in 1675) as just below the other three great comedies (an assessment echoed by others in 1684 and 1694); Langbaine's report (in 1691) that the play had been frequently acted since the Restoration with "great applause" (a claim Charles Gildon repeated in 1699); and Thomas Brown's observation that whereas fairs had once inspired "our best comedians," now the stage itself had been usurped by farcical, fair-like amusements. Inevitably, too, Jonson's play became entangled in Collier's 1698 debate with Congreve: Collier alleged that Congreve exceeded Jonson in profaneness, while Congreve, denying the charge, likened the dispute to Busy's pointless debate with the puppets. Collier, though, insisted in 1699 that even though Jonson's Littlewit had profaned religion, at least he had not (like Congreve) tarnished scripture.

Modern students of *Bartholomew Fair* emphasize such central themes as aggression, authority, carnival, deception, drama, fertility, hypocrisy, language, law, license, manipulation, marriage, pride, and religion, along with bogus power, chaos vs. order, corrupt rhetoric, failed communication, faulty judgment, human debasement, transformative games, self-mockery, and universal foolishness. The fair has been seen as symbolizing and defending theatre; as humanizing the characters (especially the condemners); as mocking not authority but its abuse; as replicating rather than repudiating capitalist economics; as collapsing the playwright's usual emphasis on judgment and distinctions; and therefore as free, freeing, deconstructive, ambiguous, and fluid, but also as an event Jonson seeks to control. For some, Jonson's drama reenacts Christian redemption; invites us to consider our roles as audience and judges; and ends with a full affirmation of (or perhaps merely a slight gesture toward) renewal and reconciliation. Its tone has been variously interpreted as energetic, farcical, funny, genial, humble, imaginative, ironic, orgiastic, realistic, repressive, satirical, skeptical, and/or tolerant. Some see the work as more accommodating, forgiving, gentle, humane, subtle, and ethically complex than Jonson's earlier plays, as well as being more accepting both of its audience and of popular art. In this work (some claim), Jonson de-emphasizes artifice, exaggeration, comic manipulators, obvious distinctions between gullers and gulled, and debts to previous writers, while his anti-Puritan satire is more individualized, lively, and better-integrated than before. Some see Jonson showing new openness to emotions and to native literature and triumphing over his earlier need to triumph. Others, however, argue that his emphasis on discriminating judgment here is more implicit but no less important than in his earlier works.

Comments on the play's structure have argued that its loose unity derives from its focus on the fair; that its superbly unclassical "plotlessness" is complex but never chaotic; that it mixes five main actions (involving Littlewit, Purecraft, Busy, Cokes, and Overdo); that Ursula connects all these plotlines; that the loose structure matches the play's realism and emphasis on surfaces; and that the work shows Jonson's debt to classical four-part designs and/or to morality plays and masques. Other suggested influences have included Aristophanes, Shakespeare, Jonson himself, and Thomas Nashe. Meanwhile, various suggested topical aspects include possible satire of Shakespeare, Inigo Jones, King James, a London mayor, the Howard-Essex scandal, current academic and political debates, a father of one of the actors, and Jonson's own recent experiences as a tutor.

Techniques discussed by critics of *Bartholomew Fair* have included exaggeration, jargon, paradox, pomposity, authorial self-parody, constant motion, local color, minimal conversation, mock heroism, paired characters, an emphasis on Christian names, a greater focus on conduct than on words, an unusual length and large cast (permitting subtle comparisons and contrasts), a tendency for the most foolish character to lead each group but for all groups to dissolve; and (especially) use of abrupt, terse, jerky, and realistic prose. In addition, the characters have provoked much comment. Thus Busy has been called the best-drawn Puritan by any English playwright, and critics have noted how his speech is repetitive and illogical but how even he is invited to the final feast. The foolish, infantile Cokes has been called particularly well developed, as has Overdo, who has been called pedantically rhetorical, monological, and authoritarian. He has been viewed as a stereotype (a disguised magistrate who learns humility) but also as a figure whose descent and sufferings prove finally fortunate to his fellow characters. Grace has been called too barren, cool, unethical, and under-developed but also has been termed one of Jonson's most appealing women – impressively virtuous and capable of resisting temptation, even if socially impotent. Meanwhile, Ursula has been seen as a comic Circe who changes men into pigs; as more honest and loyal than her genteel customers; as a mythic "great mother" representing fertility (and using vital, fleshy, physical language abounding in imagery of family, food, fruitfulness, and pleasure); and as a symbolic mother to the pregnant Win.

Most debate about the characters, however, centers on Quarlous and Winwife. Some commentators think Jonson endorses them as pragmatic, perceptive, rational, and prudent judges who, despite flaws, resist temptation, compromise intelligently with reality, and ultimately win the women. For such critics, Quarlous is a complex, theatrically self-conscious master-wit whose moral growth helps unify the drama. Other analysts, however, are much more skeptical, viewing Quarlous and Winwife as shallow, barren, ambitious, egotistical, morally frail, antisocial, ungenerous, and disloyal. Responses to these characters often dictate responses to the whole play: persons who see the gallants as finally improved (or at least untainted) generally find the comedy highly affirmative, while readers who question the morality of Quarlous and Winwife also tend to view the entire play as more darkly ambiguous.

As has been shown, such debates typify much of modern Jonson criticism, and surely disagreement will continue. Yet it is precisely Jonson's ability to provoke such continually spirited discussion that demonstrates the rich complexity of his art and its continuing relevance to our attempts to understand both his world and our own. The great comedies, the other dramas, the poems, the masques, and his prose will always help powerfully shape our views of the English Renaissance.

NOTES

1 For bibliographical data about all the works mentioned in this paragraph, see Katie J. Magaw, "Modern Books on Ben Jonson: A General Topical Index," *Ben Jonson Journal*, 5 (1998), 201–47. See also Clint Darby, "Modern Books on Ben Jonson: A General Topical Index (First Supplement)," *Ben Jonson Journal*, 6 (1999), 261–75. In addition, see Robert C. Evans, *Ben Jonson's Major Plays: Summaries of Modern Monographs* (West Cornwall, CT: Locust Hill Press, 2000).

2 The ensuing survey draws on a variety of sources, including a re-reading of nearly every modern book on Jonson. However, I also strongly benefitted from the work of previous scholars, to whom I wish here to pay sincere tribute. These include William L. Godshalk in *The New Intellectuals: A Survey and Bibliography of Recent Studies*

in English Renaissance Drama, ed. Terence P. Logan and Denzell S. Smith (Lincoln: University of Nebraska Press, 1977), 117–70; David C. Judkins, *The Non-Dramatic Works of Ben Jonson: A Reference Guide* (Boston: G. K. Hall, 1982); and Walter D. Lehrman, Delores J. Sarafinski, and Elizabeth Savage, eds., *The Plays of Ben Jonson: A Reference Guide* (Boston: G. K. Hall, 1980). Information about the earliest allusions to Jonson (which seem to me especially important) comes from Jesse Franklin Bradley and Joseph Quincy Adams, *The Jonson Allusion-Book, 1597–1700* (New Haven: Yale University Press, 1922); Gerald Eades Bentley, *Shakespeare and Jonson: Their Reputations in the Seventeeth Century Compared*, 2 vols. (Chicago: University of Chicago Press, 1945); and D. H. Craig, *Ben Jonson: The Critical Heritage* (London: Routledge, 1990). For information about the staging of Jonson's plays, see especially Robert Gale Noyes, *Ben Jonson on the English Stage, 1660–1776* (Cambridge, MA: Harvard University Press, 1935) and Ejner J. Jensen, *Ben Jonson's Comedies on the Modern Stage* (Ann Arbor, MI: UMI Research Press, 1985).

3 Here and throughout this chapter, I attempt to combine (for the first time) information from all the major collections of early Jonson allusions and report them in rough chronological order. Dates frequently refer to year of *publication*, which are sometimes slightly or significantly later than actual years of *composition*. Thus an allusion may have been composed in manuscript in 1612 but not published until a decade or more later. The earliest possible date is given when it is known.

SELECTED BIBLIOGRAPHY

Jonson's works

Ben Jonson. Ed. C. H. Herford and Percy and Evelyn Simpson. 11 vols. Oxford: Clarendon Press, 1925–52.

Ben Jonson. Ed. Ian Donaldson. Oxford: Oxford University Press, 1985.

The Complete Masques. Ed. Stephen Orgel. New Haven: Yale University Press, 1969.

The Complete Plays of Ben Jonson. Ed. G. A. Wilkes. 4 vols. Based on the Herford and Simpson edition. Oxford: Clarendon Press, 1981–82.

Timber; or, Discoveries made upon Men and Matter. Ed. F. E. Schelling. Boston: Ginn & Co., 1892.

The following plays by Ben Jonson are in The Revels Plays series:

The Alchemist. Ed. F. H. Mares. Manchester: Manchester University Press, 1967.

Bartholomew Fair. Ed. E. A. Horsman. Manchester: Manchester University Press, 1960.

The Devil is an Ass. Ed. Peter Happé. Manchester: Manchester University Press, 1996.

Eastward Ho! Ed. R. W. Van Fossen. Manchester: Manchester University Press, 1979.

Every Man in his Humour. Ed. Robert Miola. Manchester: Manchester University Press, 2000.

The New Inn. Ed. Michael Hattaway. Manchester: Manchester University Press, 1984.

Poetaster. Ed. Tom Cain. Manchester: Manchester University Press, 1995.

Sejanus. Ed. Philip J. Ayres. Manchester: Manchester University Press, 1990.

The Staple of News. Ed. Anthony Parr. Manchester: Manchester University Press, 1988.

Volpone. Ed. David Bevington and Brian Parker. Manchester: Manchester University Press, 1999.

Journal

The Ben Jonson Journal. Ed. Richard Harp, Stanley Stewart, and Robert C. Evans. West Cornwall, CT: Locust Hill Press, 1994– [annual publication].

Research resources

Adams, Joseph Quincy and Jesse Franklin Bradley. *The Jonson Allusion-Book, 1597–1700*. New Haven: Yale University Press, 1922.

Bates, Stephen L. and Sidney D. Orr. *A Concordance to the Poems of Ben Jonson*. Athens: Ohio University Press, 1978.

Bentley, Gerald Eades. *Shakespeare and Jonson: Their Reputations in the Seventeenth Century Compared.* 2 vols. Chicago: University of Chicago Press, 1945.

Brock, D. Heyward. *A Ben Jonson Companion.* Bloomington: Indiana University Press, 1983.

Burdett, John and Jonathan Wright. "Ben Jonson in Recent General Scholarship, 1972–1996." *The Ben Jonson Journal,* 4 (1997), 151–79.

Craig, D.H. *Ben Jonson: The Critical Heritage.* London: Routledge, 1990.

Donaldson, Ian. "The Cambridge Edition of the Works of Ben Jonson." *The Ben Jonson Journal,* 5 (1998), 257–69.

Evans, Robert C. *Ben Jonson's Major Plays: Summaries of Modern Monographs.* West Cornwall, CT: Locust Hill Press, 2000.

Gants, David. "The Cambridge Ben Jonson: Ruminations on the Electronic Edition." *The Ben Jonson Journal,* 5 (1998), 271–81.

[The above two articles describe the new *Cambridge Ben Jonson,* scheduled to appear in 2005.]

Judkins, David C. *The Nondramatic Works of Ben Jonson: A Reference Guide.* Boston: G. K. Hall, 1982.

Lehrman, Walter D., Delores J. Sarafinski, and Elizabeth Savage, eds. *The Plays of Ben Jonson: A Reference Guide.* Boston: G. K. Hall, 1980.

Magaw, Katie J. "Modern Books on Ben Jonson: A General Topical Index." *The Ben Jonson Journal,* 5 (1998), 201–47.

Probst, Neil. "A Topical Index to Jonson's *Discoveries.*" *The Ben Jonson Journal,* 3 (1996), 153–77.

Biography

Chute, Marchette. *Ben Jonson of Westminster.* New York: Dutton, 1953.

Kay, W. David. *Ben Jonson: A Literary Life.* New York: St. Martin's Press, 1995.

Miles, Rosalind. *Ben Jonson: His Life and Work.* London: Routledge, 1986.

Riggs, David. *Ben Jonson: A Life.* Cambridge, MA: Harvard University Press, 1989.

Summers, Claude J., and Ted-Larry Pebworth. *Ben Jonson.* Twayne's English Authors Series. Boston: Twayne, 1999.

Classical learning

Evans, Robert C. *Habits of Mind: Evidence and Effects of Ben Jonson's Reading.* Lewisburg, PA: Bucknell University Press, 1995.

Martindale, Joanna. "The Best Master of Virtue and Wisdom: the Horace of Ben Jonson and his Heirs." In *Horace Made New: Horatian Influences on British Writing from the Renaissance to the Twentieth Century.* Eds. Charles Martindale and David Hopkins, 50–85. Cambridge: Cambridge University Press, 1993.

Mulryan, John. "Mythic Interpretations of Ideas in Jonson's *Pleasure Reconciled to Virtue.*" *The Ben Jonson Journal,* 1 (1994), 63–76.

Parfitt, George A. E. "Compromise Classicism: Language and Rhythm in Ben Jonson's Poetry." *Studies in English Literature,* 11 (Winter 1971), 109–23.

Smith, Bruce R. "Ben Jonson's *Epigrammes*: Portrait-Gallery, Theatre, Commonwealth." *Studies in English Literature 1500–1900,* 14 (1974), 91–109.

Renaissance London and its theatres

Braunmuller, A. R. and Michael Hattaway. *The Cambridge Companion to English Renaissance Drama*. Cambridge: Cambridge University Press, 1990.

Chalfant, Fran C. *Ben Jonson's London: A Jacobean Placename Dictionary*. Athens, GA: University of Georgia Press, 1978.

Dutton, Richard. *Mastering the Revels: The Regulation and Censorship of English Renaissance Drama*. Basingstoke and London: Macmillan, 1991.

Foakes, R. A. and R. T. Rickert, eds. *Henslowe's Diary*. Cambridge: Cambridge University Press, 1961.

Fricker, Franz. *Ben Jonson's Plays in Performance and the Jacobean Theatre*. Bern: Francke, 1972.

Gurr, Andrew. *Playgoing in Shakespeare's London*. 2nd edition. Cambridge: Cambridge University Press, 1996.

Haynes, Jonathan. *The Social Relations of Jonson's Theatre*. Cambridge: Cambridge University Press, 1992.

Paster, Gail K. *The Idea of the City in the Age of Shakespeare*. Athens, GA: University of Georgia Press, 1985.

Smallwood, R. L. "'Here in the Friars': Immediacy and Theatricality in *The Alchemist*." *Review of English Studies*, 32 (1981), 142–60.

Smith, David L., Richard Strier, and David Bevington, eds. *The Theatrical City*. Cambridge: Cambridge University Press, 1995.

Stow, John. *A Survey of London*. Ed. C. L. Kingsford. 2 vols. Oxford: The Clarendon Press, 1908.

Drama

Barish, Jonas A. *Ben Jonson and the Language of Prose Comedy*. Cambridge, MA: Harvard University Press, 1960.

Barton, Anne. "*The New Inn* and the Problem of Jonson's Late Style." *English Literary Renaissance*, 9 (1979), 395–418.

Ben Jonson, Dramatist. Cambridge: Cambridge University Press, 1984.

Butler, Martin. "Stuart Politics in Jonson's *Tale of a Tub*." *Modern Language Review*, 85 (1990), 13–28.

"Ecclesiastical Censorship of Early Stuart Drama: The Case of Jonson's *The Magnetic Lady*." *Modern Philology*, 89 (1992), 469–81.

"*Late Jonson*." In *The Politics of Tragicomedy: Shakespeare and After*. Eds. Gordon McMullan and Jonathan Hope, 166–88. London: Routledge, 1992.

Butler, Martin. ed. *Re-Presenting Ben Jonson: Text, History, Performance*. London: Macmillan, 1999.

Cave, Richard Allen. *Ben Jonson*. New York: St. Martin's Press, 1991.

Champion, Larry. *Ben Jonson's "Dotages": A Reconsideration of the Late Plays*. Lexington: Univesity of Kentucky Press, 1967.

Donaldson, Ian, ed. *Jonson and Shakespeare*. Atlantic Highlands, N.J.: Humanities Press, 1983.

Jonson's Magic Houses: Essays in Interpretation. Oxford: The Clarendon Press, 1997.

Duncan, Douglas. *Ben Jonson and the Lucianic Tradition*. Cambridge: Cambridge University Press, 1979.

Enck, John J. *Jonson and the Comic Truth*. Madison: University of Wisconsin Press, 1957.

Flachmann, Michael. "Ben Jonson and the Alchemy of Satire." *Studies in English Literature 1500–1900* (1977), 259–80.

Harp, Richard. "Jonson's Comic Apocalypse." *Cithara*, 34 (1994), 34–43.

Haynes, Jonathan. *The Social Relations of Jonson's Theatre*. Cambridge: Cambridge University Press, 1992.

Hawkins, Harriett. "The Idea of a Theatre in Jonson's *The New Inn*." *Renaissance Drama*, 9 (1966), 205–26.

Hedrick, Don K. "Cooking for the Anthropophagi: Jonson and His Audience." *Studies in English Literature*, 17 (1977), 233–45.

Hirsh, James, ed. *New Perspectives on Ben Jonson*. Madison, NJ: Farleigh Dickinson University Press, 1997.

Jackson, Gabriele Bernhard. *Vision and Judgment in Ben Jonson's Drama*. New Haven: Yale University Press, 1968.

Jensen, Ejner J. *Ben Jonson's Comedies on the Modern Stage*. Ann Arbor, MI: UMI Research Press, 1985.

Knights, L. C. *Drama and Society in the Age of Jonson*. London: Chatto & Windus, 1937.

Knoll, Robert E. *Ben Jonson's Plays: An Introduction*. Lincoln: University of Nebraska Press, 1964.

Leggatt, Alexander. *Ben Jonson: His Vision and his Art*. London and New York: Methuen, 1981.

McDonald, Russ. *Shakespeare and Jonson / Jonson and Shakespeare*. Lincoln: University of Nebraska Press, 1988.

McPherson, David. "The Origins of Overdo: A Study in Jonsonian Invention." *Modern Language Quarterly*, 37 (1976), 221–33.

    Shakespeare, Jonson, and the Myth of Venice. Newark: University of Delaware Press, 1990.

Mack, Robert. "Ben Jonson's Own 'Comedy of Errors': 'That Witty Play,' *The Case is Altered*." *The Ben Jonson Journal*, 4 (1997), 47–63.

Maus, Katharine Eisaman. *Ben Jonson and the Roman Frame of Mind*. Princeton: Princeton University Press, 1984.

Noyes, Robert Gale. *Ben Jonson on the English Stage, 1660–1776*. Cambridge, MA: Harvard University Press, 1935.

Ornstein, Robert. "Shakespearian and Jonsonian Comedy." *Shakespeare Survey*, 22 (1969), 34–44.

Ostovich, Helen. "The Appropriation of Pleasure in *The Magnetic Lady*." *Studies in English Literature 1500–1900*, 34 (1994), 425–42.

    "Mistress and Maid: Women's Friendship in *The New Inn*." *The Ben Jonson Journal*, 4 (1997), 1–26.

Redwine, J. D., Jr. "The Moral Basis of Jonson's Theory of Humour Characterization." *ELH*, 28 (1961), 316–34.

Sanders, Julie, ed., with Kate Chedgzoy and Sue Wiseman. *Refashioning Ben Jonson: Gender, Politics, and the Jonsonian Canon*. New York: St. Martin's Press, 1998.

Shapiro, James. *Rival Playwrights: Marlowe, Jonson, Shakespeare*. New York: Columbia University Press, 1991.

Slights, William W. E. *Ben Jonson and the Art of Secrecy*. Toronto: University of Toronto Press, 1994.

Sweeney, John Gordon, III. *Jonson and the Psychology of Public Theatre*. Princeton: Princeton University Press, 1985.

Teague, Frances. *The Curious History of* Bartholomew Fair. Lewisberg, PA: Bucknell University Press, 1985.

Watson, Robert N. *Ben Jonson's Parodic Strategy: Literary Imperialism in the Comedies*. Cambridge, MA: Harvard University Press, 1987.

Poetry

Bates, Catherine. "Much Ado About Nothing: The Contents of Jonson's 'Forrest.'" *Essays in Criticism*, 42 (1992), 24–35.

Boehrer, Bruce. *The Fury of Men's Gullets: Ben Jonson and the Digestive Canal*. Philadelphia: University of Pennsylvania Press, 1997.

Butler, Martin. "'Servant, but not slave': Ben Jonson at the Stuart Court." *Proceedings of the British Academy: 1995 Lectures and Memoirs*, 90 (1996), 65–93.

Donaldson, Ian. *Jonson's Magic Houses* [see "Drama," above].

Duncan-Jones, Katherine. "'They say a made a good end': Ben Jonson's Epitaph on Thomas Nashe." *The Ben Jonson Journal*, 3 (1996), 1–19.

Evans, Robert C. *Ben Jonson and the Poetics of Patronage*. Lewisburg, PA: Bucknell University Press, 1989.

Fish, Stanley. "Author-Readers: Jonson's Community of the Same." *Representations*, 7 (1984), 26–58.

Fowler, Alastair, ed. *The Country House Poem*. Edinburgh: Edinburgh University Press, 1994.

Harp, Richard. "Jonson's 'To Penshurst': The Country House as Church." *John Donne Journal*, 7 (1988),73–89.

"Jonson's House of Wisdom." *The Ben Jonson Journal*, 1 (1994), 1–13.

Helgerson, Richard. *Self-Crowned Laureates: Spenser, Jonson, Milton, and the Literary System*. Berkeley: University of California Press, 1983.

"Ben Jonson." *The Cambridge Companion to English Poetry: Donne to Marvell*, ed. Thomas N. Corns. Cambridge: Cambridge University Press, 1993, 148–70.

Johnston, G. B. *Ben Jonson: Poet*. New York: Octagon Books, 1970; first published 1945.

Lee, Jongsook. *Ben Jonson's Poesis: A Literary Dialectic of Ideal and History*. Charlottesville: University of Virginia Press, 1989.

McCanles, Michael. *Jonsonian Discriminations: The Humanist Poet and the Praise of True Nobility*. Toronto: University of Toronto Press, 1992.

McClung, William Alexander. *The Country House in English Renaissance Poetry*. Berkeley: University of California Press, 1977.

Maclean, Hugh. "Ben Jonson's Poems: Notes on the Ordered Society." In *Essays in English Literature from the Renaissance to the Victorian Age*, eds. Millar MacLure and F. W. Watt. Toronto: University of Toronto Press (1964), 43–68.

Marotti, A. F. "All About Jonson's Poetry." *ELH*, 39 (1972), 208–37.

Martin, Thomas. "Enormity and *Aurea Mediocritas* in *Bartholomew Fayre*: The Ideals of Classical Comedy." *The Ben Jonson Journal*, 2 (1995), 143–56.

Newton, Richard C. "'Ben Jonson': The Poet in the Poems." In *Two Renaissance Mythmakers: Christopher Marlowe and Ben Jonson*, ed. Alvin Kernan. Baltimore: Johns Hopkins University Press, 1977.

Partridge, Edward. "Jonson's 'Epigrammes': The Named and the Nameless." *Studies in the Literary Imagination*, 6 (1973), 153–98.

Peterson, Richard S. *Imitation and Praise in the Poems of Ben Jonson*. New Haven: Yale University Press, 1981.

Quinn, Dennis. "Polypragmosyne in the Renaissance: Ben Jonson." *The Ben Jonson Journal*, 2 (1995), 157–69.

Rathmell, J. C. A. "Jonson, Lord Lisle, and Penshurst." *English Literary Renaissance*, 1 (1971), 250–60.

Riddell, James A. "The Arrangement of Ben Jonson's *Epigrammes*." *Studies in English Literature*, 27 (1987), 53–70.

Smith, Barbara. *The Women of Ben Jonson's Poetry: Female Representation in the Non-Dramatic Verse*. Aldershot, Hampshire: Scolar Press, 1995.

Summers, Claude J., and Ted-Larry Pebworth, eds. *Classic and Cavalier: Essays on Jonson and the Sons of Ben*. Pittsburgh: University of Pittsburgh Press, 1982.

Trimpi, Wesley. *Ben Jonson's Poems: A Study of the Plain Style*. Stanford: Stanford University Press, 1962.

van den Berg, Sara J. *The Action of Ben Jonson's Poetry*. Newark: University of Delaware Press, 1987.

Wayne, Don E. "Poetry and Power in Ben Jonson's 'Epigrammes': The Naming of 'Facts' or the Figuring of Social Relations?" *Renaissance and Modern Studies*, 23 (1979), 70–103.

Penshurst: The Semiotics of Place and the Poetics of History. London: Methuen, 1984.

Woolman, Richard B. "'Speak that I may see thee': Aurality in Ben Jonson's Print Poetry." *The Ben Jonson Journal*, 3 (1996), 21–37.

Court masques

Behunin, Robert. "Classical Wonder in Jonson's Masques." *The Ben Jonson Journal*, 3 (1996), 39–57.

Gilbert, Allan H. *The Symbolic Persons in the Masques of Ben Jonson*. Durham, NC: Duke University Press, 1948.

Limon, Jerzy. *The Masque of Stuart Culture*. Newark: University of Delaware Press, 1990.

May, Stephen W. *The Elizabethan Courtier Poets: The Poems and Their Contexts*. Columbia, MO: University of Missouri Press, 1991.

Meagher, John C. *Method and Meaning in Jonson's Masques*. Notre Dame, IN: University of Notre Dame Press, 1966.

Mickel, Leslie. *Ben Jonson's Antimasques: A History of Growth and Decline*. Aldershot and Brookfield: Ashgate Publishing Company, 1999.

Orgel, Stephen. *The Jonsonian Masque*. Cambridge, MA: Harvard University Press, 1965.

The Illusion of Power. Berkeley: University of California Press, 1975.

Orgel, Stephen and Roy Strong. *Inigo Jones: The Theatre of the Stuart Court*. 2 vols. Berkeley: University of California Press, 1973.

Parry, Graham. *The Golden Age Restor'd: The Culture of the Stuart Court, 1603–42*. New York: St. Martin's Press, 1981.

Randall, Dale B. J. *Jonson's Gypsies Unmasked: Background and Theme of The Gypsies Metamorphos'd*. Durham, NC: Duke University Press, 1975.

Sharpe, Kevin, and Peter Lake, eds. *Culture and Politics in Early Stuart England*. London: Macmillan, 1994.

Wheeler, C. F. *Classical Mythology in the Plays, Masques, and Poems of Jonson.* Princeton: Princeton University Press, 1938.

1616 Folio

Bland, Mark. "William Stansby and the Production of *The Workes of Beniamin Jonson*, 1615–16." *The Library*, 6th Ser., 8 (1998), 1–33.

Bracken, James K. "Books from William Stansby's Printing House, and Jonson's Folio of 1616." *The Library*, 6th Ser., 10 (1988), 18–29.

Brady, Jennifer, and W. H. Herendeen, eds: *Ben Jonson's 1616 Folio*. Newark: University of Delaware Press, 1991.

Brooks, Douglas. "'If He Be at His Book, Disturb Him Not': The Two Jonson Folios of 1616." *The Ben Jonson Journal*, 4 (1997), 81–101.

Dutton, Richard. *Ben Jonson: To the First Folio*. Cambridge: Cambridge University Press, 1983.

Gerritsen, Johan. "Stansby and Jonson Produce a Folio." *English Studies*, 40 (1959), 52–5.

Kay, W. David. "The Shaping of Ben Jonson's Career: A Reexamination of Facts and Problems." *Modern Philology*, 67 (February 1970).

Riddell, James A. "Variant Title-Pages of the 1616 Jonson Folio." *The Library*, 6th Ser. 8 (1986), 152–56.

"The Concluding Pages of the Jonson Folio of 1616." *Studies in Bibliography*, 47 (1994), 147–54.

"The Printing of the Plays in the Jonson Folio of 1616." *Studies in Bibliography*, 49 (1996), 149–68.

"Addendum: The Printing of the Plays in the Jonson Folio of 1616." *Studies in Bibliography*, 50 (1997), 408–09.

"Jonson and Stansby and the Revisions of *Every Man in His Humour*." *Medieval and Renaissance Drama in England*, 9 (1997), 81–91.

On Renaissance and Jonson's criticism

Castelain, Maurice. *Ben Jonson's Discoveries: A Critical Edition with an Introduction and Notes on the True Purport and Genesis of the Book*. Paris: Librarie Hachette, 1906.

Dutton, Richard. *Ben Jonson: Authority: Criticism*. London: Macmillan, 1996.

Hardison, O. B., Jr. *English Literary Criticism: The Renaissance*. New York: Meredith Publishing, 1963.

Gollancz, I[srael], ed. "Introduction." *Timber; or Discoveries; being Observations on Men and Manners*. London: J. M. Dent, 1896.

Parfitt, George. *Ben Jonson: Public Poet and Private Man*. London: J. M. Dent & Sons, 1976.

Patterson, R. F., ed. "Introduction." *Ben Jonson's Conversations with William Drummond of Hawthornden*. London: Blackie and Son, 1923.

Redwine, James D. *Ben Jonson's Literary Criticism*. Lincoln: University of Nebraska Press, 1970.

Riddell, James A. and Stanley Stewart. *Jonson's Spenser: Evidence and Historical Criticism*. Pittsburgh: Duquesne University Press, 1995.

Jonson and the arts

Chan, Mary. *Music in the Theatre of Ben Jonson.* Oxford: Clarendon Press, 1980.

Evans, Willa McClung. *Ben Jonson and Elizabethan Music.* Lancaster, PA: Lancaster Press, 1929.

Johnson, A. W. *Ben Jonson: Poetry and Architecture.* Oxford: Clarendon Press, 1994.

Intellectual background and contexts

Burt, Richard. *Licensed by Authority: Ben Jonson and the Discourses of Censorship.* Ithaca, NY: Cornell University Press, 1993.

Butler, Martin. "Sir Francis Stewart: Jonson's Overlooked Patron." *The Ben Jonson Journal,* 2 (1995), 101–27.

Evans, Robert C. *Jonson, Lipsius and the Politics of Renaissance Stoicism.* Durango, CO: Longwood Academic, 1992.

Jonson and the Contexts of His Time. Lewisberg, PA: Bucknell University Press, 1994.

Lipsius, Justus. *Principles of Letter-Writing: A Bilingual Text of Justi Lipsii Epistolica Institutio.* Eds. R. V. Young and M. Thomas Hester. Carbondale and Edwardsville: Southern Illlinois University Press, 1996.

Marcus, Leah S. *The Politics of Mirth: Jonson, Herrick, Milton, Marvell, and the Defense of Old Holiday Pastimes.* Chicago: University of Chicago Press, 1986.

Woods, Susanne. "Aemilia Lanyer and Ben Jonson: Patronage, Authority, and Gender." *The Ben Jonson Journal,* 1 (1994), 15–30.

INDEX

Index

Index

Index

More, Sir Thomas, 15
Morison, Henry, 5, 53–4, 134
Mulaney, Steve, 28n

Nabbes, Thomas, 20
Nashe, Thomas, 24, 199
Neo-Platonism, 146
New Comedy, 97
Nice Wanton, The, 67

Old Comedy, 60–1, 66
Oras, Ants, 116–17
Orgel, Stephen, 51, 189
Ostovich, Helen, 69
Overbury, Sir Thomas, 4, 127, 135, 194
Ovid (Roman poet), 9, 46, 65, 165, 177, 193
Oxford University, 44, 48, 74

Parable of the Prodigal Son , 90, 193
Parable of the Talents, 197
Partridge, Edward, 189
Pebworth, Ted-Larry, 189
Pembroke, William, *see* Herbert, William
Pepys, Samuel, 190, 192, 194, 198
Persius, 2, 61, 181, 182
Peterson, Richard S., 54, 153, 157, 189, 193
Phillips, Augustine, 72
Phillips, Edward, 190, 192, 195, 198
Philostratus, 140, 169
Pindaric Ode, 52–5
Piper, David, 12
Plautus, 46, 73, 193, 197
Pliny, 7, 8
Pope, Alexander, 54, 123, 124, 125, 130, 178, 179, 180, 181
Pope, Thomas, 72

Quintilian, 46, 53

Rabkin, Norman, 113
Radcliffe, Margaret, 41
Raleigh, Sir Walter, 15
Randall, Dale, 189
Randolph, Thomas, 93
Renaissance cities 22, 48; houses, 55; humanism, 45, 47, 163; ordering of natural world, 150; pastoral, 3, 36, 40, 101, 144; symbolism, 144; syncretism, 184;
Riddell, James A., 44, 188
Riggs, David, 34, 145, 189
Robinson, Dick, 68
Roe, Thomas, 127
Romano, Giulio, 140, 141, 142, 144

Rowe, George, 189
Rowe, Nicholas, 106
Royal Shakespeare Company, The, 95
Rudyerd, Benjamin, 3, 4, 124
Rutland, Countess of, 3

Salisbury Court, 26, 27
Salisbury, Earl of, 18, 20, 27, 41, 125, 127, 141, 150
Saturnalia, 85, 96
Savile, Henry, 4
Selden, John, 4, 5, 20, 42, 158
Seneca, 45, 137, 165, 166, 167, 181, 185
Shadwell, Thomas, 192, 198
Shakespeare, William, 7, 8, 50, 72, 74, 94, 103–18, 128, 133, 135, 142, 152, 165, 185, 187, 188, 189, 193, 194, 196, 199; affection for Jonson, 104; compared to Jonson in honor, xi, 27; personal relations with Jonson, 106
plays
    Antony and Cleopatra, 108, 116–17
    As You Like It, 95, 101
    Comedy of Errors, The, 8
    Coriolanus, 112
    Cymbeline, 117
    Hamlet, 89n, 110, 112
    Henry IV, 110
    Henry V, 72
    Henry VI, 110
    Julius Caesar, 72;
    King Lear, 50, 87, 117
    Macbeth, 111–13
    Midsummer Night's Dream, A, 88
    Richard II, 110–11, 117
    Richard III, 116, 117
    The Tempest, 108
    Troilus and Cressida, 106
    The Winter's Tale, 142
    Twelfth Night, 95
Sidney, Barbara: *see* Lisle, Lady
Sidney, Sir Philip, 3, 50, 55, 129, 131, 133, 141, 186
    Apology for Poetry, 105, 176
Sidney, Robert: *see* Lisle, Lord
Sidney, William, 131
Silva, 128, 165, 182–3
Slights, William, 189
Sly, Will, 72
Southwark, 72
Spencer, Gabriel, 5, 46, 145
Spenser, Edmund, 44, 101, 182, 185
Spink, Ian, 148